DINNER
WITH A
CANNIBAL

S A N T A
M O N I C A
P R E S S

DINNER WITH A CANNIBAL

THE COMPLETE HISTORY OF MANKIND'S OLDEST TABOO

CAROLE A. TRAVIS-HENIKOFF

FOREWORD BY CHRISTY G. TURNER II

Published by: Santa Monica Press LLC
P.O. Box 1076
Santa Monica, CA 90406-1076
1-800-784-9553
www.santamonicapress.com
books@santamonicapress.com

Printed in the United States

Santa Monica Press books are available at special quantity discounts when purchased in bulk by corporations, organizations, or groups. Please call our Special Sales department at 1-800-784-9553.

ISBN-13 978-1-59580-030-5
ISBN-10 1-59580-030-1

Library of Congress Cataloging-in-Publication Data

Travis-Henikoff, Carole A.
  Dinner with a cannibal : the complete history of mankind's oldest taboo/by Carole A. Travis-Henikoff ; foreword by Christy G. Turner II.
  p. cm.
  Includes bibliographical references and index.
  ISBN 978-1-59580-030-5
  1. Cannibalism. 2. Taboo. I. Title.

GN409.T73 2008
394'.9--dc22
  2007041548

Cover and interior design and production by Future Studio
Illustrations by Bryan Duddles

CONTENTS

CANNIBALISM: PAST AND PRESENT

FINALE: LOOKING BACK TO THE PRESENT

To my father, Carl Fredrick Sigvaard Andersen,
who taught me the wonders of reading and research.

And to my mother, Caroline Faunce Andersen,
who always said, "You are what you eat and think."

ACKNOWLEDGMENTS

inner with a Cannibal is the culmination of seven years of fascinating research. Throughout, and prior to, those years of investigation, there were friends and professionals who encouraged me, aided me, guided me, questioned me and stood by with words of knowledge and wisdom.

I wish to thank:

Ann Evans Berthoff, professor emerita, University of Massachusetts, Boston, who reviewed and edited my work as chapters took form. Her critical eye, humor, enthusiasm and encouragement were invaluable. On the day I met her she read the chapter entitled "Dinner with a Cannibal." Looking up she said, "This is the title of your book." And so it is.

Christy G. Turner II, Regents Professor of Anthropology, Arizona State University, author of *Man Corn*, and leading researcher on the subject of cannibalism, provided in-depth editing and information. His help, advice and knowledge are greatly appreciated.

Dr. Garniss Curtis, professor emeritus of geology, University of California, Berkeley, for long hours of reading, his dedication to accuracy, his integrity and, most of all, for his friendship over the course of many years.

Professor Ralph Holloway, Department of Anthropology, Columbia University, for his constant encouragement and for keeping me on track and never letting me give up.

Dr. Alan J. Almquist, California State University, Hayward, Department of Anthropology, author and former grants and programs officer for the L.S.B. Leakey Foundation, provided substantive editing and relevant comments—I owe him dinner.

Others who made a difference are the following professors, authors, professionals and mentors in the fields of paleoanthropology, archaeology, gastronomy, primatology, brain research, psychiatry, geology, genetics, law, particle physics and religion: John Morgan Allman, Juan Luis Arsuaga, Berhane Asfaw, Jean Auel, Carol Beckwith, Ron J. Clarke, Anna Belfer-Cohen, Leigh Bienen, Robert Bloominshiem, C.K. Brain, Alison Brooks, Larry Burton, Frank Brown, Daniel Buxhoeveden, Basil Cooke, John Costello, Eric Delson, Harold Dibble, Jan Fawcet, Angela Fisher, Jacob H. Fox, Birute M.F. Galdikas, Jane Goodall, Lance Grande, Jack Harris, Henry Harpending, Erima Henare, Kevin D. Hunt, Donald C. Johanson, Jean Joho, Alan Kahn, Leon Lederman, Rena Lederman, Roger Lewin, Shirley Lindenbaum, Alan Mann, Ian McDougall, William McGrew, James F. O'Connell, Yoel Rak, Rudy Raff, William Rice, Kathy Schick, Sileshi Semaw, Gabino Sotelino, Dietrich Stout, Carl Swisher, Ian Tattersall, Alan Thorne, Phillip Tobias, Nicholas Toth, Jill Van Cleave, Paola Villa, Tim White, Hans Willimann, Milford Wolpoff and John Yellen.

And in remembrance: J. Desmond Clark, Betty Baume Clark, F. Clark Howell and Raymond Dart.

To Joan Travis, without whom I could have never entered into the inner sanctum of paleoanthropology, I owe an unpayable debt of gratitude.

And to my Australian friend, Alex Harris, who, in 1998, gave me the book *Cannibals, Cows & the CJD Catastrophe*, which inspired the formulation of a hypothesis concerning the demise of the Neanderthals, which, in turn, prompted research into the topic of cannibalism that led to the writing of this book—a very large thank you indeed.

I am also indebted to Susan Heffron and Gretchen Notzold of the Teton County, Wyoming branch library in Alta, who pulled through with out-of-print volumes; Michael Harrison and Therry Frey for loaning me their unique volumes on New Guinea; Dr. Michael Huckman for allowing me time with his prized volumes, John McCarter for use of the Field

Museum's library; and David Coolidge for sending me the book *Flyboys* by James Bradley.

Last, but never least, go hugs to my husband, Dr. Leo M. Henikoff, a harsh, unflagging editor who stood by—or went fishing—through more than seven years of research, travel and writing . . . even though, during the first two years of this project, he referred to me as "The Ghoul," and in the same breath, asked when dinner would be ready.

And of course, there is my publisher, Jeffrey Goldman, whose excitement, talents and dedication to the publication of *Dinner with a Cannibal* proved to be prodigious.

DINNER

WITH A
CANNIBAL

FOREWORD

by Christy G. Turner II

inner with a Cannibal is a terrifically well-written, exhaustively re-searched, and frequently chilling story of humankind's ancient and modern murderous consumptive behavior. Inspired by her master chef father, and plentifully versed in human prehistory, Carole A. Travis-Henikoff previously wrote a highly praised cookbook,[1] followed, naturally it seems to me, by this more anthropological dietary account. Such accounts have, until recently, usually been shrouded by heavy-blanketing taboo.

It has often been said in various ways that we are all prisoners of our own experience. That which we know little or nothing about is commonly disbelieved, and sometimes considered a dangerous and taboo subject. Of all the taboo topics at one time rarely discussed in an open fash-ion—cancer, death, sexual behavior, witchcraft, many others—the topic of cannibalism remains among the last to shed its taboo imprisonment. Human cannibalism is rarely talked about except briefly in some college-level anthropology classes, although it has long been a subject for cartoon art depicting fat, pith-helmeted jungle explorers about to be cooked in a large iron pot—usually a racist jibe at tropical Africans. While I know of some other recent book-length writings on cannibalism, *Dinner with a Cannibal* is the broadest and most up-to-date work to break the hold taboo has on the subject. Oddly, starting in 1979, its taboo status actually increased because of an anthropologist named William Arens. Arens claimed cannibalism has never been witnessed by reliable observers, and therefore likely occurred only in occasional starvation or sociopathic situations. That claim has since been refuted over and over in recent years but just in rather inaccessible scholarly journals. Certainly none of these publications can be found in street-corner or airport bookstands. It is this body of recent and earlier scholarly literature that is broadly and carefully synthesized by the author.

The taboo surrounding even the use of the "C" word is itself remarkable. I have a few archaeology colleagues who can barely bring themselves to use the C word. Instead they refer to my findings, excavated at numerous prehistoric southwestern U.S. sites, which show clear evidence of cannibalism, as "extreme processing," a politically correct euphemism if ever there was one. Another Southwest archaeologist has reportedly proclaimed that use of the C word should cease altogether. Politically correct efforts at word excommunication have a long history, some rightfully so—as in the case of racial or ethnic slurs—others, simply foolish or patronizing, as in the above two examples concerning the word "cannibalism."

The modern form of the cannibalism taboo is linked to political correctness and the neutering of the relevant language. I predict that all the protestations surrounding the study and discussion of cannibalism will be swept away after the general public and interested scholars read Carole A. Travis-Henikoff's *Dinner with a Cannibal*. Why do I feel this way?

Well, for starters, the author has a deceptively well-crafted and witty writing style that carries the reader along as effortlessly as with the best whodunit. In fact, *DWAC* is a fascinating scientific whodunit: who ate whom and why? Travis-Henikoff sees cannibalism as an ancient and natural adaptive strategy that kept early humans alive until seasonally scarce food resources improved. Travis-Henikoff is not alone in her "hunger hypothesis" for cannibalism. Famed psychologist Lewis Petrinovich (*The Cannibal Within*) documented similar starvation situations. Equally famous paleoanthropologist Tim White made a compelling case for nutritional cannibalism in his study of butchered and cooked prehistoric human remains excavated near Mesa Verde National Park, Colorado. And Travis-Henikoff's scholarship is excellent, although it never gets in the way of an engaging read.

Secondly, as mentioned, Travis-Henikoff has done her homework. I found myself repeatedly taking notes on references that I had missed in my 40 years of researching the subject of cannibalism. I missed most of the literature on cannibalism detailed in biblical and other religious writings. This oversight prevented me from appreciating how important human sacrifice and cannibalism were in the early ceremonies and practices of the Judeo-Christian religions. This information has led me to think that the Spanish proclamation against Aztec cannibalism was not just a way to dehumanize the Mexicans so that they could be colonially exploited, as some historical reconstructionists would have us believe, rather there were ancient cannibalized skeletons in the Christian closet. Needless to say, *DWAC* is a taboo-buster, and its comprehensiveness and clarity of explanation are equal to the best popular anthropological writing of today— Brian Fagan, Roger Lewin, Jared Diamond, and others. It contains much food for thought, and it is meaty enough to satisfy even the hungriest of graduate students.

The story of human consumption is made all the more acceptable with the author's review of cannibalism in the nonhuman animal world. Various invertebrates, fish, amphibians, and mammals are naturally or situationally cannibalistic. As for the human story, Travis-Henikoff guides us around the world in an in-depth tour of recent, prehistoric, and ancient incidents of cannibalism practiced by diverse cultures in Oceania, Australia, East Asia, Africa, the Americas, and yes, even in pre-Christian and

Christian Europe. No major human group escapes her eye for documentary detail, history, and types of cannibalism practiced. Cooking methods, organ preferences, and other culinary facts could only be professionally detailed by someone well acquainted with the art of high cuisine. Her story is based on news reports, ethnographic accounts, documentary reconstructions, ancient writings, and fossil and sub-fossil human bone processing (cut marks, perimortem breakage, burning, cooking, etc., similar to the bone damage seen in butchered game animals). Total consumption and skeletal destruction leave not a gram of evidence in some groups, hinting that prehistoric cannibalism in those areas will not be easy to come by.

Europeans were rather good at cannibalism (including a widespread medical variant), along with the torture, rape, and burning of witches, and werewolf hunts. Cannibalism was specifically outlawed by royal Spanish decree following the initiation of the Spanish church and state inquisition in 1481. With the Inquisition came the legal enforcement of the cannibalism taboo. But, as Travis-Henikoff relates in much detail, the taboo has been violated throughout twentieth-century Eurasia—in politically driven episodes of starvation in the Soviet Union (i.e., Stalin), in large scale outbreaks of politically-motivated Chinese cannibalism (i.e., Mao), and by commanding thousands of unsupplied Japanese military troops to fend for themselves following their invasion of China. Her details about cannibalism during World War II in the Pacific paint an even grimmer picture of modern human cannibalism. Stories about isolated, starving Eskimo groups eating their dying or dead elders are trivial by comparison.

The author notes that today we and the media generally associate cannibalism with sociopathic and psychopathic individuals, invariably male loners. She notes that this sort of mentally disturbed cannibalism is very rare, and most contemporary and recent cases of cannibalism involve starvation or a culturally determined pattern of consumptive acts that often were associated with feelings of loss and grief for the consumed person. She uses Beth Conklin's recent study of the South American Wari tribe to exemplify cannibalism and cultural patterning.

Travis-Henikoff is very well versed in anthropology, especially paleoanthropology, and is personally acquainted with many of the scholars who practice this science of very ancient human life and evolution. Hence, she is able to paint a highly credible picture of human cannibalism that goes back hundreds of thousands of years. This information from bones, when coupled with genetic data on prion disease, leads to a reasonable hypothesis that proposes our ancestors were all cannibals. There is nothing to be ashamed of. Cannibalism has been one of the "tools" in the human tool kit that has enabled us to be here today, and not extinct as was the fate of so many stronger, larger, and more numerous species at the end of the last ice age when humans had spread to all parts of the world except the deep Pacific.

I predict that the reader will enjoy this book as much as I did. Who other than a gastronomic enthusiast could write such an entertaining and enlightening book on cannibalism? But it isn't just about cannibalism, and that adds to the flavor of this delightful mental morsel.

INTRODUCTION

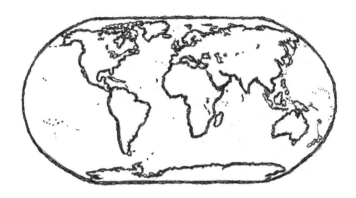

"Man, a domesticated animal still extensively raised, one wonders why, since it is rarely eaten nowadays."

—Waverley Root, from his book *Food*

Few people believe their ancestors practiced cannibalism, and some scholars deny its existence altogether, but the truth is . . . we all have cannibals in our closets.[1]

Cannibalism is the ingestion of others of one's own species and is practiced throughout the animal kingdom, from one-celled organisms to humans. The reason for cannibalism's ubiquitous nature lies in its antiquity. Recent finds of species-specific tooth marks on dinosaur bones prove occurrences of cannibalism dating back to the Mesozoic era.

Today, many people see themselves as standing outside the realm of the animal kingdom, but as living creatures with functional brains, we are not only animals, but the dominating force that holds sway over the magnificent puzzle of global biota that exists on planet Earth. We, *Homo sapiens sapiens* ("really smart man"), are the most intriguing piece of that magnificent, global puzzle; a piece that once fit neatly within the framework of the whole.

From our very beginnings, human cannibalism has been practiced for numerous reasons, many of which have been labeled. Starvation brings on "survival" cannibalism, while the ingestion of dead relatives is known as "endocannibalism" or "funerary" cannibalism. "Exocannibalism" refers to the eating of one's enemies, whereas "religious" cannibalism relates to the actual or simulated partaking of human flesh as part of a religious rite. For example, the Aztecs practicing cannibalism to keep the sun from dying versus Christian Communion.

In "ritual," or "token," cannibalism, a specified part of an adversary, ruler, or family member is consumed, as in the eating of an enemy's heart, or the eyes of a previous chief eaten by an incoming chief, or the drinking of a family member's cremated ashes mixed in a watery broth—though many would label the drinking of ash-broth funerary.

"Medicinal" (iatric) cannibalism is one of the most fascinating, as none of the medical or apothecary journals ever saw fit to identify the ingestion of physician-prescribed medicines made from human cadavers as being acts of cannibalism. Nevertheless, human flesh is human flesh, and the consuming of it by another human constitutes an act of cannibalism.

With "gastronomic" cannibalism, human flesh is dealt with and eaten without ceremony (other than culinary), in the same manner as the flesh of any other animal. The most reliable sources state that human flesh resembles beef, though it is lighter in color and texture, and, according to some, the most delicious of meats. The commonly known moniker "long pig" will be discussed in the text, but Pacific Islanders related the taste of human flesh to pork for the simple reason that prior to contact with the rest of the world, the only meat-producing mammal of reasonable size available to them was the wild pig.

Autophagy (to eat of one's self) ranges from the little boy who picks his nose to torture-induced self-consumption and truly disturbed individuals who cook and eat pieces of their own flesh.

One other form of cannibalism should be noted as it graces the pages of this book. It is referred to as "benign" cannibalism because the diner has no knowledge of what kind of meat he is eating . . . or has already eaten.

As individuals, we are a summation of our unique genetics, all we have experienced, and what we have been taught to believe. If the people within the society to which you were born practice cannibalism, burn people at stakes, make war, promote terrorism, or scarify their bodies, chances are you will do the same.

This volume investigates not only the subject of cannibalism, but when and why people ate those of their own kind and continue to do so to this very day. The *why* of cannibalism forces the examination of many surrounding subjects, from the many foods we eat, to the caves of our ancient past, to what makes us human. How do belief systems affect our lives? Are we different today from our ancestors of yesteryear? Do the memes of the societies we live in dictate our beliefs and our actions? Where do religions fit in? Are religions more powerful than kings, queens and governments? Do governing bodies use religions and/or belief systems to control the masses? Do we function instinctually, or are we mere tools of our societies? How did we get to where and how we are today? How different are we, one society to another? And how do we differ from our most ancient ancestors?

Dinner with a Cannibal presents the history of cannibalism in concert with human development, making note of religions and societies that either condoned or outlawed the practice. Through the following pages we will look at cannibalism from every angle in order to gain comprehension of the incredible, ancient/up-to-the-minute, multifaceted panoply that is the reality of cannibalism.

The interpretation of human cannibalism used in this volume is the ingestion of any part of the human form, including fluids or matter emanating from the body.

Information for this book was gathered over a seven-year period from authoritative primary sources. Research materials and investigations used for accepting the fact that human cannibalism was and is real and not uncommon, include scientific reports; firsthand accounts; anthropological and archaeological evidence; historical, anthropological and archaeological writings; recent news reports; and the analyzing of belief systems. Advice, editing, readings and contributions from leading professors, paleoanthropologists, archaeologists and scientists from multiple fields, plus physician specialists, directed and tightened the work.

I have used the names of various tribes and peoples only when the literature has been highly publicized or those listed are deceased. The main thrust of this book is to consider the human condition rather than to present a litany of everyone known to have practiced cannibalism.

Bon appétit.

Carole A. Travis-Henikoff

HOW WE GOT

TO
WHERE
WE
ARE

CHAPTER ONE

THE INCREDIBLE FOODS WE EAT

This longest of chapters begins with a light repast, something akin to an amuse-bouche that is placed before you in the finest of restaurants: something you didn't order, but the chef wants you to have, something to tickle your brain and please your palate. Following the amuse you will be served several other courses, culminating with a heavy plate of reality that calls for a bit of intestinal fortitude.

umanity's palate is more varied than that of any other animal on Earth, but our amazing menu did not happen by accident. Over the eons, repeated bouts of starvation, in combination with the evolutionary enlargement and complexity of the human brain, prompted experimentation and discovery concerning what was, and was not, edible. Today, diverse cultures hold fast to selected lists of acceptable foods, and while one culture may relish rat embryos, another passes on all but hamburgers and pizza.

Shortly after meeting Li, a college student at University of Illinois at Chicago, he asked if I would help him with his English.

"Yes," I replied, "but there will be a charge."

Crestfallen, Li said, "Oh, I have little money," then turned to go.

"Don't you want to know my price?"

Li turned back.

"You can pay me in words," I said. "The rules will be that I can ask you any question about your life, your thoughts and your country; of course, you may ask me the same kind of questions." It was the start of a wonderful friendship.

One day, Li and I decide to go out for lunch at a Chinese restaurant. As we enter, I take note that I am the only "round eye" present; a good sign, as the food should be authentic. Being a Tuesday morning, business is slow; there are no dim sum carts rolling through crowded aisles. From the menu Li and I order steamed pork ribs, steamed shrimp dumplings, squid in curry, fresh pea sprouts cooked with garlic and oil, spareribs, pan-fried spring rolls heavy with wild mushrooms, and chicken feet. I like them all, but the pea sprouts, spring rolls and chicken feet are my favorites.

Li and I find that we both dislike plastic chopsticks; they are too slippery. The best chopsticks are made of bamboo. Bamboo is a gift of the gods. With it you can do and/or build almost anything. Razor sharp knives, a house, water and food containers, cooking implements, furniture, bridges, boats, rafts, fishing poles, cups, chopsticks, you name it, all from bamboo. Bamboo is also a food and so versatile and utilitarian that it has strongly influenced all cultures that have shared its habitation. Prior to meeting the "white man," the Fore of Papua New Guinea, would dismember and de-flesh their dead with bamboo knives then steam the brains in bamboo tubes while roasting the rest of the body. Li and I get to work with our plastic chopsticks.

Our tea arrives and the discussion turns to the hot, steaming brew now known to stimulate one's immune system. In China, when someone pours tea for another, the receiver softly taps the first joints of the first two fingers of his right hand on the table as a thank you. The custom stems from when an emperor left the confines of the Forbidden Palace dressed as a common man. When the emperor, and the subject he had chosen to accompany him, entered a teahouse, the emperor turned the tables on his companion by pouring the tea. The man could not prostrate himself on the floor before his emperor as custom would have it, as doing so would have given away the plainclothes emperor, so he curled the first two fingers of his right hand and made them kneel to his Lord and Master as a subtle way of saying "I bow down to you." It is a great bit of sign language that allows one to say thank you without interrupting conversation, but take note, it is only done for the pouring of tea.

Our discussion continues on to one of my favorite subjects—food. Being the daughter of a master chef and a cookbook writer with a lifetime of study in the field of paleoanthropology—the study of human origins—I know that all things edible have been consumed by someone, somewhere on this planet. J. Desmond Clark, one of paleoanthropology's most revered, proved the point when he wrote me regarding a first draft of this chapter:

> I greatly enjoyed Dim Sum in China when we were working there between 1987–1993. It is so much better than Dim Sum in California. Yes, I have also eaten most of what you mentioned as Chinese delicacies—bees, scorpions, caterpillars and turtle—but I do not think I was offered snake, though I have eaten that elsewhere. In Africa, besides termites and caterpillars, I have tried various other delicacies. Also, locusts and mopane worms are good eating.

Li and I begin our discussion with onions. The Chinese use green onions exclusively. In the north of China, they use very large green onions that can be an inch or more across at the base, while in southern China they grow and prefer small, thin green onions. Li explains how all foods are chosen for their medicinal and health-giving properties and that the Chinese only use herbal medicines for serious illnesses. On a daily basis the Chinese regulate their diet for the sake of controlling health, sleep and fortitude. For instance, eating liver is good for your liver, kidneys for the kidneys, drinking certain teas for a peaceful continence and so on.

I tell of dining at a four-star restaurant in Spain and ordering pig cheeks—actually part of the upper neck—and how the chef took a perfect rectangle of meat, complete with its skin and fat, roasted it in a hot oven until the skin was a glowing mahogany color, brought the dish out for me to admire, then whisked it back to the kitchen where he carefully removed the mahogany skin, followed by all of the fat. The fat was discarded, but the meat and skin were each cut in half, re-stacked and served forth on a hot plate. Best pork I have ever eaten. As I speak, Li takes a piece of pork rib. I remark that the Chinese have concocted delicious ways of cooking anything edible, and how they have the broadest palates on the planet. "As far as I know, there is simply nothing you Chinese will not eat."

Li laughs. He says they have a saying, "A China man eats everything with four legs but the table."

"And you also eat fried honey bees, locusts, scorpions, raccoon-dogs, frogs, unborn rats, pangolins, bats and snakes, to mention just a few."

"Of course," says Li, "and anything else that crawls, flies or swims."

We journey on to snake meat and how it needs to be cooked for a long time. Li likes snake; he says that many believe the more poisonous the snake the better the flesh, but he has had both and to him they all taste the same. Then he tells me of a soup-based dish called Tiger Fights Dragon, or Tiger Fighting Dragon, where steamed civet cat is placed into the soup to represent the tiger and a snake is steamed and added for the dragon. Then the pot is allowed to simmer so the two can fight it out for taste. It is a well-known dish served in the winter as it is very hearty and makes the body warm.

"You mean it's a very spicy dish, right?" I say.

"No," says Li, "it's not spicy, but it makes you very hot inside. It's very good."

"Have you ever eaten dog?" I ask. I am relishing the conversation as we are getting into foods few Americans would try.

"Oh yes."

"How is it?" I ask, while thinking of my youngest child, a six-year-old chocolate lab named Sam. Li tells me dog is good, very mild in flavor, very nice.

Waverley Root, in his fabulous book *Food* says that D is "for dog; which is what you get if you order 'special beef' in Hong Kong." Mr. Root follows with a list of many other, more common comestibles starting with the letter "D."

I tell Li about my great-grandfather, who was a Frenchman from Alsace Lorraine, an area that has been snatched back and forth between France and Germany many times over the centuries. Sometime in the mid-1800s, my great-grandfather went to Paris and was invited to a 12-course meal. It was tuxedo time and there was a butler for every two guests. The whole affair was extremely formal and magnificent. About the fifth or sixth course down, a preparation of meat was served. My great-grandfather tasted it, and then devoured it; it was delicious! Not wanting to appear stupid or rude, Great-Grandfather waited for an opportune moment to quietly ask his butler what the meat was in that particular course. "Why dog, monsieur." Great-Grandfather's reaction was involuntary, and he barely made it to the gutter before losing his most marvelous meal.

Li's eyes tell me he thinks of my great-grandfather as having been naïve and un-adventuresome. This reminds me once again that our palates are trained from birth. If you are a South American Indian, leaf-encapsulated roasted larvae from a large caterpillar are as toasted marshmallows to an American youngster. Many of us love caviar (fish eggs), escargot (snails) and Mountain Oysters (sheep testicles). My great-grandmother, who married my great-grandfather after he returned pale and green from France, simply wasn't happy if she didn't have her scrambled eggs and calf brains on Sunday morning.

Li nods at this, assuring me the Chinese know the culinary worth of brains. I tell him how brains are the most caloric food on the planet. Pure butter is a wimp next to them. Even bone marrow, a favorite of our earliest ancestor—and my husband—cannot hold a candle to the succulent fattiness of brains.

I can see by the light in Li's eyes that nothing will diminish his appetite, so I continue, remarking how most cannibals had a predilection for brains, and how live monkey brains are a great delicacy in many countries. Li nods and says he has heard of this, so I tell him about my friend Will Aydelotte.

In 1969, Will was in Saigon selling various supplies to the American Armed Forces when he was invited to dine with seven others in Cholon, the Chinese section of the city. The men were greeted by the restaurant's owner, and then escorted into a side dining room where eight individual round tables made from palm centers stood. On top of each small table was a silver presentation dome. Next to and surrounding each dome was an eight-inch, sharp-sided silver spoon, a pair of chopsticks and six bowls, each containing a different sauce (one being made from beetles). When the men were seated waiters came forward to remove the domes and Will found himself staring at the top of a monkey's cranium sticking up through a hole and held securely in place with a metal clamp. To add to his displeasure, the top of the skull and the brain's dura had been removed leaving the live brain exposed. (Will said you could hear the monkeys scratching on the cage-like interiors of the tables). The men began to eat as Will watched. First the sharp silver spoon was used to carve the brain into bite-size pieces; the scratching stopped. Then the chopsticks were used to pick up a piece of brain, dip it in a sauce of the diner's choosing, and pop it into the mouth. Will was greatly relieved when the other diners finished their incredibly expensive first course and the group moved to a round table in the main dining room where *normal* foods, such as delicious, six-inch-long freshwater shrimp, along with dozens of other dishes, were offered.

If you are an Indiana Jones fan, you have seen fake monkey heads with the tops of their craniums removed being served in handsome dishes to Harrison Ford and his female sidekick in the movie *Indiana Jones and the Temple of Doom*. Hollywood being Hollywood, they got the silver dome right, but in real life the monkey must be alive and the diner never sees the face of the animal. As I recall, Indie's girlfriend faints, and I believe that if Will had been a female rather than a six-foot, four-inch man, he may have done the same.

The writer of the movie *Hannibal*, starring Anthony Hopkins, obviously took the idea for the last 15 minutes of the film from the practice of eating live monkey brains. The rude fellow who was speaking as he was experiencing a prefrontal lobotomy the hard way—should it have been a real occurrence—would have experienced no pain or sensation, since the brain has no sensory nerve endings. Brain surgeons keep their patients conscious during surgery so as to aid them in their delicate task.

As to monkey brains, it is something my great-grandmother would have been comfortable with, though I feel strongly that she would have demanded that hers be sautéed. The lethal and frightening outbreak of mad cow disease in England took brains out of meat cases and changed all recipes for "pasties," which the British had made with calf brains for centuries. In America, calf brains were the most favored, but the last brains I saw for sale were small lamb brains. Sheep, calf or monkey, the various organs of the body taste much the same from one species to the next, even when the species in question is human; just ask Hannibal or Takeru Kobayashi, who scarfed down 57 cow brains (17.7 pounds) in 15 minutes at an international competitive eating contest! His accomplishment no doubt constituted the most calories ever ingested within a 15-minute time period by a human being.

Aside from being the most nutritious of foods, brains are also good for the curing of hides when making leather. The natural enzymes, proteins, lipids and fats found in brain tissue soften and strengthen the hide. Most interesting is that in the case of most mammals, the brain/body ratio works out to be the correct amount of brain needed for the curing of the animal's hide.

Back to my friend Will, whose food thrills did not end with monkey brains. A few weeks after his most memorable meal, friends in the American Special Forces division took Will up to a mountain village where they were served a marvelous stew baked in coconut shells. When Will learned that he was eating monkey stew, he hesitated, then reasoned that we eat all sorts of animal protein and proceeded to enjoy the delicious meal with relish until the small hand of a monkey presented itself in the bowl of his spoon.

Waverley Root, on the subject of brains, tells of an occurrence of strained relations between Zaire (Congo) and Egypt when the soccer team from Zaire brought live monkeys with them to Alexandria. The Zaire team demanded the monkeys be slaughtered and served as directed in order to produce what they considered proper and nourishing food. The Egyptian cooks refused, thus damaging relations between the two countries.

I have never eaten brains, but I love sweetbreads, which can be the thymus glands, salivary glands or pancreas of veal. French chefs prefer the thymus, a gland that produces lymphocytes, which aid the immune system. Thymus glands are always harvested from young steers, as the thymus of all vertebrates (including humans) is very large from birth until pubescence, at which time it shrinks dramatically.

The finest sweetbreads I ever had were served to us in Leon, Spain; they had been blanched, peeled, poached, weighted and sliced, then lightly floured and fried to a fine crispness in hot oil. We went 60 miles out of our way to partake of another helping on our return trip back to Madrid.

Of similar taste, but less delicate, are the testes of various animals. Mountain Oysters come from sheep and are quite tasty, but bulls offer larger portions in the same packaging. In Paxton, Nebraska, at Ole's Big Game Steakhouse, we ordered Bull Balls for an appetizer, which arrived sliced, breaded and fried. Nice dish, a bit over-done, but one was sufficient for the two of us.

On the same note, my father's best friend, Stockton Quincy, owned what he called a "ranch" (complete with duck ponds) south of Bakersfield, California. Whenever we visited "Rancho NanQ," we would go to Stocky's favorite Basque restaurant. The Basques are numerous in the area as the surrounding hills are well suited for the grazing of sheep, and the Basques are renowned shepherds. Stocky's favorite dish was Mountain Oysters, and huge platters of deep-fried "oysters" would be set before us. One night, as we were dining on a large platter of testicular delicacies, Stocky looked at my father and said, "Carl, you are a master chef, where the hell do these people find these oysters? I have fished and walked over every stream in this state and have never seen the likes of an oyster." Everyone laughed, my father the hardest.

Stocky never ate Mountain Oysters again, even though they had been his all-time favorite dish; such is the power of reason, or lack thereof. I wonder what Stocky's reaction would have been to blood-filled sheep's bladder, a very healthy favorite in Mongolia.

Back in Spain in a mountain-top restaurant, on a Sunday afternoon, when all of the farmers were taking their families to dinner, we ordered one of our favorites, morcilla (blood sausage—a national dish in Spain) and caldo ("farmer's pot"), which consisted of everything the meat market couldn't or wouldn't sell: snouts, ears, lips, feet and heaven knows what else. Much of it was edible, and if I had been starving, it would have been delicious. I was glad not to see any eyeballs in the pot; I know many people love them, but they are simply not to my liking. I don't like solitary body parts that look back at me.

The farmer's pot reminded me of Claire and her husband John, who attended a formal dinner in Liberia where each diner was served a stewed monkey hand in a bowl of clear broth. A more experienced guest sitting down table from them gently spooned the hand out of the bowl and ate it with his fingers, much as you would eat a piece of chicken. As with my friend Will Aydelotte, Claire and John found the dish to be a bit beyond them.

As the waiter pours more tea, I ask Li, "So dog is good?" hoping he will say no.

He explains, "It is a dish eaten in winter like the Tiger and Dragon dish; it too makes the body warm." Knowing Li's level of English I again think he means something else; that the dish is hot due to peppers and spices, but he insists that is not the case, that these particular dishes make you warm because of the meats they contain.

Holding back my tears, I tell him about my son Brett losing his dog to some entrepreneurial Vietnamese who opened a backroom butcher shop in Seattle through which they sold fresh dog meat to other Vietnamese. Unfortunately, they were procuring the meat by picking up strays or people's pets that were in the habit of taking themselves for a walk. Brett went to the police station to pick up his dog's collar and left with a broken heart.

I tell Li of a book that claimed the Chinese only eat certain kinds of dogs and of a Chinese student who told his professor that black dogs are preferred over white ones. Li gives me an "I'm not so sure about that" look at which time I think of the Eskimos who, when starving, ate their dogs before consuming their old women, and the many other tribes scattered around the globe, including the French of yesterday, who recognized a good piece of meat.

Actually, the Chinese raise chow chows for the pot, which is why we say, "Let's go grab some chow." They also farm-raise monkeys, bats, snakes, turtles and many other delicacies for consumption. The Maoris of New Zealand raised dogs as we raise sheep—to cook and wear.

(Note: The bats the Chinese raise for consumption are known as "horseshoe bats." In 2005, scientists discovered that the lethal SARS virus originates in horseshoe bats. Animals bitten by infected bats pass the disease onto humans.)

Scanning the menu for a second time I comment that I don't see any duck tongues. I know Li likes tongue. By going through cookbooks with pictures, I have been teaching Li the names of foods. When we saw a photo of a cow's tongue ready for the pot in an Italian cookbook, Li had immediately put his finger to his tongue and said, "good."

I tell of dining in a fabulous Chinese restaurant in Toronto. On the menu was a dish listed simply as duck tongues. My husband ordered them immediately. A lovely little oval plate was placed before him with 13 little tongues neatly arranged in a graceful arch. With nothing else gracing the plate, the tongues created a simple bow of Asian beauty; they were delicious. All tongue, regardless of species, tastes like tongue. Even though they had come from a duck, the inch-long tongues tasted much like, and as good as, any cow's tongue my father had ever prepared—a bit chewier perhaps; too much quacking.

Changing animals, I mention how the French and Belgians love horsemeat (importing much of it from America), and how, on Thursdays past, the Harvard Club of New York offered horsemeat for lunch and sometimes dinner. Li nods as I go on to tell of an archaeological site, dated at 110,000 years, that proved at least one group of our European cousins, the Neanderthals, ate more horse than any other kind of meat, with the now extinct auroch (a species of cattle) coming in second, followed by a third-placed deer. Li notes there aren't many horses in China. Of course not! They ate them all!

The chicken feet arrive and I quickly grab for one with my slippery plastic chopsticks. The feet are simmered for a good long while and then roasted slowly with a sauce. They are quite delicious, the sauce being reminiscent of a mild barbecue sauce. It is polite to bite off a digit or two, chew and suck the meat from the tiny cartilaginous bones, then deposit them on your plate using either your fingers or chopsticks.

Dim sum with Li made me hungry to know more. I needed to extend my search for the boundaries of the human palate. Searching for something wild, I found *Man Eating Bugs: The Art and Science of Eating Insects*, in the bookstore in the Field Museum in Chicago. The book is a global overview of culinary insects, spiders and invertebrates preferred by various cultures. As the authors, Peter Menzel and Faith D'Aluisio, traveled the world, they sampled what they found and even collected recipes for the adventurous, or very hungry, gourmet. The book can either whet your appetite or ruin it, but most certainly, it will fascinate you.

A sampling for your dining pleasure: In Mexico you can eat meal-worms and spaghetti or mealworm quiche, grasshopper tacos, stinkbug pâté, tarantula or wasp-larvae tacos and many other delicacies, such as crickets. Throughout Asia you will find a wide variety of bugs and crawly things: water beetles, stinkbugs (that global favorite that adds iodine to your diet, and is a blessing to those living where iodized salt is unavailable), fried or raw scorpions, deep-fried tarantulas, giant female red ants, the blood and gallbladder contents of snakes, plus menu delights such as "Deer Penis with Herbs" or "Deer Penis Soup" (good for stamina and sexual prowess), flesh-colored marine worms, plump pink silk worm pu-pae, water bug larvae, cicadas, dung beetles, "Fresh" ant butter, bamboo worms, dried bumble bees (cures sore throat), and insect shit teas (no doubt medicinal).

In Thailand, there is a highly prized dish, manda, for which I have the recipe: Grate raw mango into a bowl, add hot chilies, garlic, lime juice and sugar. Mash together well, then add one manda rice-paddy beetle, mash a bit more and serve. A manda rice-paddy beetle is four inches long and one and a half inches wide; it is strong and spicy in taste—so I'm told. "Manda" is also the slang word for pimp.

In Indonesia, when important company is invited to dinner, hosts prepare dog for honored guests, with dragonflies as an appetizer. Author Peter Menzel tells of being so honored, "I wouldn't purposefully seek out dog for food, but I must admit it was good."

In South Africa, the authors found the iodine-rich stinkbugs again, along with grasshoppers, mopane worms (a national favorite) and termites. In Uganda, it was live termites (heads only—more brain food) and palm grubs. In Botswana, more live termites and mopane worms.

Back across the Atlantic in Colombia people eat ants, while in Peru they love tayro kuroworms and guinea pigs. Millions of guinea pigs are raised for food, but a select few are used to cure people of all types of medical disorders. The animals are held against the site of the malady, or, in some cases, rubbed over the entire body. Therapeutic guinea pigs are neither killed nor consumed.

On an extremely crowded flight from Seattle to Chicago, I met a priest from Peru. His ancestry was native Peruvian with a dash of Spanish. He was a multilingual, fascinating individual. We spoke of my work on this volume, South America, past and present, and the infamous healing guinea pigs, which are rubbed over "sick" areas of the body while a shaman chants his healing messages. The priest's comment: "I had disbelieved all reports of healings through the use of guinea pigs but have since witnessed many healings where the malady never returned. I have no idea what occurs and can only believe that the strong beliefs held by the patients work to promote healing from within."

Further west in Australia, witchetty grubs are so good that Australians of English descent make a party dip of them or fry them up for a tasty meal. The Aussies say they taste like a tender cheese omelette. The native Aborigines were the first to discover the delicious flavor of witchetty grubs along with honeypot ants and Bogong moths. For their apothecary, they use the innards of cockroaches as a topical anesthetic while other insects form a medicine chest of remedies.

Man Eating Bugs is proof positive of one of the points this book hopes to make. If everyone in your family, village, town, city or country does XYZ, or eats CDE, then you will look upon XYZ and the eating of CDE as being normal, rational and positive, or, at the very least, accepted practices. Because of how and where you were raised you may not wish to eat scorpions, grubs, insect larvae, tarantulas, worms, stinkbugs, grasshoppers, or maggots or drink insect shit teas, but millions of people on this planet look upon such items as delicacies.

It should be noted that worms are 90% protein and insects, grubs and larvae are also high on the charts. Our earliest ancestors, along with many of our living primate relatives, maintained their health and added to their survival by consuming such foodstuffs. All of which reminds me of the story of when my husband's son Troy was a little boy. A friend returning from Africa had brought Leo a box of chocolate covered insects. Troy walked in and saw the opened box of "candy" on his father's desk. "What are these, Dad?" he asked. Acting as though the contents of the box were the finest chocolates in the world, Leo said, "Why they're chocolate covered insects from lands far away. See, there's a grasshopper, here's an ant, here's a—" Suddenly, Troy's little hand shot out, grabbed a grasshopper and popped it into his mouth, then he chewed, swallowed and grinned up at his father, "Which one are you going to have, Dad?" Dad ate the bee.

Enough of bugs and grubs. In *The Virginia City Cook Book*, I discovered tasty items served to the 45,000 people who lived through the 1860s and 1870s in the high mountain city whose scanty remains sit as a tiny ghost town visited by millions of tourists. Thank God the "Bucket of Blood Saloon" has stood the test of time.

The billion-dollar Comstock Lode was torn out in hunks and nuggets as dray loads of gold and silver trudged towards town and the assay office. Virginia City boasted an opera house where the most famous performers of the day performed to diamond-adorned, evening-gowned women who applauded through satin gloves. Even President Grant took the time to visit Virginia City, which was then known as "the most important city between Chicago and the Pacific Ocean."

What did all those gold-fevered people eat aside from foie gras and Old Virginny Pickled Nasturtium Seeds? Brain croquettes, Dutch Nick's Marrow Toast, Katie's Fried Pigs Feet, Lou Siegriest's Wild Horse Stew, Lucius Beebe's Deviled Grilled Beef Bones, kidneys in white wine, deer liver and tripe. (Tripe: a portion of the stomach of a ruminant used as food which must be simmered for many hours. Ruminant: cud-chewing, hoofed mammals with an even number of toes and stomachs with multiple chambers; for example, cattle, camels and giraffes.) The gold diggers enjoyed pickled and soused tripe; tripe Espagnole; tripe a la mode de Washoe; and menudo, the Mexican dish made with tripe and eaten very early in the morning after a heavy night of drinking, and said to cure any hangover. And, of course, Son-of-a-Bitch Stew, which originated amongst cowhands when a steer was butchered. In Virginia City, it was made whenever a deer was shot. Either way, the ingredients are heart, liver, tongue, kidneys, sweetbreads (if an immature animal was taken) and brains all cooked together with a bit of salt pork, some onion and very little water, if any.

Son-of-a-Bitch Stew is an upscale (in quality and nourishment offered by its ingredients) American cousin to haggis, Scotland's most famous dish. To make haggis you take a sheep's stomach (a sheep is not a ruminant) and fill it with a mixture of fat, onion, some Scotch oatmeal, seasonings and the cut-up heart, lungs and liver of the sheep. Sew the whole thing up, prick with a pin and simmer in water to cover for a good long while.

Some say my Viking relatives started the custom of cooking the innards of an animal in its own natural vessel. Due to the Vikings' seafaring and invasion skills, there was a series of Scandinavian kings in Britain the redheads of Ireland can thank the Vikings for their beauty—while the Scots can boast of their haggis, which was proclaimed Scotland's national dish in 1786.

Of haggis, the great Scottish poet Robert Burns wrote:

Trenching your gushing entrails bright
Like onie ditch
And then, O what a glorious sight
Warm-reekin, rich!

The Scots love Burns; butcher shops often have portraits of the poet on their walls. In the November 21, 2002, edition of the *Chicago Tribune*, one Jo Macsween is quoted on the subject of haggis: "Really it's that poem that made haggis Scottish. It started that Scottish spirit of 'Don't give me that fancy French food. If you want to fight and be strong, you've got to have a haggis.'"

Around the globe the heart, liver and brains, to say nothing of the other organs of the body, have always been favored for their rich taste and plentiful nutrients. The muscle of any animal pales in nutrition when compared to the organs. Even school children of my generation knew that liver offers much needed iron, plus a huge dose of vitamin A and other good things. But you must never partake of polar bear liver, it will give you such an overdose of vitamin A that it just might kill you . . . all Eskimos know this.

And speaking of Eskimos, Dr. Garniss Curtis, professor emeritus of geology at UC Berkeley, famous for his accurate dating of early hominids via the method of potassium-argon dating, has a favorite story concerning dead deer. Garniss has lived behind the Berkeley hills for many decades and used to drive a little-used dirt road over the mountains as a shortcut to his laboratory. Others knew of the road, and once or twice a year someone would hit a deer. Garniss would pick up the carcasses, knowing them to be fresh since they had not been there in the morning. After getting the first deer home, Garniss tried cutting up the carcass with a chainsaw. Think of the headlines! "Famous scientist dissects cadaver with chainsaw."

It should be noted that Garniss only worked with the chainsaw for a few minutes. Watching blood and flesh flying around the garage, he quickly switched to a smaller electric saw, which worked wonderfully. At any rate, Garniss and his family would enjoy some fresh venison and then freeze the rest, including the heart, liver and kidneys.

One day a professor of anthropology, and personal friend to Garniss, called and asked, "Hey Garniss, what's the chance of you having any deer organs in your freezer?"

"Very good," replied Garniss, " I think I have three or four hearts, livers and kidneys."

After a slight hesitation, the anthropologist asked Garniss if he would offer them for the satisfaction of five visiting Inuit Eskimo chiefs who had never been away from the frozen north and did not like their meat cooked.

"Of course," said Garniss.

So it was that a one-course dinner was set before the great chiefs. In the middle of the table was a large, beautiful platter piled high with the livers, kidneys and hearts, all uncooked and in various stages of defrosting. The Eskimos were delighted. Each had brought his traditional curved *ulu* knife, and went right to work. After eating the platter clean, they said it was the first real food they had eaten since leaving Alaska. Later the anthropologist told Garniss that the Eskimos most loved the portions of meat that were still frozen solid or only partially thawed. Over such pieces they smacked their lips and nodded their heads to indicate their pleasure.

It turned out that the anthropology professor had brought the Eskimos to Berkeley in order to further his study of their language and history. They had been with him for a week. That very morning he had asked the chiefs if they were comfortable and happy. They said all was fine, but they found our food inedible and complained that they were losing weight and not feeling very well. They asked if he could get them some good raw meat, organ meat if possible, preferably from a wild animal and frozen if that could be arranged, and that is when the anthropologist called the dead deer geochronologist.

By now it should be obvious that humankind has survived by being the most adaptable creature on the planet. Only humans live pole to pole and everywhere in between. Our capacity to adapt allowed us to walk into the present. Along the way many of our ancestors died to predation, weather patterns and natural disasters, many of which produced periods of starvation. Cannibalism offered survival until other food resources became available.

When foul and persistent weather marooned several families of the Donner Party on a California mountain pass of the same name, when all stores and animals[1] had been eaten and several of the party had succumbed to hunger and the elements, the survivors were left with an age-old dilemma. Throughout human history such circumstances have offered but one way to survive. When animals go hungry and cannibalize their own, they give no thought to the act; starvation has set in and instincts lead the way.

But a human knows what he is doing, he thinks about and understands his actions, and that mental ability to recognize and understand one's actions may be the greatest difference between humans and all other life forms. This special capacity is often referred to as consciousness. And knowing we know—as far as we know—is unique to humans.

It was early spring in the southern hemisphere, October 12, 1972, to be exact, when a crew of five, 14 members of an amateur rugby team consisting of young men from Montevideo's finest families, plus 25 family members, friends and one stranger took off for Santiago, Chile, in a small Uruguayan Air Force Fairchild F-227 turboprop. The weather was foul and there had been several delays, but eventually the decision had been made to leave. Since the F-227 had a ceiling limit of 22,000 feet, the pilot had to navigate through a mountain pass and turn directly into the jet stream, a phenomenon not yet fully understood in the field of aviation. Visibility aloft was zero, the pilot lost his way, thought he was nearing his destination and began his descent, not knowing he was still in the midst of the Andes. The crash killed 13 people outright. Of the many wounded, two died the first night and two more during the next few days. Sixteen days after the crash an avalanche killed another nine, and by the time of rescue, 70 days later, three more had perished. When the odyssey ended, 16 young men returned home.

During the first few days, the survivors could hear, and sometimes see, search planes looking for them, but the crash site was nearly invisible, as both wings had snapped off after the plane had clipped a mountain crag during the last seconds of its descent. All that remained was two-thirds of the plane's fuselage and most of that was covered and buried in snow. Realizing this, the survivors made a huge cross out of luggage. One search plane saw the cross, but viewing it from on high, thought it to be a natural geologic phenomenon.

A few days following the crash the plane's meager food supplies were nearing their end; real hunger began to take hold. Before them was food and water, though a majority did not wish to recognize the food. A second-year medical student championed life by explaining how they could survive, why they didn't have to die, why they should not die—why it was their duty to survive. He argued that the soul did not stay to decay with the body, but traveled on. In his final argument, he stated that if he died, he would haunt all who refused to consume his flesh, for surely they had no true will to live. Others reiterated his statement, while some said it was beyond them.

On the tenth day a majority of the survivors, with great trepidation, ate human flesh for the first time. Many retched over their first morsel, but hunger, deep-seated hunger, was present and as the days passed, the eating became easier. Holdouts were encouraged to save their lives, and the group settled into a routine with one caveat: since one young man had lost his mother at the time of impact and had his 18-year-old sister die in his arms some days later, it was agreed that no one would partake of relatives or friends. The decision held through most of their ordeal.

On their first day of cannibalism, one of the rugby team members wrote a letter, "I came to the conclusion that the bodies are there because God put them there, and since the only thing that matters is the soul, I don't have to feel remorse; and if the day came and I could save someone with my body, I would gladly do it."

Every day at a precise time they listened to the news on a portable radio that had been found amongst the luggage. Three South American countries were sending search planes out on a daily basis. As days continued to pass, the news went from hopeful to horrifying when they heard an announcement stating the air search had been called off. The brunt of their ordeal had begun.

The exposed part of the plane's fuselage would heat up during the day, and they would put thin strips of flesh upon it to defrost and dry. Each person had a spot on the roof of the plane to semi-cook and dry his daily ration. On windless days they built small fires and cooked the meat. All preferred the meat cooked, but the weather, rather than desire, controlled the grill.

Eating a diet of nothing but protein and water caused severe constipation to set in and many became concerned. Some of the men became so alarmed as to think they would become impotent or die of bowel obstruction. Several kept detailed records, and from them we know that for three men the numbers of consecutive days without a bowel movement were 28 days, 32 days and 35 days. When the constipation broke, it was always followed by diarrhea. More and more they realized they needed fat in their diet and would dry pieces of it on their roof spots until a crust had formed. Though many disliked the fat, everyone ate some on a daily basis to ward off constipation and aid digestion.

At night the group would huddle in the fuselage with their luggage stacked and wedged in to close the open end at the back of the plane so as to block out the bitterly cold temperatures of the night. When the first wing broke off after clipping a mountain crag, it somersaulted over the fuselage and cut off the tail. The steward and navigator went with the tail section while three passengers, along with the seats they were buckled into, were sucked out of the plane. So it was that each night the chore of luggage stacking and packing would commence, and it was during the night, 16 days following the crash, that an avalanche roared through the luggage wall into the fuselage killing nine.[2]

As with all people trapped or imprisoned in a situation of monotonous and limited food supply, the evening conversations would invariably turn to food. Each person would take a turn at describing in minute detail a recipe he loved. The entire process of gathering the foodstuffs, down to the placing of the finished dish upon the table, was related so as to serve and feed the mind. When all known and loved recipes had been verbally made and mentally consumed, night after night, they switched to creating menus complete with the appropriate wines, china and stemware. A topic never discussed was that of their wives or girlfriends. No talk of sex was allowed. It was an unwritten, unspoken rule, each man knowing within that speaking of his lover would weaken his spirit through longing.

The unspoken was put down in letters to loved ones and held in the hopes of delivering them by hand. One rugby player wrote to his grandmother: "You taught me many things, but the most important was faith in God. That has increased so much now that you cannot conceive of it."

Others wrote their loved ones and likened the consuming of their friends to the last supper and the Eucharist.

In the beginning they ate only of muscle and fat, but eventually added livers, hearts, kidneys and intestines to their diet while continuing to shun lungs, skin, brain and genitals, which they deemed to be beyond their hunger. They ate on a daily basis in order to keep up their strength. It took physical effort to melt snow for water; to cut, butcher and divide meat portions; to start fires and cook when the weather allowed; re-stack and pack the luggage at night; and to care for the wounded. Those confined to the fuselage with broken legs and septic wounds were incapable of working. And as time passed, the meagerness of food allotted per day put the survivors into a state of quasi-starvation that addled their brains. Compassion for the injured turned into various forms of loathing as anyone who could not or would not pull their weight were silently looked upon as parasites.

Sympathy exists only when survival looks promising, consequently empathy left many of the sound-bodied men, with some reaching the mental state of believing the seriously wounded to be faking.

As day 50 approached, supplies of human meat ran short. A rule came down: "no more pilfering." No one obeyed the rule. Body parts that had been rejected earlier were scavenged and eaten, though some, due to recent thaws, were not in the freshest of condition, nonetheless hands, feet, tongues, lungs, blood clots and, in one case, testicles were eaten.

Aside from the fact that they had consumed most of the muscle meat, their senses were clamoring for different tastes as their bodies cried out for minerals and vitamins. Salt deprivation took some to great extremes. Body parts that had begun to rot were consumed. The small intestines (above the bowel) were the first to be eaten in poor condition. The contents were squeezed out, cut into small pieces and eaten. Some said the taste was strong and salty, probably from bile and gastric juices that aid in digestion.

At first a number of the survivors refused to touch the rotten offal, but in time all partook. With bodies starting to decay and meat supply running out, they learned that rotten flesh tasted like cheese and did not kill the consumer. Only after eating all other postcranial parts of the bodies did they overcome the closed-eyed, frozen sightlessness of their friends and get at the brains, the most nutritious of all body parts. The first to go after the delicacy cut the skin across the forehead, pulled back the scalp and cracked open the skull with an axe. They ate the brains frozen or mixed them with all other meats cut in small pieces. Stews of this concoction were the most favored and flavorful as the brain made everything taste better and easier to eat. There was one drawback: brains in a state of putridity could not be eaten, therefore, many heads were solemnly buried.

At last they had come upon what early man had known hundreds of thousands of years before and even went on to copy his ways by making soup bowls from crania. One man used his as a shaving bowl.

They were down to remnants when the fates smiled on them. The warmth of the sun, coupled with another avalanche, exposed previously hidden bodies from their snowbound freezer; they were going to make it.

With fresh, whole, frozen cadavers at their disposal you would think all rotten flesh, intestines and the like would have been discarded and buried, but many had come to need the stronger and heartier tastes and continued to eat things that reminded them of cheese and salt.

On the last of three expeditions taken in an effort to walk out of the Andes, two men left wearing human socks (cut from cadavers) for warmth and snowshoes made from seat cushions. Each man carried rugby socks stuffed with meat and fat. One carried a human arm over his shoulder. After 10 days of hiking through deep snow in the most rugged of mountains, the men reached land free of snow. By a mountain stream they spotted a man on horseback. From the other side of the river the man gestured that he would come back the next day.

After 71 days of being marooned on a mountain top deep in the Andes, the rest of the group was rescued and returned to safety. Survival was made possible by the cannibalizing of those killed in the crash, plus those who later died in the avalanche or of injuries. Many victims of the crash were never found, a fact that had limited the amount of available food. On average, each of the survivors lost 50 pounds. While they fed on the flesh of others, their own bodies fed upon themselves. The meat offered by the deceased was not enough to prevent the effects of gradual starvation, but offered enough sustenance for a few to walk out to a lower elevation and back into the land of the living.

The survivors of the Andean plane crash returned home more religious, more metaphysical and less materialistic. To this day they remember their experience as an intensely religious event and visit the site once a year. With them they take flowers and prayers for the many loved ones they lost, who, through death, sustained the lives of others.

Above all else, we are adaptable.

As we leave the restaurant, Li thanks me for dim sum, then adds, "You should come to China. Then you can eat everything but the table."

CHAPTER TWO

UBIQUITOUS FOOD

Basic instincts drive and direct a vast majority of the life forms that inhabit planet Earth. While acts of consuming others of one's own species may be prompted by various situations, "Fred" is food: end of discussion.

We are the most unique and powerful animals on planet Earth. Our top-dog status and uniqueness emanate from our highly developed and sophisticated brains, which, over time, have allowed us to overcome some of our basic animal instincts. Since our oldest bipedal predecessors lived a mere six to seven million years ago, and being that life on Earth began some three and a half billion years ago, we need to examine cannibalistic behaviors found within other species in order to understand cannibalism within our own.

In Latin, *Callinectes sapidus* means "beautiful swimmer that is savory," a much beloved crustacean that is commonly known as the blue crab listed on spring and summer menus as "Soft Shelled Crabs." Usually dipped in cornmeal, flour or tempura batter and fried until golden, soft-shell crabs are eaten in their entirety, shell and all. When fresh and properly cooked they are not only savory, they are delicious.

Softshells are caught during molting season and processed for sale prior to the new shell hardening, a chemical action that begins two hours after the too-tight old shell has been discarded. *Callinectes sapidus* males have blue-tipped claws; ladies wear red. Boys have a T-shaped abdomen flap while the girls sport a triangle that widens and becomes rounder at maturity. When blue crabs mate, a male finds a female ready for her final molt, which will take her into adulthood. Taking the receptive virgin in his claws, the male cradles her beneath him for several days, all the while looking for suitable cover where he guards her through her life's last molt. While in the soft-shell mode, mating occurs. A female may spawn several times with matings occurring during each episode. Soft-shell mothers lay 750,000 to 8,000,000 eggs, which they carry on their abdomens in a froth of foam. Less than one percent of the eggs hatch and make it to adulthood.

When the mating process is completed the male again cradles the female until her new and final shell has hardened. This is a very sage and wonderful thing to do as a spawning-aged female who has not found a mate will cannibalize any and all soft-shell females she can find. You might call it a case of extreme sexual competition.

Cannibalism is the act of any life form consuming others of its own kind. This culinary experience has been, and still is, practiced by millions of species, from flesh-eating dinosaurs such as *Majungatholus atopus* that once roamed the island of Madagascar to the *subtilis* bacteria of today. Within our own mammalian classification "there are 75 species of mammals distributed among 7 orders that practice cannibalism, either habitually or as necessity dictates."[1]

The animal kingdom, *our* kingdom, is replete with cannibalism.

Instinct, laced with chemicals, can prompt various life forms to do unseemly things when an organism is in peril or at a physical disadvantage. When my children were young, we purchased a pair of young pinto lab rats. With the onset of her first heat, the female became pregnant. We separated the rats, and when the young mother's time came she produced seven little pink-blind-furless pups that she licked and cleaned and fussed over for some time before devouring the lot of them! Through books and veterinarians I discovered what led to this outrageous behavior. First was the rat's age; she was too young. Second, her body was not producing enough milk and the pregnancy had weakened her health. The lack of milk would have caused the litter to perish through starvation, and by eating the litter she gained valuable protein and nourishment. I remember my horror, leaving the room as she proceeded with her grisly task, and finally, coming to terms with her situation. Again, gruesome as it seems, nature provided the most logical solution for the circumstance. That same rat went on to have several litters (until we forced a divorce), and was the most wonderful rodent mother I have ever had the opportunity to observe. She was also the smartest rat I have ever known—despite her shadowy beginnings.

In the realm of adults, female spiders, especially those of poisonous species, often devour their mates following copulation. According to research, spiders eat irregularly, and when copulation occurs, the body of the male guarantees nourishment for the female and the development of her young. Arachnid mavens believe cannibalized males are willing to give their all in order to ensure the passing on of their genes while helping to promote healthy, strong offspring. Of course, a male spider doesn't say to himself, "Gee, there's a great-looking female. I feel like having some fun and offering my life for the benefit of children I'll never know." It took time, lots of time, for his peculiar behavior to develop. Over the last half-billion years, countless organisms have evolved and those who devised the best strategies for survival and the passing on of their genes remained extant the longest. So it can be assumed that sometime during the ancient past, male spiders that took the chance of being devoured won the mating prize and passed their genes and bizarre behavior onto current generations.

Some examples are the black widow spider that will consume her mate after copulation—if she can catch him. The same goes for the female praying mantis (an insect). Then there is the female redback spider that always devours her mate *during* the sex act.

The male redback offers the female his head as he fastens his sperm pouch within her body; once locked-in, the pouch will continue to pump sperm even if its owner has lost his wits. The plot seems to be to keep the female busy eating while he delivers a large quantity of sperm thereby defeating some of the competition that is sure to follow once the female has wiped her mouth.

Researchers at Susquehanna University say you might have a better chance at mating and staying alive if you were a male *Schizocosa ocreata* (Hentz wolf spider). Post-mating cannibalism is common, but not inevitable. Investigators found that older, larger females are more cannibalistic than younger and smaller females and more apt to cannibalize smaller males with relatively smaller hair tufts . . . if you are a wolf spider, hair counts.

Many animals, when it comes to sex, place their lives on the line for posterity and a future they may not be around to enjoy. Nature is renowned for providing natural instincts laced with pleasure, hormones and various chemicals to ensure the continuation of her species at all costs.

Salmon return from the open oceans to their stream of birth, finding their way home via scent. Upon reaching their natal pebble beds, they spawn by scooping out a depression in the streambed with their tails. The female then deposits her eggs to be followed by a male who showers them with sperm. The sexual climax for a salmon, and many other species, results in death; a death which offers life—when the infant salmon emerge from their eggs, they feed off the remains of their parents and life proceeds downstream and back to the sea. In kind, some species of squid—as in, fried calamari—spawn en masse, then die, leaving their carcasses to feed their offspring, insuring them a high protein start in life. One of the larger species of squid (there are hundreds) prey on adults of their own kind, often consuming a *cousin* that is only slightly smaller than themselves in attacks that are so fast that one could miss the action without an underwater, high-speed camera.

Sand shark siblings devour one another while still in their mother's oviduct. This bizarre custom offers us a view of cannibalistic siblingcide practiced prior to birth. The same behavior has been found in other shark species and may have an adaptive aspect to it. If nothing else it is a case of survival of the fittest, possibly prompted by an inability of the mother's body to provide enough nutrients for the full-term maturing of an entire litter, in which case the strongest ingesting the weaker would ensure the birthing of vital, fully developed offspring.

Away from the oceans, the freshwater black bass will shower the eggs of his mate with sperm, then take up residence beside them, protecting them day and night from any and all predators. But when the fry hatch, "Dad" eats every single offspring he can catch. Fortunately, good old Mother Nature allows some of the fry to escape so you can still catch a nasty old black bass.

Within the framework of competition, female ground squirrels have been observed abandoning, or being forced out of, a burrow, often leaving offspring behind. Once a female exits the burrow, another female takes over the vacated home and cleans house by devouring the absent mother's brood, then settles in to have one of her own.

If the first mother was forced to leave her nest of little ones by the usurper, then we have an example of a female furthering her gene pool while limiting that of another, combined with the annihilation of competition through acts of cannibalism. Which relates to recently released data, gathered over nine years of documented observation, that concern one of my favorite animals, the meerkats of the Kalahari Desert in South Africa. A good portion of the field study can be viewed on the popular television show *Meerkat Manor*. Meerkats share parenting, with both males and females taking turns at babysitting and bringing treats to the youngsters.

And, as with lions, lactating females will suckle offspring other than their own. The other side of the story is that dominant females monopolize reproduction by killing and eating the offspring of subordinate females. Most interesting is the fact that pregnant subordinate females have been observed dragging pups out of a family burrow, killing them and eating them. The actions of the subordinate females are responsible for 50% of cannibalistic infanticides, with the dominant female committing all others. Though researchers observed subordinates killing and eating pups of dominant females on two occasions, the final tally showed that dominant females parent 80% of surviving pups.

Many species perform cannibalism in connection with infanticide, with lower orders of life using cannibalistic infanticide as a species-survival tactic. Scientific literature shows most researchers holding to the thought that infanticide began as a result of extreme stress brought on by overcrowding (overpopulation) and limited food resources (starvation). This supposition goes on to say that as time passed, such practices were set in place and can now be observed minus any noticeable, motivating stress-trigger. The killing and consuming of young has been observed for so long, in so many species of insects, invertebrates, and amphibians, that those who study them are shocked if they fail to see such behaviors during seasons of birthing and parenting.

Exploitation of young as a food resource is the most prevalent type of infanticide. Globally, billions of eggs and infants of myriad species are devoured daily. Where members of the same species partake of the young, the act of infanticide becomes an act of cannibalism. In multiple lower orders of life, cannibalistic infanticide is rampant; insects, spiders, amphibians and fish are just some that participate in the practice. Among many of the practitioners there is little or no parental protection of the young. Eggs are laid and left. This is frequently overcome by the laying of hundreds, thousands or even millions of eggs. Nature thus stacks the deck, knowing that a few individuals will manage to survive and grow to continue the genetic line of their parents.

The red-tufted scorpion of Mexico has been observed devouring her own hatchlings, but such behavior is believed to be an unconscious reaction to a natural feeding instinct, but big boys, who used to be little boys, will tell you of catching a mother scorpion, complete with dangling litter, and placing the "family" in a jar. As soon as Mama discovered that there was no way of escape she would set to work devouring her offspring, then commit suicide by stinging herself. In the same vein, a Spanish anthropologist told how he and his buddies used to catch scorpions and place them in a circle ringed by a ditch that had been dowsed with gasoline. As soon as the boys lit the gasoline-soaked earth, and the scorpions realized they were encircled by fire, the scorpions committed suicide by stinging themselves. If a mother with babies was placed in a ring of fire, she would first devour her litter.

If you happen to be a fly fisherperson, or, heaven forbid, a bait or lure fisherperson, you know that come spawning time, hooked-jawed male trout will eat as many fertilized trout eggs as they can, including those they themselves recently showered with sperm. But the fish dads have competition, as everything in the river loves eggs for lunch.

In the same river, big brown trout love young brown trout and at times even larger brown trout. A fisherman I know was bringing in a 14-inch brown when a monster brown came up from the watery depths and ate his catch in a gulp. Fish do not chew their food.

While many living organisms give birth and then abandon their young, other species not only watch over their eggs and/or offspring, but also see to their feeding and development.

In the jungles of South America lives the beautiful little strawberry frog. This thimble-sized frog has a bright red head and body with bright blue hind legs. After mating, the tiny female lays 6 to 10 eggs in a leaf filled with rainwater. Then she sits down to guard her precious progeny. As the eggs develop into tadpoles and exit their egg sacks she encourages them, one at a time, to wiggle onto her back. Then she climbs high into the forest canopy, going from one bromeliad to another until she finds one filled with rainwater but devoid of any other life form, such as mosquito larvae. When a clean pool is found, the mother frog slips a tadpole off her back into its own, very private, pool. When all the baby tadpoles have been laboriously placed in their own bromeliad pools, she goes about the task of feeding her growing brood. Every day or two she visits each pool. By the movement of the tadpole she knows if it is hungry. If hungry, the tadpole is fed a fresh egg from his mother, neatly deposited into his or her personal pool. This egg feeding ritual continues until the tadpoles reach maturity.

Many species provide nurse eggs for the development of their young. True nurse eggs are not fertilized and have been equated with milk offered by mammals that suckle their offspring. Professor Rudolf A. Raff of the Department of Biology at Indiana University supplied me with information concerning diminutive sea stars from Antarctica (members of the brittle stars family)—researched by Maria Byrne of the University of Sydney—among which embryonic offspring are retained within the mother's body cavity where they feed upon tissue provided for them until they are approximately 20% her size, at which time they break through the calcium carbonate shingling of her exoskeleton to join Mom in feeding upon the detritus that litters sea bottoms on a global scale. Brittle stars are brainless, having nothing more than a tiny ring of neurons, but they have been on Earth for 500 million years, offering proof that Mother Nature has always worked to keep her planet clean.

Things are more aggressive amongst life forms such as marine snails, mites, spiders, scorpions, termites, Hemiptera ants, bees, wasps, beetles and butterflies, where the strongest feed on other siblings that range in age from egg to larval stage to infant. Some arthropods can go through several molts and come close to maturity solely on sustenance derived from sibling eggs and littermates. By producing an excess of young, many invertebrates ensure the continuation of their species while increasing survivability and accelerating the growth and development of those who make it to adulthood.

Research done by David Pfenning, University of North Carolina, on the spadefoot toads of Arizona allows us to jump from invertebrates to amphibians where the spadefoot toad hops to the top of the cannibal charts. These Arizona desert-living toads are from the family *pelobatidae*, which includes amphibians that have no ribs, tiny teeth and digging tubercles on their hind feet that dig down into the ground as summer comes on and dries up the waters the toads need to survive. After hibernating for up to 10 months, the spadefooters emerge after spring rains and plop into pools of fresh water that they fill with tadpoles that dine on algae or miniscule shrimp with their tiny little sucking mouths that lead to tiny coiled up stomachs. However, should algae and/or shrimp be scarce, or overcrowding occur, some of the spadefoot tadpoles make a choice and grow into toad monsters with huge mouths and uncoiled stomachs that become large digestive bags ready to accommodate other spadefooted tadpoles—especially those most distantly related to themselves! Does this suggest genetics that recognize relatives on a toad level? Who said science was dull?

Higher up on the food chain, cannibalism is less common and is most frequently observed when males of a species devour the young. The American male alligator makes a real effort to make snacks of hatchlings, including his own sons and daughters, though some researchers claim to have observed fathers who were model parents when in the vicinity of their own offspring. Within the mammalian family, male lions perform the selfish gene act. When a protector male dies or is driven off by a younger, stronger male, the incoming king will kill and devour the youngest cubs. The females tolerate this behavior and come back into estrus, at which time they willingly copulate with the new boy on the block. Soon new cubs carrying the new king's genes are meowing, playing and nursing within the confines of a pride that is once more secure.

When truly hard times befall a pride of lions, usually prompted by drought, both the lion and lionesses will devour infant cubs in order to sustain life. Animals instinctually do whatever is necessary for survival. If the adults were to die, the entire pride would perish, as young cubs are too small and weak to defend themselves, incapable of feeding themselves and not mature enough to mate. Such incidences equate with survival cannibalism.

Recent research footage covering the lives of a pride of lions living on an island with a herd of water buffalo inadvertently discovered a cannibalistic female that routinely cannibalized the cubs of other females while "babysitting."

Whereas lions usually resort to cannibalism when under extreme duress or during times of takeover, hyenas are habitual cannibals from birth. Sibling pups will fight one another to the death moments after exiting the womb, the death struggle often beginning within the birthing chamber. The mother will watch this survival-of-the-fittest battle without interference, it being the status quo in this top ranking species.

Adult hyenas see competitor hyenas as just another meal and willingly lay siege to any opponent they can get their fangs into. The nature of these attacks is unbelievably base. In 1972, Hans Kruuk observed a straggling male hyena be chased and attacked by members of a rival group. Within a 10-minute period the victim's ears, feet and testicles were bitten off and his limbs and belly lacerated. As a final (and seemingly benevolent) assault, he was paralyzed from a bite to the spine. He died shortly after the attack. Returning to the site early the next morning, Kruuk found a hyena eating from the carcass with clear evidence that others had feasted through the night.

Male polar bears will wander by a female's den in spring when she is first introducing her cubs to the world. If it were not for the strength and ferocity of the mother bear, many cubs would never reach maturity. Research has shown that in many instances the cubs are the predator's own, and whether a cub is taken or not the male will continue to test the mother over and over again until the cubs are quite large. It has been suggested that this nasty act may have a species-related survival advantage by ensuring the strength of the species, since only strong, healthy mothers can run off a merciless, cub-eating male, while a weak or sickly mother would be more likely to bear inferior cubs. Grizzly bears exhibit the same behavior.

All of the animal cannibals described above are either carnivores or omnivores, but John A. Byers, in his book *Built for Speed: A Year in the Life of Pronghorn*, reveals the truth about the antelope of America, which is usually listed as being a strict herbivore. Pronghorn antelope mothers not only consume the placenta upon giving birth, but also eat the feces of nursing fawns. Byers suggests that feces-eating is a way to manufacture antibodies transmitted to offspring through the mother's milk. Or could it be an ancient habit of cleaning up telltale droppings that would indicate the location of an infant to packs of wolves or coyotes?

Obviously, cannibalism wears many hats. On September 27, 2002, at 6:45 A.M., John Walker and others were walking through the Berenty Reserve in southern Madagascar. Madagascar is a large island nation off the southeastern coast of Africa and home to the majority of the world's lemurs—our cousins, many times removed. Most lemurs have inquisitive monkey faces with large forward eyes, long bodies and limbs, short fox-like noses and raccoon-style tails.

As Mr. Walker and friends walked down a trail, they noticed a solitary infant lemur, *Eulemur fulvus*, sitting some 40 yards ahead of them. Suddenly another troop of *E. fulvus* entered onto the trail. A male from the troop saw the infant, rushed to it, grabbed it and beheaded it. A female then took the infant from the male and proceeded to eat the body. Mr. Walker ran to get his camcorder. When he returned many minutes later, the female was still eating of the body. Mr. Walker recorded the remainder of the event for approximately 10 minutes.

Lemurs live in matriarchal societies, which explains why the female was able to take the body from the beheading male. The male's actions were in line with his inherent duty to protect his troop from any and all foreigners and procure protein at any opportunity.

When male langur monkeys take over a harem of females, their first act is to kill existing infants. Japanese primatologist Yukimaru Sugiyama observed this behavior in 1967 and was the first to realize that the killing of infants brought long-nursing females back into estrus, thus allowing the incoming male to father the next generation. As years of observational hours ticked by, the killing of infants, coupled with the consumption of the body, was observed countless times by numerous researchers at multiple sites.

In 1960, at the suggestion of Dr. Louis Leakey, Jane Goodall began her decades of chimpanzee research at Gombe Stream in Tanzania. The chimpanzees at Gombe are known as the common chimp (*Pan troglodytes*), and differ from the pygmy chimp or Bonobo (*Pan paniscus*) in cultural ways and hairstyle more than in physicality.

Longtime studies of *Pan troglodytes* by Goodall, and *Pan paniscus* by Japanese researchers working mostly in Zaire, offer more than a half-century of documented behavioral studies on species whose genetics vary from ours by 1% to 3%.

In 1974, the Japanese documented an incidence of cannibalistic infanticide. Since that time, the killing and consumption of newborns and small infants has been observed in both species, performed by both males and females. Two cases stand out from the norm. One involved a male Bonobo thought to be the biological father of the infant he ingested. The second incident involved a female who took a newborn from another female and consumed it while the mother sat by watching. More than once the cannibalistic female put down her meal and went to the mother and put her arms around her. Was the baby malformed? Stillborn? Or was the guilty female in chronic need of protein? Taking care of a problem? Hungry? Or a brutal killer? Why didn't the birth mother do anything to stop the consumption of her newborn? In all other like cases mothers fought for their offspring and/or ran after the culprit-cannibal as he or she made off with the body.

Among the common chimpanzees, infants have been killed and eaten during attacks by males on stranger females. Were the females attacked for being in foreign territory? Or were they attacked for the easy procurement of meat? Or was the infant destroyed so as to prompt the stranger female into estrus?

Photos, videos and descriptions of male apes feasting upon infantile victims remind us of the Roman god Saturn who, in legend, consumed his sons. In the Museo del Prado in Madrid, Spain, hangs a famous painting of Saturn devouring one of his sons. Painted by Peter Paul Rubens (1577–1640), it is a large, magnificent and disturbing painting. Saturn and son fill the canvas. Saturn's aged body shows well his massive, once-youthful musculature through sagging skin. His face is fierce in the midst of attack as he steadies himself with his staff. The child, held tightly in one massive hand, is, of course, Rubenesque, his reddish hair contrasting with the gray of his father's. Three stars in the top center give way to a background of black clouds, which color our mood as we stand before this *mythical* scene. Art historians claim Rubens's painting was a pictorial slam against the Spanish government's treatment of its citizens; the Spanish Inquisition was in full swing.

The most heinous acts of infant cannibalism among apes were performed not by ferocious males, but by two females observed at Gombe Stream by Goodall. A female named Passion, and her daughter Pom, went on a four-year rampage of killing and devouring newborn infants. Passion, who was named upon the occurrence of her birth, cajoled her daughter Pom into joining her in the wanton stealing, killing and devouring of infants. At first Pom appeared to be reluctant, but in time seemed to relish the gruesome attacks in which infants were killed quickly with a bite to the head, then devoured. During the four years of Passion and Pom's cannibalistic spree, only the dominant female, Flo, managed to produce and rear an infant. Passion and Pom killed and consumed all others. In one occurrence, the mother of the infant that had been targeted was a survivor of polio and was moderately handicapped. In that particular case the mother was severely and purposefully wounded while trying to protect her infant. After four years of attacks, Passion conceived and while pregnant tried to steal more babies, but her attempts were thwarted. A short time later, her daughter, Pom, also became pregnant, and the horrible spate of murder and cannibalism came to an end.

Ms. Goodall and her associates did not interfere during Passion and

Pom's horrific cannibalistic spree, as their mission was, and is, a process of observation and study of the greater apes in their natural environment. The other chimpanzees of Gombe Stream mirrored the observers and did nothing to stop the killings nor make any effort to help the victims.

Passion and Pom's natal group is known as the Kasakela, which later split into two groups when six males and three females slowly moved away and to the south, leaving eight males in the north. Researchers named the new subgroup Kahama. Like humans, chimpanzees are territorial, and chimpanzee males do "border patrols" on a regular basis, walking single file around the edge of *their* property.

After the original group split, males from the old and new groups would perform loud territorial displays upon meeting one another along a conjoining border. Such aggressive behavior escalated into war when the Kasakela males began hunting down lone males from the Kahama group, capturing them and beating and biting them to death. By 1977, after three years of "war," perpetrated through individual killings, the entire Kahama group had been annihilated but for a few females that were taken back into the Kasakela group.

Human researchers observed some of the killings, found a few carcasses and noted "missing persons" from the victimized group, which eventually ceased to exist. Most of the victims' remains were never found, but it is not known if any form of cannibalism took place.

Years later, in 2003, researchers observed several male chimpanzees (*Pan troglodytes*) harass, kill and devour an adolescent male. The incident was a first, as all previous human observations of cannibalism among chimpanzees had involved the devouring of infants.

The proposed reason for the obliterating war between the Kasakela and the Kahama was human overpopulation, which had crowded the chimpanzees into an ever-diminishing area, which translated to less food in a reduced territory, which spelled impending starvation and death. When human pressures threatened the food supplies of the splintered groups, the males of the original group methodically took action.

Field observations made by biologists on a global scale have shown that all primates join other species in becoming more intolerant of strangers, or other group members, whenever food is in short supply.

The encroachment of humans is a known fact, but did the reduction of territory also cause the initial split? Did the six males and three females leave in hopes of finding another feeding range?

In August of 1998, British primatologist Martin Muller ran through the forest of Uganda, led by horrifying screams emanating from 10 male chimpanzees that were in the process of killing another. By the time Muller arrived, the victim had 30 to 40 puncture wounds, ribs exposed, trachea ripped out, and testicles, toenails and fingernails torn off. Obviously, the victim was dead, but the chimpanzees Muller thought he knew so well continued in the process of killing their enemy. For the first time, Muller knew fear in connection to those he loved, admired and studied.

Cannibalism and cannibalistic infanticide are so rampant within the animal kingdom that a listing of all known species and the specifics regarding occurrences would fill several large volumes. But what about us—the species *Homo sapiens*? Human beings, mankind, humankind, womankind, people . . . you and me? We will get to that soon enough, but first some glimpses at how we got to be who, what and where we are today.

CHAPTER THREE

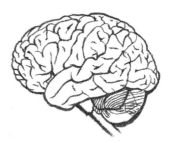

INNER WORKINGS

Human behavior is modeled by what we believe, which is programmed by the society into which we are born, coupled with the events of our lives. While human behavior is malleable, human nature is expressed through age-old instinctual responses to incoming stimuli. Sophistication is achieved when an organism overrides natural instincts in order to modify behavior.

D o our emotional and physical reactions to incoming stimuli reflect instinct or socialization? How old is the neocortex (*neo* "new" and *cortex*, the outer layer of the brain)? When we stood up and walked forth, did we evolve whole new brains? Or are our brains a compilation of ancient remnants covered over with a modern facade? Reviewing the evolution of the human brain illuminates the differences between instinct and socialization as well as between humans and other animals. With this information, acts of cannibalism can be viewed from various perspectives.

The human brain is built much as an old cabin in the woods. It starts off as a one-room, electrified structure with a bed in one corner and a fireplace taking up most of the opposing wall. There is a chair and a small table upon which sits a small, single book. Over the mantel hangs a stag's head and a rack with a loaded gun at the ready hanging just below. This original structure equates to the brainstem, often referred to as the reptilian brain.

The old reptilian brain prompts responses to physical needs and incoming stimuli. Such functions are directed by motor and sensory tracts that keep a sharp eye out for danger, your heart pumping and your lungs working. The reptilian brain doesn't ponder the present or the past—or its navel for that matter, but works 24/7 as a composite tool for survival. Other than autonomic functions, the brainstem's primary focus is self-preservation, a part of which is aggression expressed in any way that will ensure the survival of the organism in question.

As the years go by, different generations keep adding to the one-room structure. A potbellied wood-burning stove is brought in, and a large porch is added. Time passes; a bedroom, a bookcase, a back porch and a closet are added, plus some new and bigger windows, but you still have to go to the outhouse to relieve yourself. These encapsulating add-ons comprise the old mammalian brain known as the limbic system.

The limbic system is the center of emotions and sensory networks that allow for more complex life forms. The system is made up of several small parts that accomplish many tasks, from main-event memory storage and sense of smell, to gastronomical and sexual appetite. It motivates you through the day and, when functioning properly, keeps one's emotions on a positive track. It fills pregnant women with feelings of motherly love and colors an individual's emotional tone to all incoming stimuli. Through response mechanisms brought on by fear, it teams up with the brainstem for acts of aggression.

Years pass and after several ever-more-brainy generations, the reptilian brain that was surrounded by the limbic system is completely encased with the addition of two modern bathrooms, two more bedrooms, a library, a huge storage room, a sun room, indoor plumbing, and a laundry room. This new expansion is the neocortex, the crinkled-up sheet of gray and white matter that makes for a smarter, more cunning animal. In humans the neocortex is made up of six layers of neurons and offers consciousness, language, comprehension, abstract thought, problem solving and the capacity for brilliance. In *Homo sapiens*, the neocortex is large in relationship to body mass and surpasses, as far as we know, all other living organisms in the realm of mental capabilities.

Deep inside the "new" human brain sits the old fireplace, which is now mostly for decor except for when things get tough. The stag's head and gun keep their position. From the first molding of the reptilian brain 500 million years ago, to the limbic system (300 to 250 million years ago), to the neocortex (200 million years ago), to the beginning of the configuration of the human brain (five to six million years ago into the present), the human brain has kept all of its old stuff. As far as we know, it has never thrown anything out; it is the original pack rat. New rooms and equipment may override older areas, or take up most of the work in a more modern fashion, but the old stuff is still there.

Dr. Silvan S. Tomkins, after years of observing the emotional and psychological reactions of adults, studied children from their exiting the womb into their years of comprehension and manipulation. He found humans to be born with eight basic "affects," what I would call innate emotional responses; the majority are negative in nature. They begin with (1) distress (fear), starting with the birth cry; (2) anger; (3) disgust (connected with taste in infancy); (4) what he refers to as "dismell," a survival instinct based on the strong reaction to, and removal of oneself from the vicinity of, bad-smelling substances; (5) surprise, which startles and terrifies; (6) excitement (positive rapid response); (7) enjoyment (interest with less rapid response); and later (8) shame. All infants respond with a minimum of one of these eight affects to incoming stimuli.

Paring down to basics, a jocular anthropologist once described the four forces mandatory for survival as the four Fs. In order of importance they are fleeing, fighting, feeding and fornication. Such instinctual attributes are found in all life forms.

(Something to ponder: U.S. medical and legal practitioners have taken the anthropological flee-or-fight response and renamed them the "fight or flight" response. Please notice the reorganization.)

All species follow the original order of the four Fs. In order to survive, an animal, or any living organism, must avoid all threats to life by either fleeing or fighting. Fleeing, being the most prudent course of action, usually comes first. But when trapped, threatened with death or defending one's gene pool, fighting will become, or be deemed, necessary.

When there is no threat to life or limb, food must be found and consumed. But take note, even during the most glamorous dinner party the first two Fs are still on alert. Men and women in tuxedos and ball gowns may successfully hide their flee-or-fight responses, but if you watch a group of feeding baboons you will notice they are constantly looking around in a nervous manner, always scanning for danger as they eat. Even though large male baboons take turns sitting and watching for leopards, snakes or large eagles—any of which can snatch up an infant in an instant—it is not enough. Experience has taught each individual that he or she must be steadfastly on the alert. With all the watching, guarding and furrowed brows, many baboons still lose their lives to predators, one of which is our cousin the chimpanzee. With his larger and more complex brain, the chimpanzee does not dash out and grab an infant, rather he makes friends with the baboons and even plays with them. When the baboons let down their guard and opportunity appears, a young baboon loses out, and the chimpanzee goes home to share his dinner with those who earlier shared fresh meat with him, including non-related support group members and those females and family members whose favor he wishes to curry.

Though impromptu coitus has been known to occur at times of eminent peril, as in wartime when people's lives are threatened and the subconscious urge to have one's genes continue into the future is flowing, sex among most living organisms is usually performed when an animal has sustainable foodstuffs and feels relatively safe. So the act of mating comes in last on the list of survival strategies. This may appear to go against the motives of the "my-sperm-first" crowd, but nature knows all too well that an organism must be relatively safe before successful egg laying or infant rearing can take place. And one look at the abundance of life on Earth proves that periods of safety are found by all for the pleasure of continuing ones species.

Scanning *The Sex Lives of Wild Animals* by Eugene Burns, it appears that the brainier the animal, the more time is given to the pleasures of making babies. Mink stay coupled for up to 24 hours, the male hanging on via a clenching bite to the female's neck (never buy a wild mink anything), while lions mate for a minimum of five consecutive days with five to ten couplings per day, which is what you can do when you are the king—though observers say the male lion is often so lazy that quite often the "girls" have to wake him up to perform.

All of Tomkin's affects tessellate with the four Fs and may be viewed as a composite signature of our add-on brain structure, which houses modern, elaborate wiring for higher planes of thinking along with the old shotgun for survival. Over the eons neural electrochemical responses have produced repeated reactions to all incoming stimuli, which in turn, molded our character and selected out for the protection, growth, preservation and continuation of our species.

So where does all this information fit into the realm of cannibalism? Everywhere! As described in the previous chapter, "Ubiquitous Food," lower life forms practice cannibalism on a habitual and instinctual basis. As we climb the ladder of life into the realm of mammals—animals that are capable of showing emotional responses, cunning and the ability to learn—cannibalism is common, but found most often in connection with newborns or when the chips are down and the animal is faced with a life or death situation. When such circumstances present themselves, carnivorous and omnivorous animals show no hesitation to prey on those of their own kind, as the basic instincts emanating from the old reptilian brain, coupled with the limbic system, beg for any and all modes of survival, including acts of cannibalism.

But then there are humans, "us," the ones with the big brains that are easily taught what to think in accordance with the beliefs of the group in which they are raised. *Homo sapiens*—modern humans—comprehend their actions and that is when the plot thickens as programmed behavior meets instinct and culture directs the play; incidents which will be dealt with throughout the rest of this book.

Let us begin with those who fall outside the norm.

We will never know if Passion and Pom's four-year spree of psychopathic behavior, exhibited through infant cannibalism, was brought on through psychological or chemical derivation, but within the human race there have been countless numbers of emotionally, mentally and/or chemically disturbed individuals who have mirrored the exploits of Passion and Pom. Such individuals live lives of extreme and deviant behavior. There exist myriad books, trial files and clinical records spanning many centuries of human cannibalism perpetrated by pathological serial-killer cannibals such as the infamous Jeffrey Dahmer.

I will recount but one case concerning a serial-killer cannibal, as such people make up a mere fraction of one percent of the historical multitudes who practiced anthropophagy. I chose the following case because it offers an odd and sickening twist in that it is not definitively known if the killer himself ever partook of human flesh.

On May 17, 1924, some children playing on the banks of the Leine River in Hannover, Germany, found a human skull. By mid-June three more skulls had been discovered. The "butcher of Hannover" was soon to be caught.

Years prior, at age 16, a young man by the name of Fritz Haarmann was sent to the Provincial Asylum for indecently assaulting young children. He was listed as incurably feeble-minded and not responsible for his actions. However, he was smart enough to escape and make his way to Switzerland, where he lived a life of petty crime. Two years later he returned to Hannover and provoked a brutal fight with his father. Frightened of his own son, the senior Haarmann tried to appease Fritz with the purchase of a fried-fish shop. Fritz quickly put the shop into bankruptcy and enlisted in the 10th Jaeger Battalion in Alsace where he was considered a very good soldier—full of esprit de corps and so forth—but after two years he was discharged, suffering from neurasthenia—nervous debility and exhaustion coupled with vague complaints of a physical nature. In other words, a nervous breakdown. He was released from service and received a pension.

Again Haarmann returned home. The year was 1903. This time his father tried to have his son certified, but one Dr. Andrae said that although Fritz was morally lacking, unintelligent and self-centered, there were not sufficient grounds to have him put away. From that time, 1903 to 1918, Haarmann spent most of his time in prison for minor offenses.

Upon release from prison in 1918, Haarmann joined groups of homosexuals in taverns and dance halls, took slum lodgings at number 27 Cellarstrasse, and worked his way into the black market, which was still rampant at the close of World War I. Joining a black-market meat-smuggling racket, he soon put on some much needed weight and was running his own business within six months. He also became a *Spitzel*—a police informer—making it his business to know every crook, runaway and transient in Hannover. By squealing to the police they gave him a wide berth in regard to his homosexual behavior. Haarmann went so far as to adopt an official manner, observing and treating others as though he was a member of the police. Soon locals were referring to him as "Detective Haarmann."

Haarmann sold black-market meat during the day and picked up young male runaways at the Hannover train station at night. Once he had found himself a young lad, he would take him home, talk to the boy and then sodomize him. Some boys were let go, but most were killed. So the boy who was deemed feeble-minded became a businessman, a police informer, a sodomizer of young boys and a vile killer who was well known for having meat to sell when his competitors' bins were empty. Haarmann's unsuspecting customers became practitioners of "benign cannibalism," an occurrence that has happened before and since. While attending a conference in Korea, an American publisher sat with the president of Uganda who took over following President Idi Amin's exile. The president verified the well-known story of Amin serving human flesh to a large group of guests at a state dinner for foreign ambassadors. On the following day the guests were told what they had eaten—several threw up on the spot.

Haarmann's first victim was a 17-year-old runaway boy whose father was still away at the front. When the boy's father returned home, he and his wife went to Hannover to find their son, who, like Haarmann, had the first name of Fritz. The young Fritz had sent a postcard prior to his disappearance, and his parents soon found a boy who had known their son. The boy told them about "Detective Haarmann" and of Fritz making friends with him, but the police had to be pushed into an investigation of their *Spitzel*. When they finally entered Haarmann's flat unannounced, they found him in flagrante delicato with a young boy and placed Haarmann in prison for nine months. Four years later at his trial, Haarmann admitted that when the police entered his flat the head of young Fritz had been sitting behind the stove wrapped in newspaper.

Upon his release from prison, Haarmann took a new flat and picked up a 24-year-old accomplice, Hans Grans. The two set a pattern. They would lure a runaway to their flat, sodomize him and then kill him. The following morning the body would be butchered for sale. Haarmann *claimed* he killed the boys by biting them through the throat. He said it was efficient, and there were no screams for the neighbors to hear. The butchered meat was sold at the local market stalls and through other channels. Victims ranged from 10 to 20 years in age. Runner boys were often seen coming and going from Haarmann's apartment with wrapped packages of fresh meat—and why not? Haarmann was well known as a dealer in smuggled meat.

One of Grans's duties was to take the butchered remains to the Leine River and slip them into its murky waters in the dark of night. Police-ordered dredging in 1924 brought forth hundreds of bones and many skulls.

In the end there was a farcical trial where the psychopathic Haarmann defended himself and made a mockery of the court. Nevertheless, Fritz Haarmann was decapitated for his crimes. (The Germans continued to use the guillotine into the 1950s, while the French last used the blade to execute an immigrant killer in 1977.) Grans was sentenced to imprisonment for life but was later re-tried and released. His only crime was the luring of young men to their deaths. Between 30 and 50 boys and young men were murdered, butchered and sold. More than 20 victims are known for sure, with names, dates of runaway and witnesses of when they met Haarmann, who confessed to "30 or 40."

These hellacious crimes went unnoticed even though two suspicious women—friends of Grans—visited Haarmann's apartment one day when the men were out. Finding large quantities of meat they took small samples to the police, asking that they check as to what kind of meat it was. In 1923, there were no sophisticated tests such as exist in today's laboratories. The police doctor claimed the meat to be pork, which tells us something about its color, but nothing about its taste. The term "long pig" comes from Pacific Islanders who so named human flesh, as the long muscles of a human are longer than the corresponding muscles of a wild pig—the largest and most often consumed mammal found on the Pacific Islands. As to taste, admitted cannibals from around the world have stated that human flesh differs from all others and is "the best I've ever had." However, it should be noted that such quotes come from people living in areas that offer a limited variety of comestibles.

Over the centuries people such as Haarmann have given a hideous and revolting imagery to the word "cannibalism." Haarmann was a warped, sadistic psychopath whose behavior offers perceived justification to all who rail against cannibalism, but such people are rare in the global arena of cannibalism. Human cannibalism, performed by average people, shows itself in numerous, varied and unadulterated forms that have been with us for hundreds of thousands, if not millions, of years. As the most formidable species on Earth, we are still in the process of walking out of the mountains, plains, steppes, forests and caves of our past where circumstances and societal beliefs often made acts of cannibalism acceptable. Perhaps thoughts from H.G. Wells's *The Outline of History: Being a Plain History of Life and Mankind* address my point the best.

In Volume II, when he has finished with Alexander the Great, Wells explains how the stories of history must be told in order to come to a full understanding, not only of history, but of ourselves, the nature of our race—the human race—complete with its "still raw humanity." Then he cites the fact that only 70 generations have lived since the time of Alexander and that little time has passed since our ancestors "charred their food in embers or ate it raw."

"There is not much scope for the modification of a species in four or or five hundred generations. . . . We have writing and teaching, science and power, but we are still only shambling towards the light. We have tamed and bred the beasts, but we have still to tame and breed ourselves."[1]

CHAPTER FOUR

FEET TO MEAT

The human journey began with the act of standing up and walking forth.

n 1974, Mary Leakey began excavating a site known as Laetoli in Tanzania. During the first season many faunal (animal) fossils were found, and in 1975 a maxilla (upper jaw bone) of a hominid—*Homo africanus* or "African Man"—was found. Between the excavator's camp and the various sites being worked on were tuffaceous slabs of volcanic ash, many of them overlapping one another; concrete evidence of a volcano that had erupted periodically and repeatedly over a span of days, weeks or even months, many millions of years ago. These exposed remnants of an ancient volcanic eruption were pockmarked with the footprints of many animals, but the workers and scientists had simply walked by without recognizing the prints for what they were. Then in 1976, Andrew Hill arrived at the site. Andrew's story is that they were having an after-hours dried elephant dung throwing fight (dried elephant dung is pretty much odor free; grassy if anything), when he dodged a large scatological missile and found himself on his hands and knees looking down at various and obvious animal tracks. New excavations began, and as the word got out, paleoanthropologists and geologists arrived to help; Peter Jones, Richard Hay, Tim White, Michael Day, Richard Leakey and Paul Abell to mention a few. One day Abell was helping Tim White and others excavate some baboon tracks when he decided to return to camp. Walking by the site where the maxilla was found, he looked down at a tuff that was sticking out from beneath another, overlaying tuff. In the projection he saw what he knew to be the heel-print of a hominid, with the front portion of the footprint still covered by a later ash-fall. When the upper tuffaceous layer was removed the rest of the footprint appeared. Work continued and in the end the tracks of three hominids, comprising more than 70 footprints, were uncovered. The footprints of the ancient hominids parallel and join those of many other animals as all living creatures retreated from an angry, life-threatening volcano.

When a volcano really blows its top, it creates its own weather system as molten rock, ash, heat and water vapor explode into the atmosphere. The result is rain, lightning and ash that drift with the prevailing wind. The mixture of ash and rain make for something akin to a wet, fine-grained ash-cement that sets up to become a semi-fragile rock when it dries.

The Laetoli footprints present us with clear evidence of three bipedal hominids walking over a layer of fresh, moist volcanic ash that captured their footsteps for posterity 3.6 million years ago. The next time you walk along the moist sand at the edge of an ocean, take a minute to look back at your tracks and ponder our wondrous journey through time. . . . We have come a long way.

The oldest known fossils (fossilized or preserved bones) of upright bipedal apes tell us that our most ancient predecessors were walking around some seven million years ago (Chad skull dated to seven million).

Those first creatures were an anomaly in that they were the first mammals to stand erect and walk on two legs without the aid of their forelimbs. (Kangaroos are marsupials rather than placental mammals, and hop rather than walk.) Fossils from numerous sites tell us that over time more than one ape-like creature chose to habitually stand erect and walk on two legs. The motivations for upright walking are still unknown though several hypotheses exist. What is known is that of those who chose an upright stance, all but one line died out, and that most successful lineage is ancestral to us all.

Our closest genetic cousin extant today is the chimpanzee, with DNA that differs from ours by a mere 1% to 3%. We refer to chimpanzees and other great apes (other than ourselves) as knuckle-walkers. They can walk upright for short distances in a gait known as a bipedal swagger, but they are incapable of true upright walking because of their skeletal frames. Bonobo chimpanzees (*Pan paniscus*, often referred to as the pygmy chimp) are as tall as the common chimpanzee (*Pan troglodytes*), but are slightly slimmer in build with the added attraction of a fascinating, part-down-the-middle hairdo. Bonobos have been observed to walk upright far more often and for longer distances than the common chimpanzee, but by and large, their mode of locomotion is by way of knuckle walking. Along with the Bonobos' greater ability to walk upright is another physical trait that was thought to be unique to humans: mating face to face.

(It should be noted that humans did not evolve from chimpanzees. The two species split off from an unknown, though common, ancestor ages ago.)

When our earliest upright ancestors started cruising the landscape with their newly freed forelimbs, they probably continued with the diet they had known prior to the remodeling of their hips and the angling out of their femurs, processes which are necessary for bipedality. The leg bones of all apes, other than those of man, line up vertically, while our femurs angle outwards to accommodate our upright stature, which in times past, changed the design of our hipbones. However, when first born, our leg bones line up like those of our ape cousins, which is why we are unable to walk as infants. By the time we are bouncing up and down in our cribs and standing in our parents' laps, calcium has begun to build up on the inside knob of the lower end of the femur. As the calcium continues to build the femur is jacked up on one side producing the outward leaning angle neces-sary for bipedality. Have you ever noticed the bow-leggedness of toddlers? Their first year of walking resembles the bipedal swagger of other apes as the buildup of calcium is still in its infancy. The lay-down of calcium on the distal head of the femur does not cease until the age of 14 to 17 or when-ever overall bone growth stops and a person reaches their adult height.

The remodeling of bones to fit function is not a difficult thing for Mother Nature; she has performed the feat billions of times on every sort of organism over the course of evolution on this small planet.

If we look at the diets of our cousins the chimpanzees, we find them to be omnivorous. The common chimpanzee kills and eats Colo-bus monkeys for the most part, while Bonobos have been known to kill and consume up to 15 different species, including a very small species of African deer. And, as noted in the chapter "Ubiquitous Food," both spe-cies of chimpanzees have been observed in the practice of cannibalism. Though meat appears to be vital in the diets of both chimpanzees, it makes up only a fraction of their overall food intake. The bulk of their nourish-ment is derived from leaves, shoots, nuts, insects (more protein), and fruit. Leaves and other forest foodstuffs are extremely rich in fiber, which de-mands lengthy digestion. The common chimp, which eats less meat than his Bonobo cousin, has an ample girth while the Bonobo has a lean trunk. The stomachs and guts of the other apes, namely gorillas and orangutans, are the largest of the bunch, as they must process the bulky vegetarian diet they ingest, though they do enjoy an occasional meal of termites or weaver ants. Because of diet, none of our cousins possess a waist, but we do (though at my age I am fighting against the loss of mine and am pretty damn upset about the situation).

By two and a half million years ago, bipedality was a long-held trait of the modern-human-to-be line and marks the time of the first simple stone tools, a huge technological advancement. In Ethiopia, at a dig site called Gona, professors Sileshi Semaw, Nicholas Toth, Kathy Schick and colleagues from the Stone Age Institute in Indiana, unearthed stone tools in proximity to fossilized faunal (animal) bones bearing clear stone-tool cut marks. These finds offer unmistakable evidence that 2.6 million years ago it was often steak, not potatoes that our ancestors relished for dinner. (Potatoes are indigenous to South America and 2.6 million years ago the only two-legged creatures living there were birds.)

A short half a million years later—around two million years ago— things started to get really interesting as the bodies of our ancestors began to make distinctive changes in size and form. This remodeling of the body was strongly influenced by a diet more plentiful in meat. Paleoanthropologists call our remodeled ancestors *Homo erectus* ("erect man"), and their bones and advanced stone tools have been found not only in Africa but at several sites in Java (beginning at 1.81 million years), in the Caucasus Mountains in the country of Georgia at a site known as Dmanisi (1.7 million years) and at a newly found site, Majuangou, in northern China west of Beijing, with a proposed date of 1.6 million years. The date is approximate as there is no volcanic material in connection with the site. (Java dating was done by Curtis and Swisher via potassium-argon dating.)

H. erectus was obviously a traveling man and stayed the course for more than 1.5 million years, dying out at different times in different places. The last of his kind disappeared in some areas of the globe by 500,000 years ago, while on islands such as Java, *H. erectus* remains have been found in two caves dated at 50,000 and 25,000 years ago. The late dates for Java speak to a species isolated by plate tectonics and rising ocean waters. The first *H. erectus* to arrive on Java had walked there. At the time, the Malay Peninsula, Sumatra and Java comprised a continuous land mass. Many skulls were found in the late sites on Java. Some academics see both sites as providing evidence suggestive of cannibalism, which, if correct, should not come as a surprise if one looks at the global picture through a broad lens capable of peering into our deepest past.

In relationship to when *H. erectus* died out, comes the incredible find on the tiny island of Flores in lower Indonesia. Excavations at Liang Bua, a large limestone cave, have produced many bones of a tiny people that have been named *Homo floresiensis* (nicknamed "Hobbit"), with dates from 95,000 years to 13,000 years before present. What is amazing is that the bones tell of a people no more than three feet high with a cranial capacity of a mere 400 cc. That makes the Hobbit's brain equal to that of the famous australopithecine, Lucy. The incredible late date of 13,000 years has con-founded the experts as the Hobbit fails to fit their timeline for humans, and our predecessor *H. erectus*. Among the bones found to date—together with stone tools and evidence of fire—is one skull whose endocast (an inner cra-nial cast of the skull that produces a brain mold) looks more like the brain of an *H. erectus* than anything else, but for the fact that it is tiny. Thanks to my friend, Professor Ralph Holloway (the endocast man) of Columbia University in New York, I have held a replica of the Hobbit's brain; it fits easily in my cupped hands and is no bigger than a small grapefruit. As I held the tiny endocast I knew why I so love paleoanthropology. The Hobbits are mucking up the works, forcing science to do what it has always been brave enough to do, even when it would rather not: search for the truth while accepting the fact that once held beliefs based on available data must be relinquished when new information forces changes in the overall picture previously perceived.

What can be observed in Flores are "cousins," whose brains prob-ably functioned for the sole purpose of surviving. In order to survive, all life forms—including humans—must avert danger, obtain nourishment and reproduce. The arts, institutes of learning, buildings and bridges are not necessary for survival. Folk tales, recounted by modern people who currently live on the Isle of Flores, tell of a tiny people who were incredibly vicious, a people who would eat anything. The excavating scientists be-lieve the Hobbits downsized because of limited food supplies on the island. Other animals, stuck on small islands, have downsized, and on Flores an elephant that was once larger than today's African elephant dwarfed down to the size of a cow. Nature has always molded form to match the environment. The shrunken elephant is now extinct—no doubt killed by diminutive hunters.

Of argumentative interest: since only one skull has been found, some anthropologists insist that it is from an individual who suffered from microcephaly, a rare disorder that produces a diminished cranium resulting in a small brain, distortion of the face and minimal mental capacity.

Being small does not preclude survival tactics, but any human suffering from any form of microcephaly would be hard-pressed to maintain himself. Microcephaly is rarely passed on genetically, and most victims die at an early age. So how do you explain the fact that all of the Hobbit bones found thus far are equal relative to size? (Another argument for you to follow in the press.)

Back to the ancestors we have studied for decades: in *H. erectus* we see a not-so-distant relative that had perfected an array of stone tools, including large hand axes for disarticulating the bones of large animals, and a diet high in protein. With a change in diet, *H. erectus*'s rib bones snuggled in for a streamlined figure in opposition to the flared-out, large, gut-covering rib cage of his mostly vegetarian, tree- and forest-dwelling, knuckle-walking cousins.

It is nice to stand taller and develop a waist, but the most important thing we see in *H. erectus* is his enlarged brain, which measured to be twice that of his upright ancestors of half a million years before. With greater encephalization, *H. erectus* was smart enough to scavenge and kill for meat, thus gaining more protein and fat. These most efficient of foodstuffs aided in the formation of neurons (brain cells), and helped to make *H. erectus* ever more brainy and cunning as the years rolled by.

Now you can understand why the Hobbit, with its tiny brain and bones, is upsetting the apple cart. Can an organism grow bigger and smarter, then downsize and retain enough mental function acquired over the millennia to survive? Humans have done it with many animals, going to the greatest lengths with dogs, all of which are descended from the wolf; but be it a Pekinese or mastiff, a dog is a dog is a dog.

As to size and brains, the Neanderthals had brains 20% larger than ours, while our *Homo sapiens* brains have been shrinking over the last 25,000 years, all of which offers a great deal of food for thought. Calf brains anyone?

0.8 Mya, or 800,000 years ago, in the Burgos mountain range of northern Spain, there lived a group of people who were much closer in bone structure to modern humans than to *H. erectus*. Their fossilized bones are the oldest of our lineage to be found in Europe. Dr. Juan Luis Arsuaga and his team at Universidad Complutense de Madrid have named this group of more than 20 individuals *antecessor* as they believe they were predecessors to both the Neanderthals and to Cro-Magnons—us . . . modern humans . . . *Homo sapiens*.

We know the date of the bones of *Homo antecessor* through magnetic reversal. Today we speak of magnetic north, but the earth's magnetic pole has flipped from the southern end of our planet to the north end many times since the formation of our planet. Volcanic ash contains tiny crystals of magnetite made up of magnetic iron, nickel, cobalt and small amounts of other alloys. Since the earth's core consists of molten iron, it works as a giant magnet, causing grains of volcanic ash to line up as they fall to the ground. Of interest is that magnetic north (or south when a reversal has occurred) never remains in one exact location, but continually moves in an erratic path one to many miles from "true north." Magnetism coming off a bar magnet will show the same variability. While geologists have yet to prove the exact cause of reversals, they have long been able to date the timing of reversals through potassium-argon dating, which measures the rate of decay of potassium to argon gas, a process that begins whenever a rock has been liquified in the furnace of a volcano. Volcanic ash offers us a wealth of information concerning our planet by providing data concerning magnetic reversals and allowing for precise dating. Potassium-argon dating has been refined over the years—thanks to lasers—and is now good to within 1,000 to 10,000 years for dates going back millions of years.

Today there is growing evidence that the earth is heading into another reversal, but it is not known whether we will notice the event or if it will affect life on Earth in any way.

Through potassiumargon dating we know that the last reversal took place 780,000 years ago, giving us the "North Pole" we know and love today, plus a place for Santa to live. And!—the bones of *H. antecessor* were found well below the level of the last magnetic reversal, lying within the beautifully layered stratigraphy of a mountain.

H. antecessor's bones would have never been found if Spain had not decided to cut a railroad pass through the mountains. That fortuitous cut exposed what had once been a huge openair cave that has been given the name Gran Dolina. Over the last decades excavations have yielded the most numerous and amazing paleoanthropological finds ever to be discovered; the Dmanisi site in the Caucasus Mountains is now a contestant for that distinction, though the two sites differ from one another dramatically. At close to a million years in age, *H. antecessor* has proven the existence of a largebrained people whose cranial and facial bones were much like ours, and when fleshed out with clay in the laboratory look much like members of our current family. If these early humans were dressed up in modern clothes and took a ride on the subway they probably would not draw much attention to themselves, certainly less than a Neanderthal whose skull and facial features differed to a more considerable extent from ours.

Fossilized bones discovered at the lowest level of Gran Dolina are the oldest yet found in Europe and represent six individuals who were cannibalized, their bones giving evidence of early human behavior and a people new to the fossil record. Stonetool cut marks that correlate with defleshing and disarticulation, breakage of long bones for extraction of marrow, method of deposition of remains, along with other recognizable evidence, demonstrate the practice of cannibalism within the ranks of some of our oldest kin.

Yesterday, as today, the beliefs and behaviors of different peoples exhibited great variability. *H. antecessor* may have behaved much as any other predator when it came to the procurement of meat. Meat may have been just that, meat, and what kind of animal the meat was derived from may have offered no emotional consequence. Or, since *H. antecessor* is known to have made strong and useful stone tools and lived within socialized groups, they could have attached strong beliefs to acts of cannibalism.

Older than Gran Dolina by more than a million years, is a single maxilla (upper jaw bone) known as Stw 53 "Member 5." The name given to the fossil identifies it as coming from Sterkfontein Cave in South Africa, and "Member 5" denotes where it was found in the limestone labyrinth of the cave.

At the Eighth Annual Meeting of the Paleoanthropolgy Society in Columbus, Ohio, April 27–28, 1999, Travis Pickering, Tim White and Nicholas Toth presented a paper on Stw 53 and the more than 700 faunal bone pieces from large herbivores that were found with Stw 53. The focal point of the paper was the description of stone-tool cut marks incised on the upper right cheekbone of a hominid, one of our evolutionary relatives. The location of the cut marks is consistent with the de-fleshing and disarticulation of a skull. However, the faunal bones show no tool marks! But it should be remembered that humans often garner meat from carcasses without cutting to the bone. Following chapters will give examples.

Stw 53 does not prove cannibalism was practiced two million-plus years ago, and is far too old to be surrounded with a hypothesis of religious ritual or societal belief, but the site of the cut marks would have resulted in the opening of the skull and the exposing of the brain.

Fossil and archaeological evidence from many caves on many continents imply that a great many of our forebears saw nothing wrong or shameful in the act of ingesting others of their own kind. Whether they did so to fill their bellies, fully expunge an enemy, honor their dead, survive the threat of imminent starvation or pay homage to a god or gods can never be known, only conjectured. What is known is that half a century ago cannibalism was still prevalent in many areas of the world and Gran Dolina and

Stw 53 offer the real possibility that only within recent recorded history has the practice of cannibalism been denounced and outlawed.

Today, we have reached a point of discovery that opens wide doors that expose our mental underpinnings. One of the things we are learning is that our genes, in combination with our cultures—which author Dr. Alan Kahn refers to as "memetic organisms"—dictate our behavior. The word "meme" was coined by Richard Dawkins and relates to ideas, fashions and belief systems spreading through a population to the point where they can be distinguished from one society to another; in other words, cultural genes. And memes are what separate us today, as various behavioral and social differences divide us. Take incest, an act well known within our species but frowned upon as going against both instinct, which works towards the strength of a species, and the moral code of many human cultures. Instances of sisters mating with brothers, or parents mating with their children fill the pages of Greek mythology, the Bible and the histories of many a royal family. But pharaohs who married sisters, and royal families who wed too close to the original bed, produced many congenital idiots. Such scenarios were played out for the containment and/or enhancement of wealth, land and power, even though inbreeding had proved to produce some very dull boys and girls. We will never know how many feebleminded offspring were done away with, or kept locked up in dungeons or towers; history hints at a great many, but proof of number is impossible.

Interestingly, recent studies have shown that marriage between second and third cousins has been practiced, and is still being practiced, over much of the world. These studies show that careful pairing between second or third cousins can genetically strengthen a people if the original pair is genetically sound and free of diseases that are genetically passed on, and if cousin-marriages are well spaced through generations. However, in several societies first and second cousins are chosen as young brides on a habitual basis leading to various, and often fatal, congenital diseases. As to the current kissing cousins, they too wed for the sake of keeping it all in the family, and since they have been brought up in identical cultures their marriages are often successful.

In relationship to not looking at your sister or mother as mates, people seem naturally opposed to looking upon others of their own kind as food except during times of starvation, war or culturally motivated incidences. Famines, brought on by climatic variants, war or natural disasters such as droughts, earthquakes, floods, volcanic eruptions or overpopulation are obvious originators for the practice of cannibalism. However, if the substance that saved you from starvation not only sustained the life of your people, but also helped fill your need for protein, then the crafty side of humans, with their high-vaulted foreheads, would quickly find ways of repeating the repast, even after the threat of starvation had passed. And the only way to continue such a practice within an established society would be to build a belief system around the act that makes the *unseemly* palatable and proper. In other words, while the prefrontal lobes of humans, which do not fully mature until you are 24 years old(!), allow for salient decisions, such as deciding not to threaten a bull elephant, if everyone in your memetic organism (society) celebrates the eating of enemies, chances are, you will join the party.

Looking back one can envision times when natural instincts came face to face with devastating disasters, which, when stirred together well, produced various behaviors and attitudes, many of which made it through time to lodge themselves onto a modern list of human taboos.

Or, since chimpanzees have been observed in acts of cannibalism, and we now have evidence of dinosaurs dining on those of their own kind, does the practice go back far, far beyond the time when we stood up? Is cannibalism so old that it constitutes a bit of ancient baggage carried around by all carnivorous and omnivorous creatures and even some herbivores? In the rafters of the old cabin in the woods, within the old reptilian brain, is there a dusty old trunk labeled "C"?

If live monkey brains and eyeball soup are still being relished in various parts of the world, if liver once a week fills your body's need for iron and vitamin A, if gourmets and gourmands love the rich and delicious innards of mammals and fowl, and if liver, tongue, brain, and heart from any mammal or bird can be easily distinguished as being liver, tongue, brain or heart by any blindfolded chef or omnivorous eater, then the consumption of human flesh is wrong for legal, moral, mental and emotional reasons, not because human flesh would fail to offer wholesome nourishment. The human gut (past and present) would digest the flesh of a human just as it does any other source of protein, perhaps better. Recent research indicates that meat from one's own species is more easily digested than flesh from other species (a Tums-taking bit of knowledge if I ever heard one), so the problem with eating those of your own species lies within our large human brains, which, according to the teachings of our individual cultures, will cause great distress in some and calm acceptance amongst others.

Genetic findings, first published in 2003, that mark us all as descendents of cannibals, also show through genetic expression that many of our ancestors enjoyed unique dining experiences as recently as 50 years ago, which should not be too surprising as there are cannibals living today: one is in jail in Germany, three in America and two are up for trial in Africa, while a great many others roam free. And, as following chapters will reveal, many peoples who had previously performed some variety of cannibalism were forced to stop the practice during the last centuries as one invading government, memetic organism or religion after another outlawed the act of consuming your own.

CHAPTER FIVE

CANNIBALISM, DISEASE AND GENETICS

"Calf's brains form the most wholesome and rebuilding diet for all those who are weakened by excessive headwork; and the same remark applies to the brains of the ox and the sheep. The amourettes, which almost always accompany ox brains, are only the spinal marrow of the ox or the calf. This may be used in the preparation of a few special dishes; but all the recipes dealing with brains may be applied to it." —Auguste Escoffier, 1845–1935[1]

pongiform encephalopathies (SEs) are a group of 21 known diseases that cause cellular deterioration of the brain. Prominent SEs that occur in humans are Creutzfeldt-Jakob disease (CJD), mad cow disease (BSE—bovine spongiform encephalopathy), kuru and sporadic fatal insomnia. All SEs are fatal. Irregularly

folded proteins, known as prions, are found in the brains of all victims of all SEs and are considered to be the agent of infection. Prions prompt other brain proteins to mirror their misfolded shape. Then each newly misfolded protein prompts another. In time, the multiplying prions clump together and cause the death of normal brain cells. By the time death arrives the brain resembles a sponge.

Notably, prions are impervious to all methods of sterilization and can be transmitted from animal to animal, animal to human, human to animal and human to human.

I remember standing on a high kitchen stool looking down into the huge pot where more than a gallon of fresh grape juice was boiling together with pounds of sugar. I was four years old and I already knew that my mother made the finest grape jelly in the world. Of course, she had her French grandfather's concord grape vines to harvest and the know-how of not too much sugar. Hours into the process my mother would go to the refrigerator. Out of the ice tray compartment she would extract a small, near-frozen plate. While holding it in one hand, she would carefully stir the grape jelly with a big wooden spoon, lift it above the boiling mass, rim down, and allow the jelly to run off the spoon. The last time she had performed this fete was only a few minutes back; the deep purple liquid had simply run off the spoon in separate streams along its bottom edge. But this time the jelly ran off the spoon in sheets and the last drops ran together along the bottom rim and dropped slowly back into the boiling pot. Placing the cold plate under the spoon my mother allowed a final drop to plop onto the cool surface where it stood high and rounded like the yolk of a truly fresh egg. The jelly was done. The old gas stove was turned off, the jelly jars came out of the oven and the ladling process began. I stood motionless watching every movement. And I almost stopped breathing as the paraffin wax melted in the tiny pot that had only one purpose in life. Then my mother was gently pouring the clear paraffin onto the surface of the still hot jelly; how careful and precise she was at her task. My stomach was grumbling. I could hardly wait for the work to be finished so my mother could toast me a piece of freshly baked bread, butter it lightly and lather it with jelly still warm from the bottom of the pot. Everyone said my mother's grape jelly was the best in the world, even my master-chef father who had cooked for the king of Denmark.

In the same year, thousands of miles away, another child stood in eager anticipation as her mother cooked a special dish, but the cooking vessel was of bamboo and the food that was being prepared was human flesh. Strikingly, it was from a member of the child's tribe.

From the air, the highland mountains of Papua New Guinea appear to stand on end in a blue-green corrugation of tattered material. Gold miners of the 1920s were amazed to find tribes of people living in such rugged terrain, their dwellings perched on narrow mountain spines or in high mountain valley areas formerly believed to be uninhabitable. Some mountains are so steep and high in elevation that tribes separated by a single peak may never make contact. When peoples of the steep mountains were first discovered, it was calculated that some 200,000 individuals dwelled in the eastern highland mountains of the world's second largest island.

Films from the '20s and '30s show tribesmen laughing and shaking in shock and amazement as they gaze for the first time upon white men, whom they believed to be ghosts of their dead. Having dwelled in isolation for thousands of years, the mountain tribes had lost all memory and knowledge of the ocean that surrounds their island even though they possessed highly prized seashells traded up from the coasts. Like the Asmat tribes on the western end of the island, they had no chiefs, but recognized some men as being more powerful. The men adorned themselves with nose bones crafted from the bones of the cassowary bird, beaded and feathered headdresses, and penis sheaths. The women wore grass skirts, cut fingers off at the joints to show mourning and dried the hands of dead infants to wear around their necks in remembrance.

The early gold miners, and those who followed them, found many, but not all, of the tribes living in the lofty mountains of Papua New Guinea. In the early '50s, an Australian patrol officer and his translator were tromp-

ing up and down mountains of the eastern highlands when the patrol officer noticed a small village on a mountain spine to the south. Pointing to a
grouping of huts, he asked, "Who are those people?" The translator said,
"Fore" (For-ray), which the officer dutifully noted in his journal thinking it
to be the name of a tribe. But "fore" simply means, "people to the south."
As with many indigenous peoples of the world, the "Fore" had never named
themselves. Living in the wilds, far from city-states and beyond the reach of
other controlling tribes, few peoples living in isolated areas ever bothered to
label themselves. When pushed by explorers, anthropologists and government employees, nameless tribes have invariably come up with a word(s)
that translates out to "*the* people," as in *original*, often with the inference
that the intruders are not.

Today, all of the tribes in the southern area of the eastern highlands of Papua New Guinea identify themselves as Fore. The first village of
Fore sighted was the village of Okapa, one of some 160 villages scattered
throughout the highlands; a village that was in great peril.

The Fore of Okapa have become famous within many fields of science because of their late discovery and a killing disease they call "kuru"—
the shaking sickness—a spongiform encephalopathy. Kuru had been
transmitted through several generations by infected human brain and spinal
cord tissue consumed during feasts of funerary cannibalism. By the time of
discovery, the disease had spread from one village to another through marriages into other tribes that also practiced endocannibalism.

Kuru had brought the people of Okapa close to extinction, a fact
that enhanced the fame of the Fore as the study of kuru led to the discovery of prions, a more thorough understanding of all spongiform encephalopathies, two Nobel Prizes in the field of medicine and, ultimately, the
discovery of genetic markers that offer evidence that we all have cannibals
in our closets.

As set forth in the foreword, cannibalism has been practiced in a
variety of ways. Over the centuries many tribes in New Guinea practiced
exocannibalism (the eating of revenge victims, enemies or outsiders), but

as far as is known, the Fore were not among them. The Fore engaged solely in endocannibalism, the eating of kin upon the occurrence of their natural or accidental death.

The practice of endocannibalism began among the Fore during the first decades of the twentieth century. Australian anthropologist Shirley Lindenbaum, who worked with the Fore during the early '60s, has stated that the Fore took to eating their dead in imitation of neighboring tribes to the north, but regardless of how cannibalism begins within any group of people, once established as being proper, customs and beliefs are set in place until the practice is looked upon in a positive fashion. And so it was with the Fore, until 1956, when the Australian government outlawed cannibalism.

The Fore believed the consumption of tribal members showed affection towards the deceased and was the best way in which to process their grief. The body provided valuable protein, and the consuming of the flesh was a way of showing respect and love, of taking in the essence of a loved one as opposed to burying the body in sugar-cane gardens, to rot and decay. One man commented that he could not understand anyone wanting to bury a loved one in the cold, wet ground rather than incorporating the body into oneself so that the dear departed could be forever with the consumer in body and spirit.

Fore women told anthropologists that when they first tasted human flesh they found it to be sweet and asked themselves why they had not taken advantage of such good meat in the past. They even wondered at their madness, at the wasteful disposal of good food that could have enhanced the diet of their people.

As the practice of endocannibalism became accepted, dying Fore could ask to be eaten or buried in the ground; a majority chose to be consumed. In some reported cases, women not only asked to be consumed, but assigned various body parts to favored friends or relatives in advance of their demise. In all other instances the allocation of body parts was ordered by the men, commensurate with the distribution of pig meat.

Antithetical to most cannibalistic tribes, Fore women dissected the majority of corpses, carefully butchering their loved ones using bamboo knives and stone tools. And it was the women who relished the organs, especially the brain and spinal cord. Fore men did not practice cannibalism per se, nor did they share bush meat with their wives or children. When a funerary feast took place the men ate sparingly of muscle meat, shunned organ meats, and dined in seclusion. So it was that the women and children of the Fore comprised the vast majority of kuru victims.

Out of respect for the dead, Fore women rarely cleaned their hands and bodies of a relative's brains and bodily fluids during the preparation and cooking of a corpse. It was suggested by early researchers that transmission of kuru might occur when a baby's eyes, mouth or nose were wiped or touched by the loving hands of a mother who was busy working with the body of a deceased tribal member, but such transmission is difficult at best, demanding open cuts or wounds through which the lethal prions can enter. More research inferred that kuru was transmitted through the process of consuming diseased brain matter. Likewise, Fore children and infants were most likely exposed to lethal prions when fed steamed brains lovingly cooked in bamboo tubes.

The Fore did not consume all who died. Victims of dysentery or leprosy were buried, but owing to the variable and lengthy time of incubation for kuru (up to 40 years or more), the Fore never connected the disease with acts of cannibalism.

The butchering of the corpse was performed away from the village, often in the women's sweet potato gardens where up to 40 women and children would gather for the event and subsequent feast. After de-fleshing the bodies with bamboo knives, Fore women used stone axes to disarticulate the body, cracking the long bones for the extraction of marrow and the cranium for the brain. Every single part of the body was consumed but for the teeth and bile sack. Sexual organs went to the closest kin of the opposite sex.

When all meats, organs and offal had been processed and eaten, the remaining bones, and bone pieces, were placed by the fire pit. After a week or so of slow roasting, the bones would be pounded in bamboo containers and the resultant "salt" would be sprinkled over cooked vegetables, offering a healthy dose of calcium. In the end there were no remains whatsoever to be found of the cannibalism that had taken place. Authors Jennifer Cooke, Nigel Davies and Richard Rhodes all offer reports of cannibals (on a global scale) using or consuming every scrap of the body, thus leaving no trace of cannibalism for future investigators to find.

The Fore attributed kuru to sorcery, and since all victims died of the disease, kuru was the most feared form of sorcery known to the tribe. It was believed that any man could put the curse of kuru upon a woman, as none had thought to connect feast to illness. Anthropologists Shirley Lindenbaum and Robert Glasse were the first to tie events of cannibalism to kuru in the 1960s. After years of research, Australian doctor Michael Alpers[2] connected collected data and proved their insightful observations.

The last documented cases of cannibalism within tribes of the Fore were reported in the '60s, though more recent reports relate incidences reaching into the '80s. In relationship to early incidents of cannibalism, and kuru's long incubation time, one to three new cases of kuru a year were reported within studied tribes during the '80s as elderly Fore continued to succumb to the disease even though the last cannibalistic feast they themselves had attended had been in their teens.

Since the 1950s, an estimated 2,500 Fore have died from kuru. By the time cannibalism was outlawed in 1956, the population of many Fore villages had been severely depleted of women in their reproductive years. The demise of fecund women, along with a great many children of both sexes, presented clear evidence of an epidemic; kuru had taken a ghastly toll. Lacking sufficient women of childbearing age, Fore men offered bride prices for any available females from neighboring tribes.

Peoples of the world, whether they be cannibalistic or not, show affection towards clan-mates. Biology has shown that the desire to be a parent, the emotional drive to be a good or bad parent, the desire for sex, plus emotions such as altruism, pride, fear, depression, elation and so forth are based on genetics, societal imprinting and brain chemicals, which combine to prompt various behaviors. Before Western society entered into the arena of the Fore, they were a gentle, loving, egalitarian people who adored their children, giving them free reign as soon as they could walk. Everyone took care of a child in need, and each person responded to the emotional needs of others, often without the use of words. A look, a movement and someone would be caring for another or helping with a task. The Fore were so free in spirit and open to all experiences that they readily accepted and kept the name mistakenly given to them at the time of first contact.

E. Richard Sorenson, in a 1977 *Smithsonian* article entitled "Growing Up as a Fore Is to Be 'In Touch' and Free," wrote of how quickly the Fore dropped their old egalitarian ways as never imagined people, ideas, clothing, steel tools, medicine, salt and countless other modern items were encountered. The Fore had a long history of individual pursuit concerning all things economic and social and quickly discarded their indigenous ways. But many, if not most, seemed to enter an emotional and mental state of cultural shock as their world changed around them. As their world changed, the Fore traded their old habits for new. In time some could not recall how they once dressed, the making of stone tools or the eating of their dead close relatives.

The capacity of the mind to change its way of thinking coupled with the natural proclivity of humans to "upgrade" themselves to anything they deem new and better is clearly what has led many anthropologists and ethnographers to believe that habitual and/or cultural cannibalism was rarely, if ever, practiced. The denial by some Fore concerning past practices reflects a normal desire to be more "modern" coupled with the fear of disapproval by those who now overshadow their lives. It is a lesson that warns of false truths that can be expected by an investigator when interviewing current generations concerning practices performed by their ancestors, or, in many cases, the very people the investigator is interviewing. There are volumes on cannibalism that tell of cannibals coming out of their "closets" only after the interviewer proved that he or she was not connected with the government, church or any other institution that had controlled, repressed or jailed the cannibal and his people because of their beliefs and practices.

The immense literature on cannibalism offers a pattern: First, a cannibalistic people are contacted by the "outside," then overwhelmed, their lives being irretrievably changed as the more technologically adept outsiders bring in items and ideas beyond their imagination. Then, and most cruel to the psyche, they are forced to obey new laws that go against their systems of belief as well as follow the religious teachings of the outsiders, both of which forbid cannibalism. As a final belittlement, they are encouraged to whitewash their own history by being admonished to "not talk about it."

In times past it was not unusual for 60% to 80% of an indigenous population to die from diseases brought to them by explorers or conquerors, diseases for which they had no immunity. Today, with the aid of modern medicines, and few, if any, tribes left to be found, the number of epidemic deaths has dropped dramatically. The Fore present a unique case, where an indigenous population was not killed off, but saved from extinction through contact with people from the outside. If not for contact with the outside, and strict laws against the practice of cannibalism laid down by the Australian government, the Fore may well have died out. The Fore present a prime example of depopulation within a people via a disease not introduced by outsiders, which offers alternative thoughts as to how past populations of hominids and humans may have met with extinction.

In contrast to the condition in which they were found, the Fore of today are coffee growers and businessmen, there are roads leading upwards into their mountain-top lands, and they are once again a vibrant and healthy people who maintain a working relationship with doctors, researchers and anthropologists in studying the genetics and etiology of kuru and other spongiform encephalopathy diseases.

Such work has brought forth many scientific findings. In the April 25, 2003 issue of the journal *Science*, researchers John Collinge, Simon Mead and colleagues at University College London reported their findings

on extensive genetic work done with the Fore. By studying the genes of surviving Fore women who had participated in funerary cannibalistic feasts in
the years of their youth, protective genes were found in 23 of the 30 females
studied. Their report suggests that cannibalism practiced in ancient times
may have brought on episodes of spongiform encephalopathies, which, in
turn, pressured the human genome to develop protective genes against such
diseases. The genetic markers are polymorphisms; one being a mutant version of a normal prion protein gene. Natural selection would have favored all
who carried the mutated genes, as they do today. Of the aged Fore women
who carry the protective genes, none has been stricken with kuru, though
all had participated in one or more funerary feasts. The mutated polymorphisms (prions) have been found among all peoples on a global scale. It has
therefore been hypothesized that their selection for persistence within the
human genome occurred very early in our evolution. Collinge suggests the
mutations occurred prior to modern humans spreading around the globe.
Archaeological and paleoanthropological findings and research would agree.
Epidemics of spongiform encephalopathies brought on by cannibalism in
ancient populations would have produced the mutations that offer two protective genetic signatures now found in peoples from around the world. The
Japanese and some southern Asians differ somewhat in that a different signature of the same gene protects them.

Most importantly, the genetic variations found by the researchers
protect against all spongiform encephalopathies (now referred to as prion
diseases). None of the British victims of mad cow disease carried the beneficial markers, but most Britons do, which provides suggestive evidence as
to why only 134 people out of a population of 50 million have succumbed
to the beastly disease.

Further studies performed since early 2003 suggest that possession of the right genes may not protect completely against prion diseases,
but hold these diseases at bay for such long periods of time that the carrier
usually dies of other causes prior to an onslaught of misfolded prions. The
most current research suggests that with the right markers, incubation

time can extend to half a century or more.

For research performed during work with the Fore, two Nobel Prizes were awarded for findings on the complexities of kuru. the first to Daniel Carleton Gajdusek (USA) in 1976, for identification of an infectious disease process with an unusually long incubation time, and the second to Stanley B. Prusiner (USA) in 1997, for the discovery of prions, the disease-passing, misfolded proteins found in the brain tissue of all spongiform encephalopathy victims.

For millions of years our ancestors were prey to terrifying predators, starvation, annihilating weather patterns, natural disasters and others of their own kind; that cannibalism was part of the picture should not come as a surprise. Indeed, the plethora of archaeological evidence, as well as artifacts and histories, both oral and written, point to a global story as well as periodicity, as no group of people seem to have continued the practice indefinitely, though their descendants often returned to the practice for undocumented reasons (episodes of starvation or overpopulation would be the best bet).

In our current cultural atmosphere, many will continue to throw a wet blanket over any and all evidence of up-close-and-personal dining, but anyone who reads current scientific investigations and the massive and diverse volumes of available literature that began with the advent of writing will find it difficult at best not to accept the practice of cannibalism within the human species.

And should you view the Fore as primitive, you might find it interesting that the peoples of New Guinea have not only inhabited their wild island for more than ten thousand years, but were some of the world's first agriculturists. As reported in a July 2003 issue of *Science*, recent studies at Kuk Swamp in the highlands of Papua New Guinea show that purposeful cultivation occurred on the wetland margins at 10,220 to 9,910 years BP (before present), and that by 7,000 years ago the cultivation of several plants was fully developed. Such findings are clear markers for invention and social organization.

Today, the high mountains of the world have been climbed and few, if any, indigenous peoples remain unknown. Today, technology and religions raise the highest barriers between peoples, each carrying the potential for leveling the playing field or blowing us to smithereens.

CHAPTER SIX

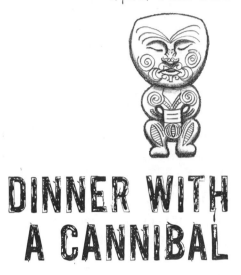

DINNER WITH
A CANNIBAL

"Subsequent to killing and eating the giant Moa bird into extinction, the Maori dined on fish, farmed vegetables, dogs, rats and an occasional human or two. . . . The greatest insult to be offered to an enemy was to eat him."[1]

n the early 1970s, my late husband, Dick Travis, purchased a carved wooden Maori lintel (a decorative horizontal piece affixed over a door or window) in the area of Rotorua on the North Island of New Zealand. In 1981, the two of us returned to New Zealand anxious to find more of these wonderful carvings, but to our dismay none could be found. Regardless of shop or gallery, no Maori carvings were available for sale. Finally a shopkeeper told us that the carvings were no longer being produced and that the older ones had been collected by the national museums, which were where we found them, each one carefully mounted behind glass enclosures and well guarded. In our search for Maori lintels, we were told by white New Zealanders that there were only about 80 full-blooded Maoris left and that the Maori would soon join the thousands of races that exist solely in text.

In the fall of 1985, I was in the city of my birth, Los Angeles, where I had the good fortune to meet Mr. Gavin Thompson, trade commissioner to Los Angeles from the New Zealand Consulate. I told him about the lintel and how much I wished to know more about the meanings behind the carving. Mr. Thompson said, "I have the perfect man for you in my office. His name is Erima Henare. He is Maori and an expert in the field of Maori art. I am sure he would be interested in your carving." I lamented that I had to fly back to Wyoming the following day, but promised to respond with a photo and letter as soon as possible. I kept my promise, but by the time I could return to Los Angeles it was February of 1986. I reread the letter I had received from Vice Consul Erima Henare. The last paragraph read, "I am pleased to see that you purchased the carving while in New Zealand and above all have an appreciation of fine art."

I picked up the phone and called Mr. Henare. We exchanged pleasantries and backgrounds. As we got into the field of anthropology, I threw in a blockbuster, "A friend of mine gave me a very precious Christmas gift, a book published in 1876 entitled *The Human Race* by Louis Figuier. Mr. Figuier states that your people were avid cannibals. I know a Fijian chief and know well the pride they take in their past dining modes. I had known your people to have consumed human flesh, but I had not been aware they had added such protein to their diet in such an ardent fashion. Mr. Figuier writes, 'the New Zealanders are openly and cynically cannibals, that they relish with extreme satisfaction the palpitating flesh of enemies who have fallen at their hands.' He also states that your women were filthy and smelled of fish oil."

After a brief hesitation Erima came back with mock disdain, "Do you realize that you are speaking to a full-blooded Maori?"

With a chuckling voice, I replied, "Marvelous. You are just the man who can answer all of my questions." A time for meeting was quickly arranged.

I arrived at the New Zealand Consulate two days later at 4:30 P.M. A Fijian receptionist greeted me and buzzed me through to Erima's office. "It will be just a moment," she said.

I looked over the library in the consulate's waiting room. It was an anthropologist's dream, and I wished I were a champion speed-reader. I was perusing a photo of a carving of a well-endowed Maori male when the door from the inner office opened and Erima Henare came forward to greet me. Erima is a tall, impressive man and more than I had expected. He is well over six feet and handsome in both build and appearance. He has great dark eyes and a head of black hair that would make a bald man pale. His hair is not coarse, but wavy, with a thickness and blackness never found on a Caucasian. His smile pleased me and I willingly followed him into his private office.

We sat and talked. Evening came on and we continued to hack our way through thick jungles of thoughts, facts and feelings concerning the delights and differences between races and peoples of the earth. Eventually we got to the meat of the matter when I asked, "Were the Maoris cannibals?"

"Of course, it is well documented. My great-grandfather said the hands and arms of young children made for the best eating. "

"Ah, shades of *Kon-Tiki* where the Orinoco cannibal said the best thing he had ever eaten was the hand of a five-year-old. Figuier quotes a chief as saying that the brain was the greatest delicacy and the buttocks the most substantial."

"A good quote. I get very upset with anthropologists who say that we ate the brain to gain the knowledge of our enemies and their hearts to gain their courage. Fiddle-faddle, we ate them because those are the best parts. Brains are rich and fatty and the heart is chewy and of great taste. The corresponding parts of any mammal we eat today will tell you the same."

I agreed and continued, "Several academics and scholars have writ-

ten and loudly proclaimed that human cannibalism has never been practiced except for instances of starvation, such as the Donner Party, and that
there is no real scientific evidence of habitual cannibalism."

"That is absurd!" Erima said in amazement. "Someone should eat
them; they could take notes posthumously."

"I love it. I gave a smashing dinner party two months ago, but there
is not a single shred of provable evidence that it ever took place. You would
have to believe my words and those of my guests."

"I don't understand the reasoning of some anthropologists. I think
they are wrong when they say that my people originated out of Asia," said
Erima, changing the subject.

"At times, I too disagree with them."

"You do? Marvelous. Where do you think we came from?"

"Possibly the Americas since your people arrived on your islands
long after people had made their way into North, Central and South Americas. Of course, the blood of the peoples of the Americas show a genetic
ancestry that links them to just north of Lake Baikal in Russia and also
with Asia."

"Still, you think my people could have migrated from the western
hemisphere. Why?"

"Prevailing ocean and wind currents."

Erima opened a book to a picture of a full-blooded Maori. "Where
would you say this fellow came from?"

"Would you believe Tijuana?" I queried facetiously.

"Right. Our art shows signs of coming from the Americas, and
we know that logs that float out of the mouths of rivers in the state of
Washington have ended up on the shores of Hawaii. The Alaskan Inuit
could be our cousins. It is common knowledge that at one time the peoples
of Oceana sailed all over the Pacific. Some say my people landed in canoes
around 1300, but I believe we go back much farther than that. We do
know that after arriving on our islands we became totally cut off from the
rest of the Polynesian peoples—our unique society proves it. We were a

highly socialized, self-governing people who delighted in war. Our skin is olive to tan, and our ancestors were of great stature. Our oral history speaks of men growing to eight or nine feet tall. Since the infusion of British blood we have grown shorter and shorter. My great-grandfather was six-foot-seven and 20 stone, about 300 pounds."

"The great height of your ancestors was probably from all that fine protein they were consuming. The Fijians are also a very tall race. I have always attributed their height to their past diet. Once they killed off and ate the land animals they started feasting on each other and up they grew. The Japanese have been ascending to unheard of heights since World War II. Scientists say it is strictly due to a change in diet brought on by the introduction of milk given to children, especially orphans, following WWII. It only took one generation of milk-drinking children to start the upward growth pattern."

Erima nodded as I continued, "I don't mean to be rude but there must have been an Englishman in one of your ancestral closets. You look too Caucasian to be full-blooded Maori."

"You are right, one of my great-grandfathers was white. I'm seven-eighths Maori." Erima showed me a picture of his father, who is extremely handsome and very Caucasian in his looks.

"Those British certainly have strong genes. When my husband and I were in New Zealand we were told that there were approximately 80 full-blooded Maori left in the world."

"Baloney. Since the war my people have gone from being looked down upon to being assimilated, but with the work of my father, others, and myself Maori are once again marrying only Maori and our population is swelling at an incredible rate. It is estimated that by 2010 we will outnumber the whites."

"How do you feel about overpopulation?"

"I haven't really given it much thought. There are 67 million sheep in New Zealand, but only about three and a half million people. It's just not a problem we have had to think about."

"How do the whites feel about your Maori population explosion?"

"They are not too happy about it. They are constantly trying to claim that the re-insurgency of Maori thought and life is a communist plot. It's ridiculous. My people have always been proud and self-governing. We would have fought off all of the British but they just kept coming. We killed vast numbers of them but they didn't fight fairly. They brought venereal diseases to our islands along with diseases of the lung. VD and TB killed thousands of my people. We became too diminished in numbers and too weak physically to continue our fight against the British intruders. But our women must not have smelled too badly, because the Limeys took to them right away."

As evening approached, hunger took over the conversation. A half-hour later we arrived at Madame Woo's and sat at the bar while they readied our table. Erima asked me several questions about my life and myself. Through this discussion I learned that he has a degree in psychology, and that Maori marriages are arranged at the time of birth by the child's family.

Madame Woo seated us.

"What about your family?"

"My father is of very high rank. I am the sixth of six children, born just prior to World War II. My father was with the famous Maori troupe. He was gone seven years and was one of the few to return. The Maoris sent 5,000 men into battle against the Germans. Rommel said that if he'd had the Maoris on his side, he would not have been defeated. A Maori warrior does not like to shoot a man from a distance; he likes to know that his enemy is dead. They used to take the bayonets off of their rifles, discard the guns and charge the enemy with such neck-slitting ferocity that the Germans came to fear them like the plague. The Maoris would do their old war chants and get themselves all psyched up. They were a tough act to stop. We lost most of our troop at Casino, Italy."

"When you were little did your mother speak to you in English or Maori?"

"Maori. I entered kindergarten not knowing a word of English and

I got a caning for going to the loo without asking permission. When I asked my older brother why I had been beaten, I could not believe that you had to ask someone if you could relieve yourself. I nursed at my mother's breast until I was seven. I would run home from school and nurse before sitting down to lunch. My father says that is why I am so good at languages."

"How many do you speak?"

"Maori, English, Greek, Latin and German. I pick up on languages with great ease. Reading and writing were difficult for me, but if I hear something just once, I've got it."

"Have you ever been married?"

"Yes. She was betrothed to me at birth. We are a very family-oriented people, and parents set marriages so as to strengthen their families. When I was young I thought the marriage they had set for me wasn't right, that I would be happier running off around the world and finding my own mate, but as our wedding date drew near, I realized how right she was for me and I fell in love with her. We had been married only six months when we attended a Maori gathering in the meetinghouse. She had an asthma attack and died. She was pregnant. The whole thing was very devastating to me. I wanted to bury her in our family graveyard, but my father rejected the idea. I couldn't believe it. He explained that though he had loved my wife very much, we were both still very young, and that in time I would find myself a new wife, and there would be no place for the new wife to be buried when she died. He said that it was best that my wife's body be returned to her family. It would soothe them and leave me open to continue with the rest of my life. She had been of high birth and they buried her in full Maori adornment. Her personal things were included; she was very beautiful."

"Tell me about the burying of your dead."

"It is done quickly. In the old days the body was bound in a seated position and draped with finery in accordance with the rank of the deceased. Women in mourning would lacerate their breasts and arms using shark teeth or obsidian flakes. Sometimes men would lacerate themselves, but it was a practice performed mostly by the women. Young boys never have their hair cut until a close relative dies, then the hair is cut and placed with the corpse. My one brother didn't get his hair cut until he was thirteen. He had hair down to his buns. When my grandfather died, my brother's long tresses were cut and placed in the coffin."

"Then, if you exhumed a body and found very long lengths of hair, you could surmise that no one in that person's family had died for a long time?"

"Right."

"Too bad hair disintegrates over time, except under unique circumstances. Tell me about your women."

"We were, and still are to a large degree, a chauvinistic society. A woman was never allowed to touch the head of a man. If the man was of rank it was an absolute taboo. A woman could actually be killed for touching a man's head, especially if she touched the head of a chief—whether he was alive or dead. I have always figured that if a woman could not touch the head of a man, then we not only didn't kiss one another, but we must have coupled in the most acrobatic ways imaginable. It's a wonder we kept our populations up."

"What about birthing?"

"That was woman's work. I know that it was done in a squatting position and that if a deformed child was born, it was put to death. Before we converted to Christianity, we also killed all homosexuals, regardless of rank or stature. If a woman was married to a man of high rank, and he died or was killed, she too had to die because if she made love with another man it would be a complete insult to the memory of her slain husband."

"Shades of India and many other lands."

"Umm. Men were allowed as many wives as they wanted and could afford. The council had to give consent, but usually there wasn't a problem so long as the man could afford them. If a chief with many wives died, there would be a lot of slaughtering going on as they all had to die for the sake of his honor. Before being put to death the wives would smear themselves with ochre and shark oil. Perhaps the man in your book came by on a day when a lot of women were preparing to meet their maker."

"What about religion?"

"Many historians, religious leaders and anthropologists say that we were polytheistic, but that's not totally accurate. We did have many lesser gods and spirits that were attached to singular areas of our lives, such as the weather, our health, war, love, etc., but we had only one overall god and that was Io. He was the one true God, the others were earthly deities and small in comparison with Io."

"Then you basically believed in one true or main god?"

"Yes. I have always thought of God as a chameleon. When Christ appeared in Jerusalem he came as a Jew. Buddha was Asian, Io was Maori. God is always a reflection of those who serve him, but he is still only one God."

"You speak as though you are a Christian."

"I am. I was baptized in the Anglican Church."

"I have always been fascinated with the acceptance of new religions presented to, or forced upon, aboriginal tribes by conquering men and missionaries. Most primitive peoples are devout in their own religions. Why do you think your people accepted Christianity?"

"I am often asked that question, and the answer lies in the fact that my people were already very religious, so religion was comfortable for them. Also, they loved anything that showed the tangibility or proof of a god, and the missionaries came with crosses, bibles, robes, goblets and churches. I am sure it seemed overwhelming proof to my people that the god of the invaders was truly powerful. I should think that it was very easy for them to convert."

"There are places today in Africa and the Amazon jungle where converts are bought with cloth, food, seed, guns and bullets. In one part of Kenya a person cannot receive health care at a church-funded clinic until they show proof of church attendance. I wonder at the true devotion of such converts."

"I am aware of these things, but I doubt it was that way when my people were converted by the English missionaries. Of course, we often joke that we should have eaten more of them."

"What about my carving? Is it indicative of carvings made prior to the invasion of the British?"

"Oh, yes. The designs have not changed for centuries. The curled palm hearts represent the continuation of life, the universe and so forth. The oblong, petal-like designs with the crease down their middles represent the most precious part of the female anatomy."

"Do tell," I said.

"That's nothing. When the Limeys landed they were all over our women, but were complete prudes at heart. You see, all of our carvings incorporated both male and female genitalia, and the male member was always carved at attention."

"Historically and anthropologically, that falls into well-documented global patterns observed in both art and behavior. Street and building signs in ancient Greece, as well as Italy, were often carved in the profile of an erect phallus, and when a young man of northeastern Africa had killed his first man, he was given a wooden brow band with an erect phallus carved on the front. Today, the same tribe no longer demands the killing of a human to gain adulthood; dancing has replaced the mandatory killing initiation of times past and a headband with an upright feather has replaced the phallus. Please, do go on."

"Those dumb blokes went all over our islands lopping off every erect piece of wood they could find. But they were so ignorant of female anatomy and art forms that they left all of the carved vaginas without a scratch. They never had a clue as to what they were looking at."

Erima went on to explain how he was captivated by American women, but that should he ever marry again it would be to a Maori, as no one else would do.

We were back on the subject of prudish, hatchet-wielding mariners and both laughing when our waitress came by to ask if we desired another beer.

"No, thank you," I said.

"You need another beer," said Erima

"No," I protested.

"Look—how often do you get to have dinner with a cannibal?"

Smiling at the startled waitress, I consented, "I'll have another beer, thank you."

AS YOU BELIEVE,

SO

SHALL

IT

BE

CHAPTER SEVEN

RELIGIOUS ACTS

"O you who believe, you shall avoid any suspicion, for even a little bit of suspicion is sinful. You shall not spy on one another, nor shall you backbite one another; this is as abominable as eating the flesh of your dead brother. You certainly abhor this. You shall observe GOD. GOD is Redeemer, Most Merciful"   —Koran 49:12

hree hundred miles south of Cairo, seven Muslim farmers set out to gather *sabakh*, a rich nitrogen fertilizer, at the base of a cliff across the Nile from the village of Nag Hammadi. As the digging began, a young man's shovel struck something hard. Further digging exposed a skeleton lying next to a two-foot-high pottery jar sealed tight with a bowl-like cap and bitumen. At first the finders were afraid to open the jar, fearing poison or an evil genie. But what if it contained gold or jewels? The jar was quickly demolished. An unrealized treasure lay within. For the first time in more than 1,500 years, six leather-bound books felt the rays of the sun. Mahammed Ali, the older brother of the boy who found the skeleton and the jar, took charge and tore the books apart so that each man would have a fair share. The young farmers were of a settled Bedouin tribe and could neither read nor write, so six of the *sabakh* gatherers decided to walk away from the find empty-handed. But the young man whose shovel had found the treasure gathered up the books in his turban, lugged them home and placed them in a shed where animals were kept. That night his mother used a few of the crisp pages to start a fire for the evening meal.

The books, now known as the Nag Hammadi Library, are a collection of 13 ancient codices containing over 50 texts, comprising the most significant group of lost Christian writings ever found. Written in the Coptic language, they contain previously unknown Gospels, a small portion of Plato's *Republic* and the now famous, or infamous, according to one's religious views, Gospel of Thomas.

Closer to our topic is how the books got from a shed-like barn in Middle Egypt to a Coptic priest and from there into the hands of scholars. At the time of the discovery, the finder's family was embroiled in a blood feud. The father of Mohammed Ali and his brother had shot a man late at night while working as a night guard protecting German irrigation equipment. The following day the father was killed by a member of the deceased's family. A month after finding the skeleton, jar and books, an informer told the brothers where the murderer of their father was sleeping by a road. Taking up their shovels they found the sleeping man and slashed him to death. After cutting open the chest cavity, they extracted the man's quivering heart and ate it in a formal act of revenge.

The time of the occurrence was December 1945. Eighteen months later, the Dead Sea Scrolls would be found in the Judean desert.

The Dead Sea Scrolls are the oldest Christian writings found thus far. Discovered in caves near the site of Qumran, they sparked decades of religious argument, wonder and intrigue, much of which continues to this day.

The Qumran text Enoch 1–36 (The Book of Watchers), interprets Genesis 6:1–4 in which God's good angels descended to earth where they were smitten by women. Their infatuation led to unnatural marriages that gave way to the birthing of giants whose strength and violence led to war, destruction and cannibalism. In response to these events God caused a great flood.

> And there was a great famine in Samaria: and, behold, they besieged it, until an ass's head was sold for fourscore pieces of silver, and the fourth part of a cab of dove's dung for five pieces of silver. Then, as the king of Israel was passing by upon the wall, there cried a woman unto him, saying, "Help, my lord, O king." And he said, "If the LORD do not help thee, whence shall I help thee? Out of the barn floor, or out of the winepress?" And the king said unto her, "What aileth thee?" And she answered, "This woman said unto me, 'Give thy son, that we may eat him today, and we will eat my son tomorrow.' So we boiled my son, and did eat him; and I said unto her on the next day, 'Give thy son, that we may eat him': and she hath hid her son." And it came to pass, when the king heard the words of the woman, that he rent his clothes; and he passed by upon the wall, and the people looked, and behold, he had sackcloth within upon his flesh. (2 Kings 6:25–30)[1]

Even the jackals draw out the breast, they give suck to their young ones; the daughter of my people is become cruel, like the ostriches in the wilderness. The tongue of the sucking child cleaveth to the roof of his mouth for thirst; the young children ask bread, and none breaketh it unto them. They that did feed on dainties are desolate in the streets: they that were brought up in scarlet embrace dunghills. . . . They that are slain with the sword are better than they that are slain with hunger; for these pine away, stricken through for want of the fruits of the field. The hands of women full of compassion have sodden their own children; they were their food in the destruction of the daughter of my people. (Lamentations 4:3–5, 9–10)[2]

And from a new-age edition of the Bible the last passage reads: "With their own hands, compassionate women have cooked their own children who became their food when my people were destroyed."

Following the report of postwar cannibalism in Lamentations, events of cannibalism are thoroughly condemned, and those who chose life over death are banished and abused. The "Lord" had warned of a conflict that would lead to famine and starvation; he had told his people they would come to a point of eating their own if they did not follow his words. What the Lord God failed to tell his followers was that he would punish those who, under dire conditions, chose life over death.

The biblical story recounted above offers testimony that war, famine, starvation and cannibalism are a string of events that have encircled people and brought them to their knees over and over again throughout the ages of our existence.

And thou shalt eat the fruit of your own body, the flesh of thy sons and thy daughters, which the Lord your God has given thee, in the siege and in the straitness, wherewith thine enemies shall distress thee. . . . The tender and delicate woman among you, which would not adventure to set the sole of her foot upon the ground for delicateness and tenderness, her eye shall be evil toward her son and toward her daughter. And toward her young one that cometh out from between her feet, and toward her children which she shall bear: for she shall eat them for the straitness, where-with thine enemy shall distress thee in thy gates. (Deuter-onomy 28:53, 56–57)[3]

Deuteronomy, Chapter 28, begins with the Lord promising his people all things marvelous, from fine crops and sturdy children to victory over every plague, vermin and enemy. Then the Lord God lists all that will occur should his people fail to honor and love him; including the horrors of verses 53, 56 and 57. It is a sobering read, suggested for all who wish to know the illnesses, events and terrifying occurrences known to the times that occur repeatedly throughout the Old Testament. And while some might argue that the readings from Deuteronomy do not relate to actual occurrences, Lamentations erases the argument.[4]

The Old and New Testaments are litanies of troubled times, past, present and future. Even the burning fires of hell mirror the actual burn-ing of firstborn children in the tophets of old, such as those sacrificed to Moloch.[5]

In Micah 3, the god of the Bible tells his people that the old ways must be put aside, that cannibalism cannot be tolerated, and that penalties will be put upon them if they do not change their ways. Those words, and other like statements found in the Old Testament prompted future genera-tions to look upon all cannibals as savages, and were used as excuses by Ferdinand and Isabella when they decreed that all cannibals were to be put to the sword or the flames of Inquisitor priests.

While overt acts of cannibalism are confined to the Old Testa-ment, the New Testament commands the practice of symbolic cannibalism to all who believe in Christ.

"Verily, verily, I say unto you, He that believeth on me hath everlasting life. I am that bread of life. Your fathers did eat manna in the wilderness, and are dead. This is the bread which cometh down from heaven, that a man may eat thereof, and not die. I am the living bread which came down from heaven: if any man eat of this bread, he shall live for ever: and the bread that I will give is my flesh, which I will give for the life of the world."

The Jews therefore strove among themselves, saying, "How can this man give us his flesh to eat?"

Then Jesus said unto them, "Verily, verily, I say unto you, except ye eat the flesh of the Son of man, and drink his blood, ye have no life in you. Whoso eateth my flesh, and drinketh my blood, hath eternal life; and I will raise him up at the last day. For my flesh is meat indeed, and my blood is drink indeed. He that eateth my flesh, and drinketh my blood, dwelleth in me and I in him. As the living Father hath sent me, and I live by the Father: so he that eateth me, even he shall live by. This is that bread which came down from heaven: not as your fathers did eat manna, and are dead: he that eateth of this bread shall live forever." These things said he in the synagogue, as he taught in Capernaum. (John 6:47–59)[6]

Human beings, as a collective group, show an innate need for something to believe in. For most it is a religion, a belief system that soothes the soul and instructs the individual on how to live and what to believe. We speak of religious experiences, of moments of enlightenment and wonder, moments of intense understanding that change our lives and shape our personalities. The ubiquitous nature of such feelings and experiences offers a basis for our natural proclivity towards systems of belief.

Strict religions regulate life and behavior with punishments (actual or threatened) for those who step out of line. But rigid rules also create a protective netting that binds adherents into a symbiotic, like-minded group where each individual feels secure in the knowledge that he is not alone, but part of a social entity. The basic need to be an ac-

cepted member of a nation, religion, group, tribe, clan or family is funda-
mental to the human condition.

　　While all religions set forth codes of behavior and customs to follow, the variety of belief systems found around the globe is astounding.
Prior to the Judeo-Christian era, religions tended to be animistic or multi-
theistic, and most involved various forms of sacrifice and/or the partaking
of animal or human flesh. While harsh survival tactics and cannibalism,
along with a great deal of sacrifice, can be found in the Old Testament, the
Christian religion stands upon the overt sacrifice and symbolic partaking
of Christ's body and blood.

　　Few Catholics or Christians of today think of taking Communion
as an act of cannibalism, but as a spiritual intake of what Jesus represents.
However, had you lived in the early part of the thirteenth century during the reign of Pope Innocent III, you would have been bound to a stake
and burned alive should anyone have heard you utter a single word of disbelief concerning the transubstantiation believed to occur at the moment
of Communion. Through transubstantiation, the bread of the Eucharist
actually becomes the physical flesh of Christ, while the wine is truly transformed into his blood.

　　Symbolism was not enough for Innocent, who, himself, was anything but innocent. During his time (and for centuries thereafter), the
bread of the Eucharist was laid out in the form of a man (rather than a bowl
of wafers), and those who did not accept the religious views of the times
met with the brutal flames of an ignorant age.

　　Religious ritual, or a mental certainty, the taking of Communion
attests to accepted practices within our human past, which brings forth
a question. Why would Christ proffer himself through simulated cannibalism if cannibalism had not been practiced in previous or then current
times? There are no laws against walking to the moon as no one has managed to do so. Gods and governments do not write or pronounce laws
outside the realm of possibility or known practice. If humans had never
practiced cannibalism, if human sacrifice and cannibalism had not been

practiced for eons, Christ's order to "take this bread, it is the flesh of my body; take this wine, it is my blood," would have baffled those around him, even if he had spoken in metaphor. The many who were disturbed by his words and left his side may have held fast with their Judaic God of what is now referred to as the Old Testament, who had ordered against cannibalism after his people had repeatedly resorted to the practice following times of war and starvation. But 12 stayed, saying they knew the truth and would abide with him; and as centuries rolled by, few stepped forward to question his words.

Mentally and emotionally, how much difference is there between primitive tribes who believed their deceased loved ones could only proceed into an afterlife through the consuming of their bodies, and the unity and commitment felt by millions at the moment of Communion. As human beings our emotional reactions are basically similar to one another, and while one group may actually eat of the flesh of the dead, believing that doing so will allow their loved ones to continue their existence on the other side, others partake symbolically and emotionally in order to be at one with their god and gain eternal life.

Regardless of religion or system of faith, devout believers of all faiths hold firmly to the tenets and words of their convictions and to the belief that their god is *the* one and only God. When peoples of the world were separated by geologic constraints and watery expanses, the differences between us caused little strife, but once man ventured forth to gain desired or needed lands and resources, it was one god against another.

How many wars have been fought in the name of "God"?

Systems of belief define and separate people. Aside from setting rules to live by, religions mold societal ways, prejudice and hate, being capable of promoting either good or evil.

The rugby team members who survived a plane crash in the high Andes Mountains and partook of their dead in order to survive through the weathers of winter went on to live full and useful lives. All agreed that the experience had strong religious overtones; that in eating the flesh of their friends and family they were humbled and enlightened through the ultimate gift of life brought to them through the death and flesh of others; many likened it to the Eucharist and the last supper.

CHAPTER EIGHT

MURDER AND MEDICINE

In 1578 Li Shih-chen wrote extensively on the use of human bodies for medicinal purposes. Human meat was thought to cure tuberculosis while various organs were used to cure illnesses of corresponding organs. He also wrote at length on the use of human sweat, urine, sperm, breast milk, tears, "dirt," nails and teeth as medicines.

King Robert II, "the Pious" (996–1031), of France, fearing for the salvation of souls and the stability of his kingdom, ordered the burning of 13 heretics at Orleans in 1017. Over the next century, empresses, emperors, kings and bishops ordered heretics to be hanged or burned at the stake. From Constantinople to the countryside of France, nooses and fagots ruled the day. And when the

Bishop of Soissons incarcerated a variety of heretics in 1114, a Christian mob stormed the prison, took the accused out of town, and burned them. In an effort to bring some semblance of law and order, Pope Alexander III in 1163 commanded the clergy, with the assistance of lay princes at the Council of Tours, to search out heretics and convict them through sworn testimony to be taken by Inquisitor priests. Those found guilty were to be imprisoned and their possessions confiscated by the church.

The Council of Tours was formed principally to renounce the Cathari, a prosperous religious sect whose followers emulated Christ and the ways of the Essenes. At the time many Catholic prelates lived corrupt, lavish lifestyles and saw the growing numbers of Cathari as a threat to their very existence.

In 1252, Pope Innocent IV, via his bull *Ad exstirpanda*, placed all Inquisitors above the law, and in 1257 the church sanctioned the use of torture and death for those found guilty of heresy. The Inquisition was *legally* in force.[1]

While the initial impetus for the Inquisition was to blot out those who held beliefs not in concert with the Mother Church, overpopulation may have been another motivating force for culling the "unwanted." Between AD 1100 and 1300, good weather produced bumper crops of grain and babies. For 200 years, the weather was so good that fine wines were produced in England and sought after by European wine lovers; the French banned their import. During the same period of time, wars, plagues and the Crusades took millions of lives; nonetheless, the population of Europe trebled, crowding cities and stressing the land and its owners.

As the Inquisition spread across Europe, what had begun as harsh measures used to pressure people into obeying the edicts of the Church grew into a widespread killing machine that persevered through 650 years of sexual and physical abuse, maniacal forms of torture, beheadings and burnings. During those same centuries, war and famine hit Europe repeatedly. While the Inquisition raged, open cannibalism was practiced in Ireland from 1588–9, and again from 1601–3, when famine took over the land. And in 1594, Parisians made bread from human bones (for starters), after Henri IV laid siege on the city of love, leaving it spoiled, soiled and without a baguette to be found.

The fantastic paintings of Pieter Brueghel, born in Brussels circa 1564, portrayed through pictorial metaphor the times in which he lived. With the Inquisition in full swing he used his pencils, brushes and colors to mock and demean the horrors of the day.

Adriaan J. Barnouw, in his 1947 book *The Fantasy of Pieter Brueghel*, writes on Brueghel's drawing *The Temptation of St. Anthony*:

> The rotten fish in Brueghel's picture represents the Church of Christ, and its head, of course, the papacy, the source of the corruption within the body of the Church. The process of decomposition has gone so far that drunkenness, man-slaughter, and murder are rife among its members. . . . [2]

In another work entitled *Justice*, priests of the Inquisition mete out various cruel and lethal punishments, as they administer "Justice." A poor man, with hands bound behind his back, bends his head to kiss the crucifix as the executioner readies his sword. A priest stands by praying for his soul.

In Barnouw's written text, he details the multiple images within Pieter's picture of justice, except for a man who is being stretched on a rack while molten metal is poured into a funnel that has been placed in his mouth and held by an attendant. There are no gloves on the man pouring the liquid, nor on the holder of the funnel, but Pieter has placed a candle under the container to prove the heat of its contents.

Another artist of the times (his career as an artist began in 1475), was Hieronymus Bosch, who painted strange and weird scenes with half-human, half-animal (sometimes half-fish, half-bird or half-fruit) creatures representing and performing the beliefs and atrocities of the day: wars, re-ligion, plagues, famines and cannibalism, including scenes that show the spit-roasting of humans and the sautéing of dismembered human parts in large frying pans. By painting fantastic, seemingly illusory scenes, Bosch managed to paint reality without putting himself in harm's way. The Spaniards call Bosch, El Bosco, and the Museo del Prado in Madrid has a fabulous collection of his phantasmagorical works that speak to the times.

The first centuries of the Inquisition witnessed punishments that varied from one area to another. One or more of the following awaited those convicted of heresy: fines, confiscation of goods and property, exile, servitude, infamy, imprisonment, torture, hanging, beheading or burning, or a combination of the above.

During the thirteenth century, torture and death became the norm as the Inquisition vanquished the Knights Templar, who had become immensely wealthy after finding *something* in Jerusalem; so wealthy in fact that they had become the leading bankers of Europe from whom many popes and theologians had borrowed huge sums of money with which they lived thoroughly debauched lives. Through the articles of the Inquisition, the Knights were burned in groups bound to a common pole, but not one of them gave up the secret they had sworn to protect.

And then things got worse. By 1480, the Tribunal for the Persecution of Heresy, (the Inquisition), had long since eliminated the Cathari and the core of the Knights Templar, so it turned its attention to witchcraft. Lovely young women soon became the favored victims of the Inquisitors. During "stripping," females were habitually and repeatedly raped prior to being tortured by vicious attacks on the breasts and genitalia using pincers, pliers and red-hot irons. Things got so out of hand that the general populace publicly objected to the sexual molestation of young girls, women and boys. (Girls of 9 1/2 could be brought up for Inquisition, whereas boys had to reach the age of 10 1/2.) People didn't seem to mind the torture, hangings, beheadings and stake burnings, but they found sexual foul play a sin; not astonishing when you take into account the fact that during the Inquisition, physical pain (torture) was viewed as a means of achieving spiritual ecstasy. Phrases such as "glorious wounds" in relationship to torture can be found among texts written during the thirteenth and fourteenth centuries.

Throughout humanity's past, death was ever present, life was short and religion was the only hope offered to the masses. The modern concept of individual rights not only didn't exist, but was inconceivable to the mind of the common man.

The Church often found it was difficult to prove heresy, but if a person could be labeled a werewolf or witch, they were automatically taken to the dungeons. It was common for peasants, as well as many who governed, to believe in and blame werewolves and witches for the kidnapping, sexual abuse or deaths of others. From ancient Grecian times on through medieval times, the belief in werewolves was ubiquitous over most of Europe. Rapists, thugs and murderers—or anyone who failed to fit the common mold, or had properties desired by the church—were labeled as such. In the midst of the Inquisition, the Church used such long-held beliefs to demand the rounding up and destruction of all werewolves.

Of course, werewolves, as in seemingly real werewolves, did and do exist. Congenital generalized hypertrichosis is a rare genetic marker responsible for the werewolf syndrome. The disorder covers the entirety of the upper body from the pelvis up with hair. While making one distinct from others, being excessively hirsute does not affect one's mental capacity. Over the last centuries victims of hypertrichosis often took jobs in sideshows. The hypertrichosis gene can be found lurking on the long arm of the male chromosome . . . of course. In all fairness, there were professed werewolves—as there are today if you read really funky tabloids—nevertheless, thousands of people with no known association with *Canis lupus*, or a genetic throwback gene that may mirror our ancient ancestors, were destroyed by the Inquisition.

Those prosecuted as werewolves or witches were put on the rack, had chunks of their flesh pulled from their bodies with red-hot pinchers, and suffered the breaking of their limbs prior to beheading, an operation performed whether the victim was dead or alive. After beheading, the remains of "the beasts" were burned to ashes. The final act of burning was considered crucial for the total annihilation of the evil that had allegedly inhabited the subject.

Through the centuries, hundreds of thousands of Europeans were proclaimed to be heretics, werewolves or witches by papal courts and reigning royalty; the vast majority lost their lives.

A truly tragic indicator of just how ghastly the Inquisition proved to be is the case of Giordano Bruno (1548–1600). Born near Naples, Italy, Bruno was a contemporary of artist Pieter Brueghel. He studied under an Augustinian friar and joined the Dominicans, but left the order after being suspected of heresy. A philosopher, writer and poet, Bruno was one of the most outstanding thinkers of the Renaissance. He countered Aristotelian thought and the authority of the Church in regard to nature and human life. In 1591, Bruno was invited to Venice to stay with a young nobleman by the name of Giovanni Mocenigo, who wished to learn Bruno's "art of memory." Two years later, in 1593, Bruno announced his intention to return home, at which time Mocenigo became so distraught that he denounced Bruno to the Inquisition. Bruno was imprisoned for seven years in Rome, where he was convicted of heresy, apostasy, blasphemy, and misconduct. After refusing to recant, he was sentenced to death. He told the judges, "You perhaps tremble more in pronouncing the sentence than I in receiving it." Giordano Bruno, one of the world's great thinkers, was burned at the stake on February 17, 1600.

Possibly the best known victim of the Inquisition was a French farm girl born around 1412 who followed the mental war cries of her God and led the Bastard of Orleans, La Hire ("The Rage") and the infamous "Bluebeard" in battle. We know the young girl as Joan of Arc, who was burned at the stake for refusing to deny the vocal messages she claimed to have received from God. The date of her death was May 30, 1431.

Bluebeard was also burned at the stake for the serial sodomy and murder of young boys.

As the centuries rolled by, there were bishops and priests who spoke out against the Inquisition, making note of the fact that the "retribution" exacted against suspected heretics went against everything Christ had preached. Unfortunately, they too were tortured and burned at the stake for their words of courage and compassion. It was a dark time.

In 1816, Pope Pius VII abolished the use of torture, but the articles of the Inquisition still reside within the laws of the Church.

Some historians claim that England and Scandinavia escaped the forces of the Inquisition, but there were Inquisition-style executions in Scandinavia, and in 1553 Mary Tudor, later referred to as Bloody Mary, was proclaimed Queen Mary I of England. A devout Catholic, Mary felt it was her god-given mission to restore Catholicism and papal supremacy to her country. To earn her nickname and fulfill her God-directed "mission," she set in motion her own Inquisition by having countless Protestants burned at the stake, hanged or beheaded.

The horrors perpetrated through one century after another ruled the minds of most. Martin Luther, and other offshoot Christians, did not oppose the Inquisition; heretics were heretics or werewolves or witches and needed to be dealt with.

The word Inquisition should send shivers down your spine, but if you had lived during those brutal times and never been accused of heresy, you, like the majority of those around you, may well have agreed with the handling of the "guilty." Illiteracy was the norm, and life was mean; meaner than most can imagine. Life was also short, and if you didn't make hay while the sun shone, you missed out on life itself. With wars, foul climate swings starting in 1325, famines (often coupled with cannibalism), and plagues constantly at one's door—to say nothing of the muggers and murderers who lurked in every street, lane and alley—going to a beheading or the burning of a heretic, witch or werewolf seemed like a holiday, which is exactly how the masses treated such events. There were vendors and musicians, contests and jugglers; it was carnival time. The populace would hold their children on high so they could watch the severing of a head or the lighting of fagots, which would lead to the immolation of a heretic or some fair lass—a lass who was often too beautiful in comparison with the rest of her contemporaries to be anything other than a witch! Any person who was different, insightful, brilliant, prophetic, psychotic, criminal in nature or act, scheming or manipulative—in fact, anyone, of either sex, who did not fit the pattern set in place by the Church, royalty and their peers—was apt to die a horrid death on a platform surrounded by an enthusiastic throng of shouting, jeering humans.

If you are shaking your head in disgust, allow me to remind you that mere decades ago, hundreds of Americans congregated, not once, but many times, to witness the hanging of an African American suspected of raping or murdering a white.

Ignorance can, has, and often does rule.

During the Inquisition, Columbus set his course for "the New World"; flotillas followed in his wake. Aboard a majority of the ships that set a westerly course were Spanish Inquisitor priests who proceeded to implement their training by burning recalcitrant natives at the stake for refusing to convert to the one true God, especially if they happened to be bisexual, homosexual or cannibals . . . all by royal edict.

In Mexico City, 1649, Don Juan de Manozco, Visitor General of the Holy Office of the Inquisition of New Spain (Mexico) and member of the council of His Catholic Majesty, King Philip IV (Spain) burned "heretics." Some were strangled before burning, but the unrepentant were burned alive.

Records suggest that limited numbers of Native Americans were burned at the stake. Perhaps the natives of the Americas only had to watch a few of their own burn to death to get the picture. Many Native Americans practiced various forms of cannibalism and many tortured captives—often with red-hot firebrands—but more important to them were customs of proving themselves by being strung up by ropes connected to spikes pushed through and under the muscles of the back or chest, or by exposing their bodies to hot coals. But to be burned at the stake for baffling religious reasons held by weird-looking intruders left no room for the exhibition of courage or strength of will, and rather than experience a humiliating death that went against all they believed in, they joined the church.

While Inquisitor priests were doing their duty in new lands far across the sea, the Inquisitors of Spain were roasting Jews on spits over hot coals for not sharing the religious beliefs of Isabella and Ferdinand.

When the Inquisition began, Spain was not yet a nation. With its founding, Ferdinand and Isabella set up their own Inquisition, selected their own Inquisitor priests and confiscated all property and wealth belonging to anyone accused of heresy; Rome saw little profit from the Spaniards. And when the royal twosome put forth a ruling stating that all cannibals could/should be put to death, they set in motion the destruction of incredible societies and the abolishment of cannibalistic practices among many peoples of the world in order to fill royal treasuries with galleons of gold.

The Inquisition reminds us that we all have monsters in our closets and serves as a prime example of how insensitive and cruel humans can be towards others. But the primary reason for bringing up the Inquisition is that during its centuries of abuse medicinal cannibalism was condoned and practiced from one end of Europe to the other, as well as in lands far and wide.

Many are repulsed by the mere thought of cannibalism, considering it the worse of human behaviors. But few have looked into the subject without prejudice, or reviewed it in comparison with the many other abysmal propensities of humans. Besides, who is to say with any assurance that medicinal cannibalism had no merit? Perhaps the most provocative finding within the field of medicinal cannibalism is that the word "cannibalism" is never found in medical texts—old or new. Even the words "anthropophagy" and "autophagy" are shunned.

In Europe, the most common form of cannibalism occurred whenever someone lost his head to the executioner's axe. At beheadings, people suffering from epilepsy, palsy or other crippling diseases would crouch beneath the cutting block with their drinking bowls held high to catch the blood of the condemned as it was firmly believed that human blood reduced seizures and cured many illnesses. Of course, commerce must be maintained, and it was the right of the executioner to demand payment for a bowl of red.

A Swiss physician and alchemist by the name of Paracelsus (1493–1541) prescribed "maiden's zenish" (menstrual blood) as an application against gout. Born Philippus Theophrastus Aureolus Bombastus von Hohenheim (!), he adopted the name Paracelsus ("surpassing Celsus," who was a second-century religious scholar known for his tract on medicine *De Medicina*) as he considered himself above the ancients. Paracelsus insisted on following the wisdom of the common folk. He should have stuck with the name "Bombastus."

Human blood may or may not cure seizures or gout, but blood sausage (usually made with the blood of pigs or cows) is a common dish in various parts of the world; in France it is known as *boudin noir*. It is quite delicious and very healthy, being full of iron, vitamins and minerals. Many societies cook with or drink the blood of a wide variety of animals. The Masai of Kenya drink cow's blood with a bit of urine and ash thrown in to impede coagulation, while the Chinese make pork-blood jelly with chives, a dish prepared in some American/Chinese restaurants. Pork-blood jelly can be found on menus written in Chinese, but rarely on those printed in English—but you can ask for it. Closer to home, a friend of mine had a grandmother who used to make a marvelous blood pudding with the blood of a freshly slaughtered chicken. While collecting the blood she told her little granddaughter it was for the making of chocolate pudding; you see blood turns milk chocolate brown when gently cooked.

In the Ituri Rainforest of the Congo, reports from witnesses claimed that the blood of Pygmy victims was quaffed by Congolese rebels prior to the cannibalizing of the flesh, whereas the Fijians drenched their newly made war canoes in human blood then ate the bodies of the blood donors. But blood can also be seen as a curse and bring about the creation of customs that go back to our hunter-gatherer days. The "curse" comes from a hunter's aversion to menstrual blood. My favorite story concerning the blood of menses comes from Alaska.

While living with a group of Inuit Eskimos, an anthropologist was taken by a hunter to track seals through blowholes in the winter ice. The distance to the ocean ice fields was great and the men took turns riding in the dogsled. On the horizon appeared a last solitary copse of rock and scraggly trees. The dogs were close to the copse when the Inuit hunter pulled on the leathers and screamed at the dogs to turn and stop. Every foul word known to the man escaped his lips as he flung his arms as if to clobber an invisible foe. The anthropologist asked what was wrong. What was wrong was that a menstruating woman had passed through the copse, and the scent of blood had been left on snow and rock. The dogs and Inuit hunter could smell the blood, while the city-dweller looked puzzled. The hunter explained that they would have to go 10 miles out of their way to avoid the woman's blood scent or they would become prey to polar bears and their hunting efforts would produce nothing. The two men traveled 10 miles out of their way in safety, and the hunt was successful.

Animals (especially sharks and vultures) can smell blood from amazing distances and no woman should ever go into bear, lion or cougar country during her cycle; in grizzly bear country, it is asking to be attacked.

Science has proven that molecules of blood, dead skin cells, hair, and other minute parts of our body are not only shed on a constant basis, but create a wake of refuse that trails behind us as we move. The bulk of the dust that builds up on the furniture of your house is composed of dead skin cells. Humans, like all other animals, are natural organisms constantly in the process of regeneration.

During our walk towards today, menses blood produced cultural practices. Because carnivores naturally follow the scent of blood, and any hunter carrying such a scent would himself become the hunted, women were placed in bleeding huts until their menses had ceased, at which time they bathed themselves thoroughly before rejoining the community. It has been observed that when women live in proximity to one another (as in sororities), they cycle together. If such occurred in ages past, it would have placed many women in the bleeding hut at the same time, and it has long been hypothesized that women became the verbal ones because of forced togetherness, whereas men tend to be nonverbal since chattering while hunting assures an empty stomach.

But I digress. During the years of the Inquisition, blood was only one of the human parts used for medicinal reasons. Mummies, found and dug up from the sands of Egypt, were transported to Europe along with reports that the flesh of mummified humans was magical and health enhancing. You guessed it: "mummy" became the rage in Europe. Small packets of mummy went for a tidy price, and everyone felt the better for it—even princes carried small leather pouches of it in their saddlebags. Centuries later in Egypt, mummies were used to stoke the furnaces of steam engines that raced the rails belching ancient smoke. Better steam engines than medicine since the heavy salts and chemicals used to mummify the Egyptian dead make poor medicine for the living.

Unfortunately, the mummy supply from Egypt dwindled; something had to be done. People were enraged that their doctors were unable to obtain their precious mummy. So it was that over the course of many centuries there was another kind of health-enhancing mummy for sale— freshly cured human flesh—which was actually better for the patient then the old mummies from Egypt. The freshly cured, smoked or pickled human mummy was listed in the official 1618 *London Pharmacopoeia* and other medicinal listings from all over Europe, the latest found being the Merck pharmacy listings from Darmstadt, Germany in 1909.

Young men who had lost their heads to the axman, had been hanged until dead or had fallen in battle were gutted, hung and cured in the exact manner used to cure a ham (the hindquarter of a pig). But the corpses of healthy young men who had been hanged were the most sought after by mummy makers. When a man is hanged, the rope (hopefully) snaps the neck, at which time there is a cessation of autonomic signals from the old reptilian brain. One of the results from the shut-off of autonomic neural commands is an automatic erection. When flaccid, the muscles of the penis are constricted, prohibiting the organ from being engorged with blood, but when stimulated the muscles relax, blood flows into the organ and an erection is achieved. When hanged, the muscles of the penis relax allowing for an automatic erection. The belief that an erect phallus signals strength and vitality, as opposed to a desire for sex, is far older than the written word, and the makers of mummy must have viewed the reaction as proof of a young man's health and vitality.

There were various recipes for making mummy. Some soaked the body in honey, wine, herbs, flowers and all other things possible to enhance taste and potential benefit, while most hung the body in a smoke-house to cure. We can assume that the medicine was expensive, as some of the curing processes took weeks or months. Everything changes, but nothing changes—bought any well-aged cheese lately?

The reason for making mummy was the belief that if you were ill and weak, what you needed was some healthy flesh to compensate for and replace your weakened flesh, thus ridding you of disease. The finest physicians would prescribe mummy, which usually came in neat little squares of human "ham." The word "cannibalism" was never used in connection with the making of, or the taking of, mummy, and since it was a *medicine* prescribed by a physician, it was accepted as a good and beneficial product, no questions asked. And, since a majority of non-lethal illnesses—given time—are cured naturally by the body, the taking of mummy would have appeared to work, and the practice of curing corpses in order to fill prescriptions continued for centuries.

For the making of fine medicines from human tissue, it was reasoned that the flesh had to be procured from strong, young, healthy individuals—virgins were preferred. Likewise, it was believed that to eat of the old or ailing would make you sick. Choosing choice young meat from freshly killed victims was actually wise, as flesh from infected bodies could have been fatal. Another factor to consider is that the bodies used for the making of mummy were *cured*, not cooked. There was no roasting or high heat used to kill pathogens, so healthy, young individuals were a wise choice for the production of good mummy. Besides, every chef knows that the younger the animal, the finer and more delicious the meat.

Actually, the taking of mummy may have worked as a great pla-cebo. Research has shown time and again that the placebo effect promotes healing by strengthening the immune system, so believing in the potency of mummy may actually have helped the healing process. Nevertheless, it was a practice of ingesting the flesh of one's own kind, which constitutes an act we call cannibalism.

Aside from the antics of Bloody Mary, the British made mummy, and their physicians prescribed it on a regular basis, but the British, along with some of their continental neighbors and those of northern Africa, also pickled human corpses for the dinner table rather than the sick bay. This toothsome data-bite comes from a paper written and given by Dr. Louise Noble in 2003, entitled "The Ingestible Corpse: practices in cannibalism in early modern English culture," in which she states that the corpses of female virgins were the most highly prized and that menstrual blood was collected for the production of medicine. Also noted was the fact that jars of human blood (regular and menstrual) and urine sat upon the shelves of most apothecaries in centuries past. . . . Jolly good!

There is no doubt that Europeans, in concert with peoples from around the world, believed in the regenerative powers of human flesh, which makes the curing and ingesting of mummy no different from those who believed in benefits gained from the eating of dead relatives, or the consuming of an enemy. Globally, people, at various times, have believed that such dining practices gave them strength, power, virility, and even wisdom. Belief in perceived benefits, whether psychological or physical, would have equated to an enhanced feeling of wellness, which is probably why countless tribes of people took to taking specific organs from a fallen foe and consuming them in order to gain the strength and bravery of the victim or to annihilate the possible return of an enemy's spirit. Actually, if the diner's environment offered limited protein, a meal of human flesh may have added to his or her physical well-being, especially if the liver or brain was consumed. During the times of the Inquisition, brains were also made into medicine, but only master chefs could perform the trick as brain tissue decays far more rapidly than muscle tissue and cannot be cured (dried perhaps).

The Inquisition lasted over 600 years, during which lived Shakespeare, Leonardo da Vinci, Galileo Galilei (who recanted his scientific findings in order to escape the flames of the Inquisitors) and Voltaire (who stood up for a French nobleman convicted of blasphemy; nonetheless the man was tortured, beheaded and burned to ashes along with a copy of Voltaire's *Philosophical Dictionary*). Hundreds of other brilliant minds from the fields of science, music, art, and letters lived through and died by the Inquisition. Some of them, such as Giordano Bruno, who refused to recant, were burned at the stake for their brilliance.

But whereas Europe had several hundred years of murder and medicinal cannibalism, interspersed with bouts of survival cannibalism following devastating wars and plagues, China was busy accumulating a 4,000-year written history of dealing with human flesh. And since the Chinese have always chosen their foodstuffs with an eye to well-being and medicinal value, it is not surprising they saw human flesh as a primary source for medicines. Organs, meat and body fluids were used to cure the sick and infirm. Commensurate with their ways in dealing with animal flesh, they ate the liver for liver problems, the heart for heart problems, etc. As you will learn in following chapters, members of the Leopard Society in Sierra Leone collected the blood, liver and entrails of their victims for the making of magical medicines and potions prior to consuming the flesh of their victims.

Over the millennia, the peoples of China practiced every form of cannibalism, but they also devised a form of cannibalism that researchers say can be found nowhere else. Chinese scholars refer to this unique type of cannibalism as learned cannibalism, which derives from two religions: Confucianism and Buddhism. In the practice of learned cannibalism a person cuts off a piece of his or her own flesh, usually from the thigh, to be simmered in a broth and fed to a dying parent. The practice is known as *ko ku*, or *gegu*, and is performed most often by a daughter, but sometimes by a son. Chun-fang Yu of Rutgers University says the result was always a miraculous recovery. Learned cannibalism is iatric (medicinal), and its rationale comes from Confucian filial piety coupled with the compassion of Buddhism.

The whole of documented Chinese history being rife with cannibalism prompted Lu Xun (1881–1936) to write *Diary of a Madman* (1918) in which he condemned the practice that had persisted throughout Chinese history. Almost as if to prove his point, events of hate-filled cannibalism were witnessed during the civil war between the Communists and the Nationals when motives of revenge bounced off mirrors of the past allowing enemy hearts to be consumed. And a turnabout saw the Japanese dine on the flesh of Chinese prisoners following the Japanese invasion of Manchuria in 1937. Still later, in the 1960s, during Mao's Cultural Revolution, southern Chinese took to cannibalizing enemies of the state. (See "Politics and the Color Red.")

In today's China there are apothecary shops where various human fluids and parts can still be found; old beliefs die hard—yesterday, I knocked on wood.

The Chinese may win the prize for having the longest written record for the practice of cannibalism, but the custom spans the globe and reaches deep into the most ancient caves of our human past, from Gran Dolina in Spain, circa 800,000 years ago, to a cave at the southern tip of Africa, circa 110,000 years, to Neanderthal caves in France and eastern Europe, 30,000 to 100,000 years, to *Homo sapiens* in Germany and elsewhere. There seems to have been no means of stopping cannibalism. Mary Roach, in her book *Stiff*, remarks on the grand bazaars of twelfth-century Arabia where one could purchase portions of "mellified man"—if you had enough cash and something in which to carry the product home. Human remains were steeped in honey for a prescribed length of time for the production of mellified man, which was used as a topical ointment or ingested for medicinal purposes. (*Mel* comes from the Latin word for "honey.")

Today a bizarre form of medicinal cannibalism is still being practiced in order to maintain the health of the planet, rather than that of the cannibal. The practice is a form of assault sorcery performed by shamans in Guyana, South America. The cannibalistic ritual is known as Kanaimà, a lengthy process in which the victim eventually experiences a horrifying death. Three days after killing the victim, the sorcerer-shaman inserts a stick into the rotting, buried body, extracts some of the decomposing flesh and gobbles it up or uses a reed as a straw through which three sips are taken. Should a sorcerer-shaman fail to take three bites or sips, he will be left vulnerable to revenge from the victim's family.

In 1992, while working on a research project in Guyana, anthropologist Neil Whitehead of the University of Wisconsin-Madison touched a ritual urn in a cave; following the incident he became violently ill. Believing that he may have been poisoned by a Kanaimà (shamans who practice the rites are also known by its name), he spent several years researching the sorcerer-shamans of the area, often paying them to reveal their long-held secrets.

Whitehead's investigations produced amazing results. Kanaimàs are highland Guyanese shamans who often announce their intention of attack with bird-like warning calls. When first attacked, a victim is weakened by a blow; usually a painful spinal injury. The condition lingers until the Kanaimà returns to mutilate and slowly kill his victim in torturous ways. Months or years can pass between the initial assault and the time of death through ritual sacrifice.

Whitehead found that the motive of the Kanaimàs is not revenge, but an appeasement to the gods, a sacrificial offering to ensure the bounty and fertility of the cosmos. The sorcerer-shamans see the entire grisly process as a gift to divine beings that will ensure that plants, fish and animals will be sustained. In other words, through violent acts of murder and cannibalism, the survival, health and fecundity of their people and the cosmos will be assured.

How did (do) people formulate such ideas? Did various types of cannibalism spread from one people to the next, or did bouts of starvation plague us from the beginning, prompting the only course of action that would ensure the continuation of life? What primal beliefs led from survival cannibalism to extraordinary acts of cannibalism that seem impossible in the world of today? What went through the minds of Inquisitor priests? In paintings they all wear looks of pure piety. Why did people believe the body had to be destroyed? Did our ancestors actually derive some benefit from the consumption of human remains? Did learned cannibalism cure dying Chinese parents, or even offer them a slight reprieve? Was habitual cannibalism conducive to the development of the great height and stature of both the Fijians and the Maori? From purely nutritional, psychological, anthropological and medical points of view, such questions are salient.

Be careful when opening your closet; there's no telling who lurks within.

A bit of mummy, Mommy?

CHAPTER NINE

MESOAMERICA

In The Rite of Spring, *Russian composer Igor Stravinsky takes us back to archaic rituals performed by Slavic tribes to honor the gods of harvest and fertility. Written with uncontrolled passion, Part I, "Adoration of the Earth," surges forth with brutal strength as spring forces life to resume. With pounding, primitive rhythms Stravinsky propels the listener into the swollen rivers of existence, setting the stage for Part II, "The Sacrifice," which denotes the selection of a young virgin who is forced to dance herself to death to ensure the return of spring and abundant crops. Though Stravinsky rounded the edges of history by allowing the virgin to dance herself to death, the vivid, pulsating chords of music, combined with scantily clad dancers directed by the ever erotic choreographer Nijinsky, provoked such lusty reactions from the French audience on opening night, May 29, 1913, that a riot ensued, complete with shouts, catcalls and fisticuffs.*

enotes (pronounced suh-NO-tays) are sub-surface caverns, caves and tunnels that can be found beneath the northern end of the Yucatán Peninsula. These wondrous underground systems were formed after the peninsula arose from the surrounding seas millions of years after a meteoric blast hit the area 65 million years ago; a blast that devastated much of the earth, and annihilated the dinosaurs and 65% of then extant life forms. Rainwater falling on the new land for thousands of years caved out the cenotes as it percolated through the land causing the dissolving and erosion of limestone laid down in the oceans of the past.

A mere three million years ago, through the process of plate tectonics, the northward-heading continent of South America created a land bridge when a protrusion of land on its northwest edge slammed into a southwestern extension of land jutting out from the continent of North America, thus creating Mesoamerica.

With the availability of a terrestrial avenue, prehensile-tailed monkeys traveled as far north as southern Mexico while giant sloths made their way into western areas of the United States. And as armadillos and opossums invaded Texas, large cats, bears, camels, mammoths and numerous rodents headed south, the mammoths traveling as far south as Chile, where their excavated bones offer dates of 12,500 BP, along with evidence of interaction with humans who knew a walking meat market when they saw one.

If you look at a map of Mexico, you will notice a fat thumb of land jutting out from its southeastern side into the western reaches of the Caribbean. That thumb is the Yucatán Peninsula. Today, most of the cenotes of the Yucatán Peninsula are only partially filled with water, while some labyrinths are flooded with rain and tidal ocean waters. But during the last ice age the cenotes were often dry, with rivers of water running only through their deepest channels. These spectacular caverns offered more than water to early man and he used them in many ways. Carbon dating of an ash layer found on the floor of a cenote cavern shows that 10,200 years ago an unnamed, ancient people built a huge bonfire. The finding and dating of the ancient ash layer provides the oldest evidence of human occupation on the peninsula. Were the bonfire-makers predecessors of the Olmec or Maya? Either way, by 1500 BC, the Mayas occupied the entire Yucatán Peninsula, Belize, Guatemala and parts of Honduras.

Two skeletons rescued from watery graves within the cenotes demonstrate formal Mayan burial practices complete with funerary pottery. But in small niches, on hidden ledges, in tunnels and on cavern floors other skulls and post-cranial bones have been found that offer evidence of appeasing the gods through sacrifice. Archaeological divers have risked their lives squeezing through tight passages and shifting currents to find prizes of historical information laid down through thousands of years of ebb and flow. The majority of human remains are from early Mayan times when sacrificial victims were cast into or had their remains placed in the cenotes to ensure the continuation of the cosmos, the coming of rain, the growth of plants and an abundance of life.

In a crevice of a large cenote, a singular skull was found with clear stone-tool cut marks indicative of de-fleshing. The skull had been hacked at with a stone knife in order to remove the muscles of the head from the top of the skull down over the face. The skull was that of a male around the age of 25. At birth his malleable infant head had been bound to boards so that his cranial appearance would set him apart as royalty; a tradition followed centuries later by the Zapotecs of central Mexico. The young man's skull is prized as being the first of the cenote finds to provide evidence of sacrifice and postmortem de-fleshing dating to 3,500 years ago.

While archaeologists were plumbing the waters of the Yucatán cenotes, an exposition was being staged by two museums, one in Frankfurt, the other in Main, Germany. The topic: Blood: Perspectives on Art, Power, Politics and Pathology.

One of the exhibits was entitled, "Sacrificial Blood"

The Maya society was fundamentally shaped by its belief that human sacrifice is the most valuable good that can

be given to divine power to maintain the eternal equilibrium among cosmos, human world, and underworld. Embossed discs and clay figurines depict captives and sacrificial
scenes, but the most impressive relic of the ritual is a sharp
obsidian knife . . . manufactured from volcanic glass for the
sole purpose of excising the sacrificed human's still-beating
heart to emphasize a ruler's power.[1]

Though some archaeologists have hypothesized that bloodletting and human sacrifice only occurred during times of drought or war,
newly found evidence attests to Mayan chiefs appeasing their populations
and maintaining their power through regular spectacles of sacrifice during
peaceful times of plenty. Mayan art shows the piercing of tongues, earlobes
and penises, the collecting of blood onto parchment for use as burnt offerings plus the cutting open of human chests using elaborately knapped
stone daggers followed by the ripping out of still-beating hearts.

In *National Geographic*, cenote archaeologist Terrazas explains,
"Most rib fractures from accidents occur from the outside in, but ripping
out the heart caused breaks from the inside out."

Looking over the rib bones of a partial skeleton brought up from a
cenote, Terrazas adds, "This is a good indication of intentionality."[2]

The cenote finds validate pictorial and written histories through
physical evidence while furthering our knowledge of Mayan culture in ancient times. For all of their brutal ways, the Mayan glyphs present a calendar
that extends back five billion years. Our current cosmologists put the earth's
age at 4.6 billion. The ancient Maya were an amazing people.

When did this all begin? When was death, the life of a human, first
deemed a duty, a payment, an offering?

The Olmecs built the oldest archaeological sites known along the
eastern coastal areas of central Mexico. You may be familiar with their large
stone head sculptures of round-faced warriors, one of which weighs in at
approximately 10 tons. It is not known if the Olmec people ever assigned
a name for themselves. Others gave them the name Olmec—the "people

who use rubber" or "rubber people"—as the Olmecs were the first known people to fabricate rubber from tree sap harvested from rubber trees that grew in the hot lowlands off the Gulf shores of Mexico. By 1600 BC the Olmecs were manufacturing heavy rubber balls for a brutal game played within the confines of ball courts with slanted walls. The rubber ball used in the game was dense enough to injure or even kill a player, yet bouncy enough to be bumped about by padded knees, hips and elbows; hands could not be used. Over the centuries, the game *tlachtli* spread from one society to another and was played throughout Mesoamerica and as far north as Arizona. For decades I read the nuances of *tlachtli* as played by the Aztecs, the Zapotecs, and others of more recent times, always doubtful when one scholar after another insisted that the winning team or captain was always put to death by decapitation or by a long stone blade thrust through the heart. I looked at the ceramics and saw the artifacts, but why would you fight to win when the prize was death!? I knew the Aztecs sacrificed people atop their pyramids and practiced cannibalism, but I found it hard to believe that anyone, let alone an entire team, would play to win a game that promised death: especially a game that continued to be popular for thousands of years. Only when I began my research in earnest did the obvious come to me. It was all about belief.

A short distance from the inner west entrance to the Art Institute of Chicago, a life-size ceramic torso and head of a young man stands safe within a glass case (Veracruz, circa AD 1450–1500). The realistic figure wears the skin of a recently sacrificed victim, whose heart, referred to as "precious eagle-cactus fruit," had been cut out with an obsidian or chert blade atop a pyramid while four priests bent his body taut over a narrow stone. The victim's heart, still oozing blood, had been held high and ritually offered to the sun in order to quench its thirst. The body had then been thrown and tumbled down the steep steps of the pyramid to those waiting to flay the skin from its torso. Peoples of the eastern hemisphere flayed human skin from live victims in a process known as "death from a thousand cuts," but among the Aztecs the skin was carefully removed postmortem by cutting around the neck, biceps and lower abdomen (or mid-thigh), then down the back to a point where thin obsidian blades could be worked under the skin. When the "shirt" was free of the body, the slit that had been made for the extraction of the heart was stitched back together. The human shirt was then slipped onto a ritual impersonator of the God of Spring, Xipe Totec, an ancient god assumed from the Toltec who worshipped him pre-1100 AD. Impersonators ranged from teenage boys to young men and warriors who had been given the honor of wearing a human "shirt," which was stitched up the back once fitted onto the impersonator.

The shirt-wearers ran through the streets, danced in courtyards and visited family and friends to ensure a year of plentiful crops. But the sacrifices and ceremonies weren't enough; those honored to wear human shirts had to wear them until they dried and fell off of their own accord, much as with the dried husk from an ear of corn, as the living bodies of the impersonators were representative of the seed (new life) waiting to sprout. The aroma and discomfort was a sacrifice unto itself, but the ritual was an honor much sought after since the wearers of human shirts were believed to have become the actual god, Xipe Totec—The Flayed One, the god of rebirth, growth and regeneration—the agrarian god of the Aztecs.

In drawings and paintings made before and after the arrival of the Spaniards, impersonators of Xipe Totec were shown wearing full body suits of human skin with the victim's hands and feet still attached and dangling from the form of the wearer. On careful inspection it can be seen that the skinners were so expert at their craft that scrotal sacks are intact and that flesh face masks were also worn with openings cut for the eyes, nose and mouth. The skinned bodies of the "flayed ones" were consumed.

Diego Duran, a Dominican priest of mixed heritage who grew up in Mexico in the years immediately following the Spanish conquest of Tenochtitlan:

> . . . the flesh of all those who died in sacrifice was held
> truly to be consecrated and blessed. It was eaten with rev-

erence, ritual, and fastidiousness, as if it were something from heaven.[3]

During such agricultural ceremonies, captives, slaves and Aztecs alike were ritualistically killed, flayed and consumed. Various volumes list the numbers sacrificed in the tens of thousands. At the time of Spanish contact in 1519, the cult of Xipe Totec was widespread throughout Mesoamerica, even among tribes who were enemies of the Aztecs.

The Aztecs offered fresh blood to the sun on a daily basis with the addition of 167 high holidays of religious sacrifice and cannibalism where tens, hundreds, sometimes thousands of people were sacrificed.

Following the Spanish invasion, Spanish priests and artists, in tandem with Aztec artists and scholars, sat down to record the history, religion and cultural practices of the most ardent cannibals ever documented.

Some of the rituals performed by the Aztecs were so heinous that a majority of twentieth-century scholars glossed over the many written accounts or cast them aside altogether, even though they had been dutifully noted 500 years ago by those who were there, people who had witnessed the blood letting and carnage and had learned the language of the Aztec so as to compile their beliefs and practices. Every conceivable excuse has been used in an effort to nullify the words of past writers. Most claim the priests of the time were trying to defame the Aztecs as an excuse for their destruction, but Ferdinand and Isabella had already decreed that both heretics *and* cannibals should be annihilated through death, so there was no reason to make things up out of thin air when they already possessed the power to destroy all they deemed unworthy or in the way to riches.

And heretics they were. The Aztecs had their own politics and gods, coupled with strong systems of belief, all in opposition to Christianity. Montezuma, his predecessors, and his priests used political power to fuel ardent religious beliefs, and belief was what it was all about. For an Aztec, every moment of every day was taken up by religious thought and the gods he believed in demanded sacrifice; the sky was an immense mouth, the earth a jaw, and the consuming of human flesh was necessary to keep the cosmos on an even keel.

Aztec warriors truly and firmly believed that when sacrificed to their god, they became that god, or, at the very least, at one with the god to which they were sacrificed. Finally, I understood the game of *tlachtli*; now striving with all your might to win a game and be given the honor of mortal sacrifice made sense.

But not everyone was a warrior. A majority of those sacrificed on the great pyramid were enemy slaves taken in battle or slaves who were sent to the great city of Tenochtitlan from other areas of the empire as tax payments. Captive slaves were often held in servitude for several years prior to climbing the great pyramid, while those sent as tax payments were quickly used to appease the gods. The only civilian slaves offered to the gods and tables of the great city were those who had been fired by three consecutive masters . . . the Aztecs may have been served by the finest slaves ever to attend to the needs of a master.

For an Aztec warrior the most honorable of all deaths was to die in battle or become a god through voluntary sacrifice. An amazing fact is that captured enemies fell in line with sacrifice. At the taking of a prisoner an Aztec warrior would say the traditional words, "He is as my beloved son." And the captive would reply, " He is as my beloved father." Some captives were treated royally prior to their day of sacrifice, and few cried or struggled to get away as their captors led them up the steep stairs of the pyramid. Should a captive stumble or weaken, his captor-warrior would help or drag him up the massive stone steps to the awaiting priests. Upon reaching the sacrificial platform, many were ordered to dance prior to having their bodies bent backward over a narrow stone with priests holding fast to both arms and legs. When the body was well bowed, the head priest raised his obsidian knife high above his head, then plunged it down into the lower portion of the victim's chest, turned the blade, reached in and up and tore out the heart.

Incredible as it may sound, many Aztec warriors marched captive slaves to their deaths only to offer themselves a few years later in order to be at one with their god, an act that may seem incredible until one considers current events. If a young mother of today can strap a bomb around her body in order to kill innocent people, then surely an Aztec of yesteryear, believing firmly that he would be at one with (or actually become) his favored god, could climb the great stone stairs of a pyramid and meet death face to face at the hands of ritualistically clad priests and a cheering audience.

Though some writers have stated that only captives and captive slaves were slaughtered, the Aztecs themselves gave testimony that their own men, women and children were routinely sacrificed. Females were sacrificed in one-third of the yearly festivals while "human paper streamers" were children given by the their parents to be sacrificed to the god Tlaloc, the Rain God. The most beautiful children were picked, with those born with cowlicks being the most prized; children with two cowlicks were sought out and purchased for sacrifice. The human paper streamers were formally decorated and carried through the streets on feather-bedecked litters by men who cried throughout the procession. The wailing of the men usually encouraged the children to cry, which brought great joy to the men and all in attendance, as only the tears of children could guarantee adequate rainfall. When the festivities were over, the children were buried alive.

Hearts being ripped from living victims atop magnificent Aztec pyramids is the practice most noted in texts, but not all lives were taken in high places. In the massive plazas that spread out from the base of the pyramid were ornate temples built for the sole purpose of human sacrifice, and in each stood a skull rack, a *tzompantli*. (The largest rack to survive the centuries can be viewed in the Natural History Museum of Mexico City.) In one temple, people with skin sores were sacrificed—a prudent health measure in a time without antibiotics—while in another victims were "killed like deer"; whether the writer was speaking of the manner in which people were killed, or the number is unknown. Victims killed in these lesser buildings were put to death in various ways; they might be drowned, shot repeatedly with arrows, have their eyes gouged out or thrown live into fires—horrifying practices repeated over the course of history in varied corners of the world.

Among the written records concerning the capital of Tenochtitlan, there is no mention of fattening captives in cages. It was Cortez who found people locked in cages and being fattened for the kill in a village populated with enemies of the Aztecs—Cortez let them out, then enlisted the villagers to join him in conquering Tenochtitlan.

Starvation can be ruled out as being the driving force behind the ingestion of human flesh among the Aztecs. One codex after another tells of the amazing array of foodstuffs, both plant and animal, available to all. Aside from fruits and vegetables, they dined on dogs, turkeys, wild birds and an occasional deer. In general, the Aztecs ate well, lived well and birthed more than enough offspring to feed the gods. And while there is nothing in the literature to suggest purposeful breeding, the fecundity of the people of Mesoamerica is noted in many historical writings. Perhaps due to an abundant population, Aztec children could be bought for the purpose of consumption or to be used as a wager when betting on a ball game. The flesh of children was considered to be the finest. In contrast, children who were offered or purchased for sacrifice to a god were usually buried in mass graves and rarely consumed. Young maidens, not long past childhood, lost their heads, followed by their hearts, to feed the sun or honor a god; in many cases following a *visit* with Montezuma.

While the people who stood before a bonfire more than 10,000 years ago in a cenote on the Yucatán Peninsula are unknown to us, Mayan temples, pyramids and deciphered glyphs present us with an amazing history going back several thousands of years. In contrast, the recently discovered Olmecs offer but a glimpse of long ago through ball courts, archaeological sites and their fabulous sculptures. As to the Aztecs, we know a great deal.

Leaving Aztlán, located in the northwest of Mexico, a rabble-rousing and desperate group of people headed south. After being chased out of one area after another, their chief, Tenoch, had a vision in which the god Huitzilopochtli instructed him to settle his people on a swamp island in the middle of Lake Texcoco, upon which he would see an eagle clutching a serpent, perched atop a cactus. His vision fulfilled, Tenoch and his followers enlarged the island and built the City of Tenoch—Tenochtitlan; the year was 1325. By 1376, a great pyramid and many temples had been erected to honor many gods. The people of Tenochtitlan fell in line with more ancient peoples of Mesoamerica in their belief that the sun was living through the last of five eras and if not fed on a daily basis all would be vanquished. So began daily rituals of offering human blood to the sun in order to quench its thirst and fuel its radiance.

By the time of Cortez's arrival, an estimated 25 million people lived in Mesoamerica. Tenochtitlan was the largest city and the empirical seat of power, with an estimated 500,000 inhabitants. In 1486, the dedication of a great temple built to honor Tenochtitlan's war god saw the sacrifice of 20,000 people over a period of four days. There has been much controversy over the numbers and the time it would take to kill 20,000 people, but research using specially fabricated lifelike dummies and freshly knapped stone knives has substantiated the possibility. The debate will no doubt continue, but what is known is that people were sacrificed on a daily basis, and that festival days saw the death of hundreds, and, on special occasions, thousands.

Sacrifice and cannibalism aside, the Aztecs were an amazing people. They were superb architects, engineers, cosmologists, gardeners, farmers, builders, tradesmen, and above all, warriors. Their vast varieties of art were magnificent. The heavens were well known to them and they lived by two elaborate calendars, one 365 days, the other 260 days. Aside from the intricacies of its government, the size of its armies, its incredible gardens and immense pyramids, the capital city of Tenochtitlan had the most complete and elaborate zoo in the world, carnivorous species being provisioned with the remains of human carcasses. The Aztecs are said to have told the Spanish chroniclers that only the arms and legs of sacrificial victims were offered for consumption by humans, and that the rest was carted off to the zoological gardens. Other texts speak to broader palates.

The ancient Aztecs inhabited various parts of Mexico from 150 BC onward, and like most civilizations they waxed and waned through the centuries. By the time the Spaniards arrived, they were the Mexica, though in most writings available today they are referred to as the Aztecs, which I will continue to do in this writing. While the earliest Aztecs practiced sacrifice and cannibalism to some extent, the tribes encountered by the Spanish in the 1500s lived by and for such practices. Whether or not over-population gave rise to an increase in the elaborate rites of the Aztecs may never be authenticated, but there can be no question that without ample fecundity within neighboring tribes and within their own populations, the Aztecs could never have offered so many quivering hearts to so many gods. It is difficult to prepare a proper feast without sufficient supplies; fishes and loaves are not always available.

In 1521, Cortez began his annihilation of Tenochtitlan. After mass slaughter and destruction, Tenochtitlan fell to the Spaniards and enemy tribes who joined them as allies. Upon the rubble of Tenochtitlan the Spaniards built Mexico City—currently the most populous city in the world. In its day Tenochtitlan was one of the largest, and perhaps the most beautiful cities in the world, for at the height of its existence the famous and grandiose cities and temples of the Middle East were already of the past; robbed, pillaged and left to ruin. Cortez's men described the city as being so beautiful that it was as a dream, unreal in its magnificence. Indeed, it was a city of monumental ceremonial centers and sacred spaces covered with and governed by cosmological symbols and beliefs. Tenochtitlan was the high seat of Aztec power, a vast, controlling center that reached out to a majority of those who populated Mesoamerica.

According to the *Codex Mendoza* (1541–1545), there were four hundred towns and five regions that paid tribute to Tenochtitlan. Throughout the empire rituals of renewal involving sacrifice and cannibalism were made to numerous gods. Townships, within running range

of Tenochtitlan, sent festival offerings of human flesh to Emperor Montezuma via relay runners.

The warrior chiefs who founded the Aztec Empire may have been
bloodthirsty power-mongers, but they were also wise. Like themselves,
the peoples they conquered and assimilated practiced human sacrifice and
ritual cannibalism. The new rulers chose not to change the people's ways,
rather they combined religious beliefs with cultural practices and molded
them to their benefit. They expanded on what had already been in practice
and swept their gathering subjects into a religious fervor of sacrifice and
cannibalism promoted and protected by a cover of political and psychological domination that fostered itself through generations.

The two calendars of the Aztecs meshed every 52 years. This powerful astrological event allowed the ruling Aztecs to re-establish the central
power of Tenochtitlan with the "New Fire Ceremony." From childhood,
people waited anxiously through the years, hoping to experience the emotionally charged nocturnal ritual remembered by elders and memorialized
through art.

The ceremony was held outside the city of Tenochtitlan at a sacred
site on the "Hill of the Stars." On the night of the New Fire Ceremony,
people destroyed their household goods and extinguished their fires, then
waited in darkness and anticipation with all eyes focused on the summit of
the hill. Then it happened. Upon the chest of a sacrificed warrior a new fire
was lit. When well kindled, it was carried down to the center of the city and
placed in the shrine of the founding eagle-god of Tenochtitlan. From that
central place the new flame was distributed to all parts of the empire. For the
Aztecs, even fire, the magic that took away the night, had to be sacrificed
and born again. Every ritual spoke of renewal and continuance, and the only
way to ensure renewal and keep the sun to its daily promise of return was
through death, be it human or flame.

The Aztecs joined all others of the planet earth in believing their
customs and beliefs to be sacred and correct. When the Spaniards first
arrived, there was no effort made to stop or hide their religious festivities.

Later, when the Spaniards made their first assault on Tenochtitlan, the Aztecs captured some of Cortez's men and treated them as they would any other captive. A priest wrote of Spanish conquistadors watching as their friends were dragged up the stairs of the great pyramid, of their being made to dance, and then having their hearts cut out and their limbs severed from their bodies to be eaten.

With the killing and cannibalizing of Cortez's men, the Aztecs quickened their own annihilation as the Europeans took to slaughtering them without remorse, not only for gold, land and power, but also for the purpose of obliterating a people who consumed human flesh, a practice *their* religion, priests, king and queen professed to be the worst of sins.

But how could a few hundred soldiers, along with enlisted enemies of the Aztecs, conquer a huge population of warriors? Upon his arrival, Cortez, with his Spanish conquistadors, approached Montezuma as a peaceful conqueror, and since his arrival had been prophesized through a dream, he was accepted. Only later were guns, swords and enemies of the Aztecs used against Montezuma and his people, and by that time the most efficient weapon of all—disease—had taken its toll as a majority of the populace fell ill. In the end, colds, measles and smallpox proved to be more effective than muskets, swords and enemy tribes (horses should also be remembered here; they terrified the Aztecs and won many a battle for the Spaniards).

When war, slaughter and disease had decimated their populations, demolished their great city, destroyed their beautiful and bountiful gardens, polluted their waters and killed their leaders, tens of thousands were left to starve. But the Aztecs held to their religious beliefs. Though edible corpses lay everywhere, the Aztecs refused to eat of their dead. Only in religious context, when a proper subject had been sacrificed and a priest had sanctified the flesh for consumption, would an Aztec partake of his own kind. Such is the power of belief.

CHAPTER TEN

THE LOST CULTURE OF THE WARI

Cannibalism has never been performed by people devoid of thought or feeling, but by those who follow their every emotion without restraint.

There is no way of knowing when our brains took on complex thought or gained the ability to think ahead or recall our past through memory. What we can surmise from 80,000-year-old burials, 1.5 million-year-old hearths, and myriad artifacts left by ancient predecessors is that it was a very long time ago. With complex thought processes the world can be viewed in many and varied ways and the mortal fact of death can be perceived.

Burmese kings of long ago had people buried alive beneath the gates of their capital so the spirits of those buried would forever guard the city. Further south, in the Pacific, Fijians placed human sacrifices beneath massive corner pillars erected during the building of a chieftain's house. Such houses were often constructed in connection with the completion of one of their 80-foot war canoes. Of all the boats ever made with stone tools, the Fijian longboats were the largest vessels to ever ply the waters of the South Pacific. The Fijians "christened" their immense war canoes by drenching them, stem to stern, with human blood. The bodies of the blood victims were then roasted and consumed to complete the celebration. Within 40 years of the British landing on the shores of Fiji, the art of building 80-foot canoes had been lost, never to return.

After being set adrift by mutineers, Captain William Bligh, along with a small crew of loyal men, purposely skirted the Fijian isles, knowing that to land and take on much needed water and food would be an act of offering oneself up as a main course. He noted his knowledge of the cannibalistic Fijians in his diary along with the fact that as he and his thirsty mates passed the last large island, several longboats of hungry Fijians pushed into the sea and gave chase. Fortunately, the wind, currents and the distance already gained saved the lives and fate of Bligh and his men.

When looking into a subject such as cannibalism, it is important to understand belief systems that underlie the behavior of others. The practice of burying people beneath gates and buildings as protection against evil foreigners is thousands of years old. The oldest archaeological sites of the Far and Middle East have turned up human bones from beneath the rubble of dozens of ancient edifices. Those sacrificed were put to death for the same reason—to keep enemies from entering the space they were bound to protect. The custom illustrates long-held beliefs of spirits emanating from the dead; and people who believe in ghosts cannot view death as being final.

How do cannibalism and a belief in spirits enter into the same picture? If you believe the dead continue to exist in an altered state, then you are going to protect your deceased and treat them according to your beliefs through ritual. It therefore follows that if you lose "Igor" and his body to an enemy, Igor is lost forever and must be revenged. In satisfying that re-venge it would be reasonable to believe that if you consume the body of an enemy, his spirit will not only be quelled and vanquished forever, but you, the warrior, might be imbued with the power, courage and strength of your enemy through the eating of his heart, liver, brain or whatever. The final prize is that you have protected yourself and your people by annihilating an enemy as well as his malevolent spirit.

A cannibal taunt from New Guinea, shouted across ravines to an enemy: "I ate your brother yesterday, tomorrow I will shit him out!"

Now, turn the above thinking around. If you love your kinsmen and live in a tightly knit group where every individual is an emotional part of you, then the consuming of their body at the time of their natural death would be a way of keeping them with you, of processing into yourself their very essence and that which would naturally rot and decay.

Survival cannibalism as practiced by the survivors of the Andean plane crash is easily understood, but the two most common types of can-nibalism are labeled exo- and endocannibalism. Exocannibalism is the prac-tice of killing and ingesting your enemy, whereas endocannibalism is the custom of dining upon your friends and relatives following their natural or accidental demise. These two forms of cannibalism can be viewed as being worlds apart in regard to emotional satisfaction and methods of obtaining human flesh. Of the many peoples known to have practiced cannibalism within a framework of cultural belief, all were found to have practiced ei-ther exo- or endocannibalism, but never both—until now. Contemporary Amazon tribes, known as the Wari, practiced both exo- and endocannibal-ism prior to contact from the outside.

Beth A. Conklin, a young anthropologist, spent 19 months (1985–1987) with tribes of people known as the Wari. Through close contact, Conklin learned the Wari's language and customs. As friendships multi-plied and deepened, the Wari shared with her the ways of their past. Previ-ous anthropological studies of the Wari had been short-term, as the Wari appeared to be a quiet, saddened people who exhibited no outward signs of ever having had a complex society or belief system. Conklin's patience and caring uncovered an unknown wealth of information.

In the 1950s, Brazilian businessmen, desirous of the Wari lands for commercial development, hired assassins to go into the jungles and kill off as many Wari as possible. Using machine guns and repeating rifles, the assassins wiped out entire villages; every man, woman and child. Wari warriors had never killed more than a few men at a time, and their primitive weapons were no match for a hail of bullets. The businessmen thought little of their actions; after all, it was well known the Wari were cannibals and Queen Isabella had decreed way back in the late 1400s that cannibalistic tribes could, and should, be eradicated. Of the Wari who escaped the bullets, many fell to diseases introduced from the outside.

During the 1960s, government workers and missionaries forced all surviving Wari to abandon cannibalism, don clothing, live in government housing and go to church. These actions so overwhelmed the remaining Wari that they fell into bouts of depression followed by attitudes of sullenness. When forced to wear Western clothing, they stopped painting their bodies in intricate designs, and since their old societal ways were forbidden, they no longer performed ceremonies handed down through generations.

Prior to contact from the outside world, Wari warriors had killed their enemies out of revenge, packing the meat back to their villages for consumption; exocannibalism. But when a village member died, they practiced an elaborate form of endocannibalism, complete with ritual mourning followed by the processing and eating of the body. Most interesting are the differences in how they treated the bodies of their family members as opposed to those who were killed out of vengeance.

The Wari would avenge the taking and/or killing of one of their own by raiding and killing one or more of the offending tribe. When a man killed an enemy, everyone present in his war party was automatically considered as the killer of the man. Simply being present provided a man another notch on his nonexistent belt and allowed an initiate the consideration of having been proven a man. Once a short verbal ceremony was performed over the corpse, the Wari treated the victim's body as game meat. In most cases, they took the head, arms and legs home for consumption. One old man told Conklin, "We ate the enemies (*wijam*), because we were angry (*mana*) at them." Others told Conklin they treated the bodies of their enemies as game in order to express and act out their hatred.

Regarding cannibalism, Conklin notes that both the public and scientific communities have repeatedly held to traditional emotional reactions towards cannibalism, such as fascination and revulsion, emotions that restrict a full understanding of the subject. With a friend to confide in, the Wari willingly explained the ritual and emotional aspects related to their funerary feasts, as well as their feelings towards, and treatment of, enemies. Through personal stories, and the telling of their history, the Wari told how hatred, vengeance and aggression were replaced with emotions of love and mourning during their highly ritualized ceremonies of funerary cannibalism.

The belief systems of the Wari, as with most people, were unique. The Wari believed that all bodily fluids passed from one person to another by contact, i.e., breast milk, sweat, semen, saliva, tears, urine, feces—anything that exits the body—was believed to pass through and become part of the person who had been touched by such. Thus your babies, husband, wife and core family members were truly a part of you, and as such could not be eaten by you at the time of their death as it was deemed sinful to eat of oneself. Thus the consuming of the dead was left to tribal members outside the natal group of the deceased.

When a person died, it was common practice for close family members to lie with or on the body (often in a group), hug, kiss and even mate with the deceased. Tears and wailing were profuse as the people poured out their grief. The death of a family member brought such deep grief to the Wari that in order to carry on with their lives they annihilated everything ever owned or made by the deceased. All personal items of the deceased, including their possessions, hut and the crops they had planted were burned or destroyed. At the same time, paths they habitually walked down were scratched out and new ones were made. If a neighbor's door looked out to the house of the deceased, the doorway was thatched over and a new one was cut.

When a Wari died, word would be sent out to all neighboring villages where any known relatives resided, as the body could not be consumed until all close family members were assembled. When a child died, the body could be processed, roasted and consumed the same or following day as the child's immediate family was already present, but in the case of an older person it might take a week for family members to arrive. Because of this ritualistic law concerning family presence, the consumption of older people meant partially or completely rotten meat was served forth at the time of the funeral. In such instances, the cannibalism that, by custom, had to take place was extremely difficult for all involved.

In Conklin's book, there are drawings made by Wem Quirio, which graphically depict the ritualistic process of endocannibalism as practiced by the Wari. We see the roasting rack, two men holding up the body of a dead warrior, dancing with the corpse while singing his death songs. We see the butchering of the bloated body with another man waving a woven mat so as to blow away the fumes of decay. Even the firewood was specially prepared and adorned. Most funerary rituals, such as fire and rack building, dancing and singing, butchery and so forth, were performed by men who wore red macaw feathers standing tall from the back of their heads in honor of the dead. Women made *pamonha*, a dense cornbread wrapped in leaves and roasted along with the body and eaten to offset the constipation that so often ensues when an all-protein meal is consumed without vegetable matter. The accompaniment of *pamonha* also helped the diners perform their grisly task.

The organs of the deceased were wrapped in leaves and tied for roasting. The head, arms, legs and horizontally halved torso were dissected from the body and roasted in their natural state.

The Wari, whose folklore always featured bodily fluids, looked upon the fluids that emanated from corpses as being foul and corrupt and spoke openly about the stench surrounding the preparation of the body. But, as horrid as the fluids and odors might be, those fluids were sacred, a part of the family so to speak, and male family members would often wiggle under a decomposing corpse so that the precious fluids would fall first on them rather than the ground since to have any part of a family member's body decay in the ground was unthinkable.

The men who worked with and butchered the body for roasting smeared their hands and arms with black genipap and their bodies with strong-smelling red annatto in order to protect themselves from the putre-faction of the corpse. Likewise, diners would cover their hands and face with genipap so as not to be sickened by the foul odors of the roasted flesh.

When the body was taken from the family for butchery, the in-tensity of wailing and crying that had begun at the time of death would increase in volume and continue until the body was consumed; a process that often lasted 12 to 24 hours. By the shouting of lies and loud wailing, the spirit of the deceased was chased away to continue its journey. This tormenting of the spirit went on until the entirety of the corpse had been consumed, for if the body were not fully consumed, the deceased's ghost would haunt the tribe forever.

When the roasting of the corpse began, family members would race forward and try to throw themselves into the flames. Guards were sta-tioned to ward off all serious suicidal attempts, but the effort gave powerful proof of love and suffering.

The more decayed a body, the longer the roasting time and the longer the wailing and begging by family members as they encouraged the diners to partake. There were many trips into the jungle to vomit, but the diners persisted until the spirit of the dead was persuaded to travel on.

A man participating in his first funeral of a close relative might sing a song about "never having seen this fire before," while another who had lost many relatives might sing, "I never want to see this fire again."

The Wari mirrored the majority of religions through their belief in transformation and rebirth. They firmly believed that the body of a loved one had to be consumed or the deceased would fail to reach the otherworld and accept the reality of their death. Only when death was accepted could the deceased be transformed into a wild pig and offer themselves to the arrows of the Wari in order to feed their family for a last time. The final transformation came with the eating of the wild pig, which liberated the spirit of the loved one to a final and better place.

At the conclusion of a Wari funerary feast every single bone and bit of the carcass, along with the cooking rack and any other items used in connection with the ritual were placed on the remaining embers of the fire and cremated to a fine ash. Then the whole of the litter was scraped into a hole and covered with soil. The topsoil was then pounded until the location of the hole was indistinguishable from any other piece of ground, at which time the spot was covered with the family's sleeping platform. When all was said, wailed and done, there was no visual or tactile evidence that the deceased had ever existed.

The Wari removed all traces of the existence of a departed loved one for personal and emotional reasons, but here, again, we find the complete obliteration of all evidence of cannibalism. It is little wonder that materialistic proof of cannibalism, ancient or recent, is so difficult to come by.

It should be noted that the Wari would not consume a body whose liver looked unhealthy, or if the person had died of a pulmonary infection; such corpses were cremated until nothing but ash and bone remained. In such instances all other ceremonies were carried out to the fullest, the only difference being that the body was cremated rather than roasted and consumed.

Conklin's careful research exposed detailed information concerning customary cannibalism performed by caring people, who, like most peoples of the earth, loved their families and hated their enemies. As to universal beliefs in an afterlife, or the existence of "spirits," I offer the following.

A Yanomamo Indian from the Amazon jungles of Venezuela was taken by an anthropologist down river from his remote village by canoe, then driven in a motorized vehicle for many hours to a huge cement runway situated on a military base. When the Yanomamo got out of the car he was completely baffled by what was beneath his feet. He crawled around touch-ing and sniffing the cement until instructed to board a military transport, which took off and flew through the worst storm anyone aboard had ever lived through; only the jungle-dweller took the ride in stride. And in Cara-cas everything fascinated or befuddled the Yanomamo, but only one thing frightened him; as a matter of fact, it terrified him. At night the headlights from oncoming traffic seemed to him like evil spirits of the dead rushing headlong to get him. Every time he entered a cab after sundown, he would curl up on the floor and begin to shake and moan about evil "ghosts." His reaction is startling as he wasn't frightened by the lights of the city or the lamps in the hotel, even though he had lived his entire life having only seen artificial light from a flashlight or lantern. But something about headlights rushing toward him reduced him to a huddled mass. What had this man of the jungle seen in the darkness of the night?

When this intelligent, kindhearted warrior returned to his people, he received a welcome similar to that of Marco Polo upon his return to Venice, Italy, in 1295. No one would believe his stories, and his native language possessed few words to explain the wonders of the modern world. As isolated jungle-dwellers, the people of his village had never seen or expe-rienced anything that related to what he was trying to describe; his stories were literally beyond their imaginations. After a week or two of trying to describe what he had seen, the native stopped talking about his journey into the modern world as to do so would have cost him the loss of both position and face.

Marco Polo handled a similar situation differently. The Mongol em-peror, Kublai Khan, had held Marco Polo, his father Niccolo and his uncle Maffeo for 17 years in open and elegant imprisonment; the great Khan said the Europeans offered spice to his royal court. Finally, in 1291 or '92, (the exact date is unknown), the emperor allowed the Polos to leave so long as they saw to the delivery of his niece, the "Blue Princess," to an awaiting husband in Persia. With golden passports, jewels, the princess and an en tourage of 600, the Polos left China in 14 junks whose length averaged 100 feet—extremely large boats for the time. When they reached Sumatra, the weather turned against them, forcing them to camp along the coast for five months during which time they built "castles of beams and of logs."

The reason for settling along the wet and insect-infested coast was that the coastal people, the Sumutrans, were friendly, whereas the people who lived beyond the coast were, in Marco's words, "such as beasts. . . . For I tell you quite truly that they eat flesh of men."

The people the Polos managed to avoid for five months were the Bataks, who possessed a calendar and possibly an alphabet and also cannibalized their enemies in order to capture their spirits.

Today the Bataks number some five million and are as open about the cannibalism of their ancestors as my Maori friend. From a July 2001 *National Geographic* article can be read the words of Andreas Lingga, director of a Batak museum: showing his palm to the interviewer he says, "My grandfather said this was the most desired part. It wasn't the sweetest, but the elders thought palm flesh had medicinal properties."

A Batak woman, Ningrum Sirait adds to the pot, "It's a joke now to warn somebody, 'Don't play games with us; we eat people.'"

And they did. In 1834, two missionaries from New England were taken to be enemies and were devoured. But in 1862, a German Lutheran, Ludwig Ingwer Nommensen, arrived fully prepared. Ludwig had learned the Batak language, and to this day, on Sundays to be exact, the Batak rent the still air with one solemn hymn after another.

Marco Polo was never silent. After writing down his family's adventures, Marco collaborated with a writer of romances by the name of Rustichello, who, many think, left out many occurrences described by Marco that failed to speak of heroism. For example, on their journey home the Polos were forced to give up a huge portion of the wealth given them by the Mongol emperor Kublai Khan and the lords of Persia to a Trebizond ruler west of Turkey who did not honor golden passports or anything other than ransom.

Marco's book was entitled *The Travels of Marco Polo* and was an immediate success among those who could read in medieval Europe. Some 150 versions were written and transcribed, with no two alike. Though Rustichello penned most of them, they all constitute the work and narrative of Marco Polo, who set out with his father and uncle at the age of 17 to travel the world. Twenty-four years later, the three returned with jewels sewn into the rags on their backs and tales of far-off places with names never heard, events never imagined, bizarre customs and descriptions of items no European had ever seen or heard of. As Marco lay dying at the age of 70, friends begged him to recant his stories before meeting his God, to which he replied, "I did not write half of what I saw."

It took 80 years for others to travel the route of the Polos and return to verify the truth of Marco Polo's words. Though the Polo books contain some exaggerations, such as Marco and his family teaching warring tactics to the Chinese—tactics the Chinese had used prior to the arrival of the Polos—the geography, places, peoples, customs and foods listed in the books can be found and verified to this day.

People, all people, hesitate to believe in—or flat out deny—the existence of anything they cannot imagine, see or experience for themselves. The exceptions are religious teachings and myths that are programmed into our minds from early childhood.

In times past, societies in which tribes raided one another for revenge and/or women were the norm rather than the exception, and cannibalism was part of the process for many. Man has been a hunter for at least two and a half million years. *She* gathered and often provided the bulk of the foods needed for survival, while *he* hunted and/or scavenged for meat and protected his group to the best of his ability. Today, there are some who will tell you that females also hunted; small game, perhaps—but helping in the hunt of large animals would have been a difficult thing to do when you were pregnant or nursing and expected to gather foodstuffs such as fruits, nuts and tubers; gather wood; dress and cure hides; and care for younger members of the group, all at a time when sexual dimorphism between men and women was greater than today. We women were, and are, exceptional enough without making us into risk-taking, big-shouldered, spear-throwing killers of large game.

The stone tool kits of our early ancestors tell us loud and clear that both males and females knew how to skin and butcher that which was killed or scavenged. Blood and entrails were a natural part of our early life as they are today in the lives of doctors, nurses, veterinarians, undertakers, pathologists, coroners, butchers, hunters, chefs, soldiers in war and people who still live within the grasp of nature. But when did *you* last kill, clean and butcher the animal that provided the meat you so lovingly roast up all brown and redolent with intoxicating aromas, which will provide protein for the sustenance of both the body and the brain that controls it?

Those who deal with dead bodies on a regular basis become accustomed and knowledgeable in their work; the butcher learns his anatomy as does the physician, and it is a lousy chef who doesn't know how to skin, dissect, disarticulate, trim, bone and filet all manner of flesh.

In 2002, my husband and I were at a friend's ranch in Colorado for a hunt. Our friend has many acres, no predators and a population explosion of deer. One morning five hunters set out to help cull deer; all five brought back a buck. The deer were hung, gutted and tagged with government tags and paperwork. The organs were separated and I was given three of the livers. I prefer wild liver for its taste and the fact that the animal has never been administered drugs or hormones, both of which are known to lodge in the liver. Using a white trash bag as an apron, properly cut for the exit of my head and arms, I set to work skinning and deveining the livers. I was carefully working a knife tip under the "skin" of one of the livers so I could work my fingers under it to de-sheath the liver, when I happened to look up. What I saw was a row of three hunters, big men who had gone out and made their kill, staring at me with wide eyes and slack jaws. I am a small blonde female so perhaps the incongruity of the scene caused the unanimous reaction. Or was it the fact that few people in the world today ever interact with the actual preparation of the food they eat?

As hunter-gatherers, we knew each variety of animal we ate, and when the husbanding of animals began, the ancient knowledge of bodies—their structure, tissue (both connective and muscle), organs and intestines—carried over to the butchering and use of domesticated animals. Once a person understands the skeletal and physical composition of mammals, birds and fish, any mammal, bird or fish can be dealt with in kind.

CHAPTER ELEVEN

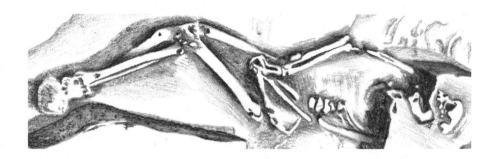

THROUGH A DISTANT WINDOW

". . . then hot gum leaves are pressed on the bridge of the baby's nose, to make it flat, for a thoroughly flat nose is essential to good looks."[1] From our most ancient past into the present, we humans have looked after our appearance.

Some 60,000 years ago a group of people crossed unknown waters to land on the island continent of Australia. At the time of their journey, Australia, the three Americas and many of the Pacific Islands were devoid of human footprints. Genetics suggest the group originated in southern India, but the evidence is inconclusive. If correct, those early explorers would have had to cross the northern portion of the Indian Ocean to reach the Andaman Islands, then travel down the curving length of islands currently known as Indonesia.

Or, they could have skirted the entire coastline of the Bay of Bengal, which runs for thousands of miles in a huge inverted V and then crossed over to the Indonesian islands. Whichever course they took, they had to face expanses of open waters when they reached the Timor Sea or the Torres Strait. If they made it all the way to New Guinea, they would have crossed the Torres Strait, but the Lesser Sunda Islands are closer to their proposed starting point and look more promising on maps of today; a few minutes with a good atlas should stir the imagination. Those intrepid people were the ancestors of Australia's Aborigines and represent the oldest known seafarers in sapient history.

The original people of Australia made their heroic journey during the last ice age, an extreme cold-weather snap that waffled over a span of 100,000 years. Warmer weather brought a rather abrupt end to the Ice Age some 10,000 years ago, causing sea levels to rise dramatically as during the Ice Age so much of the earth's water was tied up in continental ice sheets that the world's oceans dropped 300 to 400 feet. With such spectacular drops in sea level, many expanses of water were narrowed dramatically exposing new lands and shorelines. During millennia of maximum glaciation, the weather was milder, making the seas calmer than those of today. Heat drives wind, wind produces surface currents and weather, so when a planet cools there is less air turbulence, fewer storms, less wind and calmer seas. At such times, early man on makeshift rafts of bamboo or wood—or possibly seagoing canoes joined together—could have journeyed to far places, which might have been impossible if distances and weather patterns had been such as those we know today.

Those courageous seafarers of long ago landed on the shores of a harsh, beautiful and varied land inhabited by plants and animals, most of which differed from those they had known previously. Over the following millennia the first Australians developed unique cultures and ate a majority of the larger fauna to extinction, much as the first Americans would do thousands of years later. Scientific studies echo Aboriginal myths that speak of coming to a land of lush vegetation surrounded by lower seas that later rose; the eating of megafauna to the point of extinction is said to have been prompted by death-defying droughts. Whatever the past, in time higher seas marooned those who had braved them while droughts and man-made fires turned forested lands into desert. Man's poor use of the land, combined with natural disasters, worked to mold the lives and beliefs of the ancient mariners.

Legends of the Australian Aborigines speak of their coming to Australia from a land somewhere to the northwest. One tells of their being forced from their original homelands by fierce ants. Though this could speak of a plague of huge deadly ants, as legends go it could also speak of a prehistoric race as fierce as hordes of killing ants. Though a critical ant problem could force a people to move, to face the extreme dangers of the open sea rather than avoiding the danger by moving to another land site, suggest a people surrounded and hounded by an enemy that offered but one avenue of escape.

In regard to the focus of this volume, a question: did the Australian Aborigines create their complex mythologies, laws and customs after their arrival on the shores of Australia, or did they bring them from the lands they left? Within the chapters of this book can be found similar practices wrapped in robes of various colors. Do the binding threads reach back to truly ancient behaviors and attitudes that were ubiquitous within ancestral peoples during times unknown?

"Mungo Man," a lovely skeleton found under the mud of a dried-up lake in the hot interior of Australia, has been dated at 60,000 years. The dating of Mungo Man continues to be controversial—some claim older dates, while others claim younger—but, regardless of when Mungo Man met his maker, the Aborigines of Australia offer us invaluable lessons on how we lived and survived through times of our communal past.

The myths, legends, tools and wondrous art of the Australian Aborigines speak not only to their culture, but tell us loud and clear that we, *Homo sapiens*, have always been a storytelling, child-teaching, artistic, holistic and inventive species; that art and craftsmanship did not suddenly arise

40,000 years ago in a European cave, but in many lands far and wide.

Imagine an ancient people walking through calf-deep, muddy run-off waters following a downpour. The mud dries and they giggle at the natural socks nature has provided. Surely the first art was the painting, decorating and scarification of the body; first with mud, then clay, chalk, manganese, ochre, then on to shell or obsidian blade. The hands of Mungo Man, the skeleton aforementioned, had been crossed over his penis and his entire body had been smeared with red ochre prior to burial.

Evidence of like practices, along with art and artifacts, has been found on other continents. In 2003, an archaeological dig exposed fresh-water snail-shell necklaces in Blombos Cave, situated on the shores of the Indian Ocean 200 miles east of Cape Town in South Africa. The necklaces have been dated at 75,000 years, adding more than 30,000 years to the evidential timing for personal adornment. Also found within Blombos were abstract engravings on bone, finely worked bone tools and weapon points; inferred evidence of cannibalism was also found. And excavations at a Klasies River mouth cave, South Africa, dated at 120,000 years, uncovered mounds of faunal bones in concert with a *Homo sapiens* skull and bone pieces that show stone-tool cut marks indicative of anthropophagy.

Further north in Europe, burnt manganese nodules and lithics were uncovered in a Neanderthal cave dated to 60,000 years ago. The only reason for collecting and burning manganese is to soften it for crushing so as to mix it with animal fat and use the resultant pitch-black product for the painting of the body or a hide, or for crushing to a fine powder for the blackening of flesh during scarification or tattooing. The stone tools found in connection with the burnt manganese nodules were microlithics, tiny stone cutting blades still sharp enough to pierce or slice the skin. Numerous Neanderthal sites present evidence of cannibalism. The pièce de résistance (to my mind) is a group of fine throwing spears from 400,000 years ago, discovered in Germany. The spears offer clear evidence that man was already wise enough 400,000 years ago to sharpen and harden over fire the proper end of a spear; the end that had grown closest to the ground, the end that would produce the sharpest, most perfectly balanced weapon. One of the spears is unbroken and still sharp enough and strong enough to pierce the body of a horse.

Sixty thousand years ago, all peoples of the world were hunter-gatherers. And hunter-gathers, per se, do not develop written languages, though etched bones from ancient caves found on many continents depict both animals and what appear to be calendars and/or tallies of animals killed. The etched bones shout out at us concerning early mental abilities, but the art of writing, the act of inscribing facts and thoughts for future generations to read and learn from, is a mere 6,000 years old. People without written languages teach and review their wisdom, cultural beliefs, laws and histories through art, legend, storytelling, cycle songs and myth, often intertwined with elaborate rites of initiation. Rites and initiations may vary from people to people, but all are purposefully harsh and/or difficult in order to train the initiate for the rigors of adulthood. Through the words of elders, individuals learn the history and rules of his or her tribe. These methods of learning are found within all cultures.

Joining the rest of humanity, the Australian Aborigines lived through dangerous and perilous times. Through experience and observation, people came to recognize that when the mind experiences a frightening situation it goes on full alert as the flee and fight responses automatically heighten the senses, thus allowing for memory retention of all incoming stimuli. Difficult, often scary, initiations, in combination with strict training and tribal law, produce competent people capable of sustaining themselves and surviving to pass their genes on to future generations.

Initiations are the oldest identified method for imparting knowledge, gaining acceptance, or achieving a desired position within a group. Initiations for children entering puberty have been found within every known culture, while in many of today's modern cultures, rites that demand ceremony and performance in order to enter the world of adulthood have been abandoned, leaving many teenagers in doubt as to what exactly is expected of them.

There were distinct differences amongst the innumerable tribes of Aborigines that once inhabited Australia, though ancient basic beliefs seem to have persisted within various cultures. When putting their adolescents through the rigors of initiation, diverse demands were placed upon the young, but three tests showed commonality:

1. Overcoming hunger: Each initiate had to go for a two-day walkabout without food. When they returned they were brought before a fire where a sumptuous repast of kangaroo steaks and other delicacies was being prepared. The initiate had to take only a small portion, eating nothing more until morning.

2. Overcoming pain: Both boys and girls had to submit to having their noses pierced and their bodies marked by scarification. Finally, the initiates allowed themselves to be laid down over hot embers thinly covered with boughs.

3. Overcoming fear: Last came the test of fear where the young were told awesome and hair-raising stories about ghosts and the "moldered"—the Evil Spirit or Devil-devil. After the stories they had to sleep in a far-off place, usually near a tribal cemetery. During the night, elders, wearing grotesque clay and bark headdresses would silently appear and wander through the reclining adolescents while making eerie and frightening sounds. The initiates had to remain calm and show no signs of fear or troubled sleep.

Those who passed all three tests were admitted as fully initiated members of the tribe. Those who failed were never allowed to marry, or sire or bear children. With harsh living conditions and a land that provided for limited numbers, Aboriginal sex laws were very strict, and failure to obey could bring a sentence of death. Elders and relatives arranged marriages, often at the time of a girl's birth.

While both boys and girls went through the three-part initiation, boys continued on separately through harsher lessons on their way to manhood, while girls underwent more scarification. Females received rows of quarter-inch-deep cuts, each an inch in length, down both sides of their backs. The procedure was done in preparation for marriage and acceptability; a mussel shell was used as a cutting tool. Scarification differed from tribe to tribe. In W.J. Sollas's book, *Ancient Hunters and Their Modern Representatives*, published in 1911, there are two beautiful photographs of a young Australian Aboriginal woman whose scarifications line her stomach rather than her back. On her upper arms are several raised scars from self-inflicted wounds made during times of mourning the death of a loved one.

Aside from scarification, girls were taught the multiple tasks they would have to perform as adults since women did most of the work and carried all burdens on walkabouts. The men walked ahead carrying only their weapons, ever ready to defend the group or procure fresh meat.

Over the centuries the original peoples of Australia grew in population and separated into tribes that scattered themselves over Australia's vast and widely varying expanse of lands. Each tribe, or clan, took the name of an animal; for example, a group might be the Wallaby clan. Men of the Wallaby clan would say, "I have a Wallaby Dreaming," meaning that his totem was the wallaby and by that totem he was distinguished from all other clans, and that the governance of laws and rules laid down by the Wallaby clan were those he adhered to. Whatever a man's totem, he believed himself to be descended from the universal animal father, i.e., Wallaby, who was the ancestor of all other Wallaby men. No man, of any tribe, could kill or partake of his totem animal.

"Dreamtime" is ubiquitous among all tribes of Australia, a fact that speaks to its early beginnings. Dreamtime is not about dreaming, but is a term given to an all-encompassing belief system that sets forth the creation of the universe, the earth, its plants, animals and people. It offers explanations and stories of gods and spirits, and all things that exist on Earth. Dreamtime is full of spirits that continue to inhabit sacred places and tells its people how to care for the land and its animals. Dreamtime is a cosmic library so all encompassing as to foretell the future of our planet.

Paleoclimatologists have plotted times of drought that have occurred around the globe over the last several millions of years. Their work shows that droughts plagued a majority of our ancestors at one time or another. If you are a band of people who plant no crops, nor husband any animals, you must find water and collect food on a continual basis. When drought hits, foodstuffs die, animals move on or die as well, and in time you and your people are left with nothing to eat. Fire may warm you and keep dangerous animals at bay, but it cannot feed you. As surely as the taming of fire began with the picking up of a fiery brand ignited by lightning, cannibalism surely found its beginnings in starvation. And of all places on Earth where drought and starvation could attack, Australia was prime for the task.

In 1606, a Spaniard by the name of Luis Váez de Torres sailed between Australia and Papua New Guinea, on waters now known as Torres Strait. Prior to that, Macasson traders from Indonesia sailed down across the Timor Sea to harvest sea cucumbers and sometimes trade with the Aborigines. In 1770, Captain James Cook skirted much of Australia's coastline before landing in what he called "Botany Bay." You know Botany Bay; it is the current site of a town called Sydney. Though Dutch and English explorers reached Australia prior to Cook, it was only after Cook's landing that any real outside activity began to encroach upon the natives of the earth's largest island continent, a land they had inhabited, undisturbed, for millennia.

Accounts of cannibalism among the Australian Aborigines, written over recent centuries by explorers, doctors, anthropologists, geologists, clergy, government employees and laypersons alike, are prodigious. While some are braggadocios and must be discarded, there are far too many texts written by men and women of letters and honor for the entire library of writings to be dismissed. The most reliable tell of revenge killings and the eating of women, children, and sometimes, men. During times of starvation, older women were treated, killed and consumed in the same manner as game, and if a person was seriously injured, he too was killed and eaten. Infant cannibalism was widespread and many tribes consumed all firstborns to ensure the future fecundity of the mother. (See Chapter 12: "Infanticide.")

In the 1830s, there were many reports of cannibalistic infanticide among Aboriginal tribes of the Geelong and Colac regions of Australia. The Victorian Methodist Church created the Buntingdale Mission there in an effort to put an end to such practices. As head of the mission the reverend Joseph Orton wrote,

> They are frequently in the habit of devouring their own offspring . . . When they have a second child unable to walk, from the great inconvenience of carrying them in the course of their wanderings, sometimes one will be sacrificed and eaten by the parents.

In 1938, Daisy Bates published *The Passing of the Aborigines*, a compilation of 40 years of research gathered while living among the Aborigines of Western Australia. Daisy was, without a doubt, the most staunch friend and advocate the Australian Aborigines ever had. In her introduction she wrote,

> . . . for cannibalism never died out among these wandering tribes. They will kill and eat from revenge, or from primeval motives beyond our understanding. . . . Infant cannibalism was practiced where it could not be prevented.

Revenge and other killings were performed through custom, belief or need, while cannibalistic infanticide was seen as benefiting the mother, and/or aiding in the survival of the tribe. The Australian Aborigines were full-time, nomadic hunters-gatherers when Captain Cook went ashore. Anything that could add to the sustenance and survival of a group or individual was put into practice. The Aborigines' belief that an infant was not yet of this world allowed them to continue in their life's journey. People of the past, who lived in hostile lands where survival was at all times difficult, developed similar behaviors on a global scale.

Early writers, and later, professors, government officials, historians, clergymen and immigrants, observed that the Australian Aborigines thoroughly enjoyed human flesh, though some claimed the shunning of brains. Of male carcasses, the thigh was considered the choicest portion, whereas the breasts of a woman were most favored for their fat content. But the most sought after morsel was kidney fat or the kidneys themselves, which were regarded as the center of life. If a man was cannibalized out of revenge, the killer would carry some of the victim's flesh around with him in a "basketwork," or "dilly-bag," for good luck and strength. The flesh was rolled up in grass, and it was said that if a man felt weak in body or mind, he would take out the flesh of his enemy and take a bite, thus feeding both mind and body while protecting himself from the spirit of his enemy.

In times of starvation, older women (*gin*) were killed in secluded spots. One man would grab the woman from behind and bend her over while folding her arms across her chest. A second man would slay her by hitting her on the head with a *nulla-nulla* or wooden sword. The body was then disemboweled, cut up for roasting and taken back to the clan.

Children (toddlers and older) were dispatched quickly by picking them up from behind by the ankles and dashing their heads against a rock. Some newborns were allowed to die as opposed to being killed.

In *Women of All Nations*, N.W. Thomas writes,

> . . . a superfluous baby (other than the firstborn) is put out of the way as soon as it is born, either by actual violence or by the less humane method of withholding all food; but no half measures are allowed. In many parts the corpse was eaten by the brothers, sometimes by the grandparents.

In the paragraph prior to the above quote, Mr. Thomas wrote something that is intriguing in regard to his own people of the British Isles:

> . . . though a (Aboriginal) woman may bear six or seven children, she rarely rears more than two. The remainder is not accounted for, as with us, by a gradual process of

semi-starvation, by doses of gin, or by any of the other numerous civilized methods of reducing the too numerous mouths in the family . . .

Thomas wrote his words a century ago when anthropologists, writers and historians made note of everything they found and observed. At the time, keeping one's numbers in check was globally accepted, but take note that he acknowledged semi-starvation of an infant, but found the withholding of all nourishment to be "less humane." Again, people accept what *their* society condones.

Many accounts of cannibalism among the Aborigines suggest that foreigners were a favorite prey, especially the Chinese, who arrived with the intent of setting up a new city and port, but ended up working long hours for little pay. Stepping back, foreigners can be viewed as easy, unsuspecting prey and good revenge victims as they were, after all, invaders, another vicious bunch of ants to deal with. But people do not take up the practice of cannibalism because strangers have sailed to their shores; they cannibalize the invaders because they have cannibalized others in the past. If you find a particular form of religion being practiced within a newly discovered tribe of indigenous people, they did not suddenly create their religious beliefs for an anthropologist or student of religion to analyze and write about. While some religions emanate from the writings of a single individual, most religions develop over decades, centuries or millennia, one rule or myth piling atop another to form a system of belief. Religions evolve from notable events, revelation, anomalous occurrences and spiritual needs, and for the controlling of a people or the consolidation of long-held beliefs. With the passage of time, religions that are sustained are massaged to conform with whatever is deemed to be correct by current hierarchies, thus forcing the evolution that can be documented within all systems of belief. In the same manner, cultural practices of cannibalism do not suddenly appear within a society, but gradually gain acceptance through multiple occurrences.

The Aborigines of Australia killed foreigners for revenge, for the fouling of Aboriginal fishing holes, the taking of lands or the killing of Aboriginal people. A tribe known as the Merkins had a word, "*talgoro*" meaning "human-meat-waiting-to-be-taken"; what we would call a "marked man."

The killing and cannibalizing of foreigners can be viewed as a known defense mechanism performed by tribes prone to aggression and cannibalism. Victims were usually clubbed to death and taken away, but others were captured, tied to trees after their shin and arm bones were broken—thereby rendering escape impossible—then killed and eaten one at a time (no refrigeration). Those last to go were forced to watch the fate of their friends.

Various accounts suggest that the incidences of cannibalism escalated following Cook's landing and intrusion into Aboriginal lands. Prior to contact from the outside, events of cannibalism may have been connected mainly with revenge killings, the accepted practice of cannibalistic infanticide and during times of drought and starvation. It is also probable that, as with the many tribes of the Americas, some groups practiced various forms of cannibalism, while others did not. Wherever peoples are separated by space and dialects, beliefs and customs will differ; only survival cannibalism is ubiquitous.

The Australian Aborigines created extraordinary mythologies, art, laws, customs and religions as they grew to know and understand every facet of the lands they inhabited. They were, and are, an exceptional people with incredible talents and insights and a mythology that is both astounding and sage. Having lived with no outside intervention for thousands upon thousands of years, the Aborigines of Australia allow us to look through distant windows to view ourselves and perceive why we are the most proficient survivors on Earth.

Unfortunately, of the multitudinous tribes of Aborigines that existed at the time of Cook's landing, few remain. Disease, killings and the taking of lands decimated one tribe after another. In 1987, an elder of the Gagudju tribe spoke of the white man coming, of his making changes without looking or listening, of introducing things and thoughts and laws too quickly, of never understanding or listening to the land, and most of all, scarring, marring and changing the "Dreamtime," i.e., the history, and future form, of planet Earth.

Over the last decades there has been an almost complete whitewash of Aboriginal history through the auspices of political correctness in Australia; as if saying nice things about a people's past will obliterate the harm done to them. The current bias towards whitewashing history has done nothing to help the last remaining Aborigines, who are worse off today than ever before.

As noted previously, recent DNA studies have shown that we all have cannibals in our closets, though many continue to argue against the genetic evidence brought forth by Collinge and Mead. The reaction of the antagonists is natural. History has proven repeatedly that it takes time to shatter strongly held beliefs. Regardless, the histories of all nations offer like truths that infer that there are cannibals lurking in all of our ancestral closets. Such truths do not make you, me, or anyone else, a bad or lesser person. Humans have performed deeds worse than cannibalism . . . such as hunting and shooting Australian Aborigines from horseback for the sport of it.

CHAPTER TWELVE

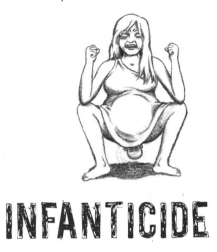

INFANTICIDE

"Some Africans believe that if your baby dies, you must bury it far away from your house, with proper magic and incantations and gifts for the gods, so that the baby does not come back, time after time, and plant itself inside your womb only to die a short time after birth. This is a story for people who need to find an acceptable way to lose a multitude of babies."[1]

Cycles of life and death are common to all living organisms. Though grieving has been observed within many higher organisms, it is only the complex brain of humans that allows for full recognition of a cessation of what we call life. With comprehension of life's cycles came beliefs in reincarnation or an afterlife, one or the other of which is noted in most religions, as well as oral and written histories.

It has been known for more than a century that when sperm meets egg the result often ends in a natural abortion. While many fetuses are expelled from the body one to seven months following conception, a majority of natural abortions occur when a zygote—a fertilized ovum in its early stages of cell division—is flushed from the body during menstruation so soon after conception that the mother remains ignorant of ever having been pregnant. But, while nature continually strives for perfection, she never achieves it. There is no perfect flower, beast, fish, bird or human, but left in the hands of nature a species will evolve to be the most fit to survive within its given environment. In her constant striving for perfection, Nature expels fetuses that register abnormalities, but she does not get them all. Every day infants are born mildly or grossly deformed in body and/or brain, while others arrive with life-taking defects or diseases. Through the eons animals of every kind, including humans, have dealt with the problem in varied, yet similar ways.

Statistics show that a century ago, 50% of first births resulted in the death of either the infant or the mother, or both. In the United States, if you could go back a mere century, you would not recognize yourself.

In highly industrialized societies of today, doctors save fetuses that would have been considered natural abortions 30 to 40 years ago. In the United States, new laws disallow decisions considered wise and rational a few years back, while in many areas of the world, such decisions are not made by doctors, but by mothers, and in some instances, fathers.

Before broaching the subject of cannibalistic infanticide we should first understand the practice of infanticide within the realm of history. Human infanticide occurred yesterday, occurs today and will occur tomorrow. In the United States, the feat will occasionally be done by a grievous mother incapable of taking care of her infant, a woman whose body chemistry codes against mothering, a young girl caught in a labyrinth of social statutes or a mother who is hungry, destitute or has more than she can manage. But the majority of infanticides in America will be performed by a boyfriend who will lose control of his emotions when another man's child will not stop crying, when each cry screams out to him, "My father lay with your woman. . . . I am proof that you are not first. . . . I am first." Multiple studies on infanticide within technologically developed societies show a majority of documented infanticides perpetrated by incoming males, who, much as male langurs of Madagascar, eliminate the progeny of past (or current) competition.

On a more global scale, occurrences of infanticide are most often committed by the mother at the time of birth. Mildred Dickeman found that infanticide was practiced among various cultures on a global scale. Hunter-gatherers, horticulturalists and stratified agrarian societies all used infanticide for purposes ranging from eliminating deformity, to population control, to maintenance of social structure.

When deformity prompts infanticide, an infant may be so disfigured as to have little chance of survival, while in other cases the deformity may be mild, but would cause ridicule and societal abuse within the mother's family, group or tribe. In many tribal societies deformity of any kind is not tolerated, thus the child is sent back to the other side. Those who live in harsh and wild places without the crutch of modern medicine, live lives equivalent to those of our ancestors in that only the fittest survive. What may sound cruel and merciless to many produces a healthy genome that allows a people to survive and multiply within the confines of a harsh environment.

Within ancient and/or primitive societies, infanticide occurred for many reasons, but regardless of why a newborn was let go there were belief systems to protect the emotions of the mother and her people. If we could go back far enough, we would all be sitting around campfires, telling our stories and stating our beliefs in order to teach the young, remind the forgetful and re-entrench the power and ways of the gods. In that far away time, death would not be a stranger and the ways of nature, combined with myths and firm beliefs, would teach us and keep us strong enough to survive.

Newborns have been placed on ice flows, in the shadows of forests or under a cover of freshly turned earth in the belief that babies are still connected to the underworld, the world of spirits. In many cultures a newborn is not a human being but one who stands between two worlds, an entity who can easily return to the other side. And returning a malformed or unwanted child to the other world will ensure it a chance of being born again at a better time, in more perfect form. While malformed or sickly infants have been let go with great regularity, other situations can prompt the same response: limited food supply, poverty, the burden of too many children, lack of safety or male protection, crisis situations or poor health of the mother, are only some of the answers to the question of whether an infant will be loved and cared for, or let go for the sake of the living.

In today's world, where mothers live in crowded cities of cement and tarmac, infants are often placed in a plastic bag and left in a trash can; the beliefs of the mothers are unknown.

Surprisingly, biologists and anthropologists who study infanticide have found that the practice does not work against a population, but for it. By spacing children properly a woman can produce more children of healthier quality over her reproductive lifetime. In societies that mandate abstention from sex during times of pregnancy and nursing, mothers will say a child was stillborn so as to keep her marriage intact. Biologically this is a sound decision, for without a husband the woman and her children would be hard-pressed to survive. By doing away with one child, she protects her marriage and ensures a home for the next.

Many tribal societies allowed their young boys and girls free rein to experience and express their sexual desires. Should a pregnancy occur, the young mother would smother and bury the newborn. This was done without remorse as it was known and accepted that the girl's mind and body were not ready for marriage and parenting. Within these same communities, once a girl was married, everything changed, as the laws of matrimony were stringent and strictly obeyed.

Some readers may recall the American teenager who attended a prom, gave birth in a restroom, killed the newborn, disposed of it and went back to the party. The laws and societal beliefs of the United States did not take kindly to her behavior.

Where infanticide is, or was, commonly accepted, children who are allowed to live are cherished and nourished. Welcomed infants receive every symbolic ritual, marking, ornamentation and blessing, all in the hopes of their survival. Every effort known to the mother and her people is extended towards the health and protection of every accepted infant. Still, death lurks, and in many cultures newborns are not given a name until they pass their first two days, month or reach their first birthday. Names are special, usually handed down generation to generation—identifiers not to be wasted. Mothers of nameless infants are well aware that many newborns perish within the first or second year so it is best to reserve Grandfather's revered name for a child that is likely to survive. Nameless infants are often given temporary names until the time of their naming day. The pygmies of the Ituri Rainforest in central Africa, who are being cannibalized by Congolese rebels as I write, do not name their infants until the first 48 hours have passed, while in other tribes in other parts of Africa, an infant is not considered a person until it can walk and talk; then, and only then, is it looked upon as being human.

In years just past, the Bushmen of the Kalahari did not look upon a child as a true entity until its second birthday or when it could keep up with the family's wanderings. Should a mother conceive during another child's infancy, the existing infant was destroyed, as the rigors of life in the desert were too harsh for a woman to care for and nurse a child while pregnant. This cultural practice worked towards the health of the mother, the spacing of offspring and against overpopulation in an environment where food at all times is precious.

So it is that infants born within the thousands of cultures that crowd this blue and tan planet, filigreed with a moving mosaic of white weather patterns, are received in different ways, their lives, treatment, acceptance and naming ruled by the beliefs of their natal society.

There is yet another form of infanticide that was practiced through-out history, though seldom mentioned. In countless wars fought over the course of thousands of years, infants and toddlers were dispatched with a vengeance, often to free up fecund women for the taking, but chiefly to kill off the genetic line of the enemy. From the Greeks and Romans to the Yanomamos of the Amazon basin, infants and toddlers came in second to men on unwritten lists of who to kill.

Cannibalistic infanticide has been practiced within many societies, but a pure form of cannibalism related to the birthing process, but not commonly viewed as cannibalism per se, is well documented.

In various cultures the placenta is washed and kneaded to extract excess blood, then cooked in various ways. It is a dish usually eaten by the mother, but in some instances it is served to the father. Culturally, it follows that if your mother eats the placenta from the birth of your baby brother, you will grow up *knowing* that the nutrients within a placenta will help your body regain its strength following the rigors of childbirth, and will thus view the practice in a positive way.

In places where the placenta is not consumed by a parent or rela-tive, it is often seen as the baby's companion or twin and considered to be a health-giving, appetizing food. Therefore it is preserved and saved, then fed to the child on auspicious occasions such as the child's first birthday, a custom noted from Africa to Alaska.

Going a step further, people from diverse areas of the world have practiced cannibalistic infanticide when firstborn, naturally aborted, de-formed, or stillborn infants were consumed by the mother, father, both parents or close relatives as with the Australian Aborigines. In all cases, continent to continent, societal thoughts ran along similar lines. In situa-tions where a mother took a fetus or newborn back into her body, it was firmly believed that the newborn was still a part of the mother's body, rath-er than a separate individual. The ubiquitous thinking was that through the intake of the issue the future fecundity of the mother would be assured and another, more perfect, healthier child would be born. The practice was encouraged by many societies in the conviction that the nutrients offered by the body would strengthen and refortify the mother, the same justifications cited by those who consume the placenta.

Among several tribes of Australian Aborigines, mothers customarily consumed all firstborns, but they were not alone. Along the river Uruguay, young mothers of the Chavantes tribe were encouraged to consume their firstborn infants in order to re-absorb their souls. It was believed that the health of very young mothers would be ruined by bestowing "soulstuff" to a child through the process of birthing and caring; however, older women were also of the habit.

The Australian Aborigines arrived on the shores of Australia some 60,000 years ago, while the ancestors of the Indians of Uruguay reached South America around 13,000 years ago. Since these peoples have different genetic roots, it can be assumed that the practice under discussion has truly ancient beginnings, or that widely separated peoples took pre-menarcheal girls as brides and came to similar conclusions that led to practices of cannibalistic infanticide.

How long ago did our human ancestors observe the obvious? That pubescent mothers are rarely physically or mentally up to the full-time task of mothering? In our hunter-gatherer days, deformed, sick or weak infants, as well as young mothers unable to care for their progeny, would have constituted a burden to the group, and left "husbands" (marriage was an unknown concept) with unavailable sex partners, food gatherers and burden bearers. So the ingestion of newborns by first-time mothers may have been seen as providing multiple benefits.

Today, more than 49 countries worldwide face significant child bride problems. Men who demand virginal brides, families unable to feed their many children, the strengthening of bonds between families or high-ranking tribal members, and laws against females inheriting land all contribute to prepubescent, uneducated girls being given in marriage to teenage boys or men decades older than the child bride. The "husbands" are theoretically supposed to wait until the bride has reached her mid-teens before consummating the marriage; a "rule" that is rarely followed.[2]

Tribes of people who populated the Fertile Crescent prior to the times of biblical writings are said to have sacrificed and consumed their firstborns. The sacrificing of firstborns can be found in the Bible, but the consuming of firstborns is not clearly stated. However, the Lord God of the Israelites did demand the firstborn of both man and beast. This being so, when God ordered Abraham in Genesis 22:2 to "take now thy son, thine only son Isaac, whom thou lovest, and get thee unto the land of Moriah, and offer him there for a burnt offering upon one of the mountains which I will tell thee of," there is no astonishment or questioning from Abraham as the practice of sacrificing firstborns had already been well established.

In kind, the writings and folklore of the Yuan of southern China speak to the killing and consuming of all firstborns. (See Chapter 17: "Politics and the Color Red.")

Infanticide and cannibalistic infanticide have been documented in the annals of Chinese history. Until recently, a majority of female infants were put to death on a regular basis as girls constituted unwanted breeders and were of no worth in comparison to a son. Of the female babies allowed to live, many were raised to the age of seven to twelve, at which time they were sold as servants, slaves, wives or prostitutes.

Today, infanticide is less common in China, but abortions are not. Though it is true that a fetus has not one neuron (brain cell) until 50 days and no functioning nerves until 70 days, the following may be unsettling. In an article in the Hong Kong *Easter Express* on April 12, 1995 (as well as other publications), a Chinese reporter presented well-documented data on the consumption of fetuses in a clear and decisive manner. Included in the article was an event where she was offered several tiny fetuses by the nurses she was interviewing. They said she looked ill and was therefore worthy of treatment.

According to her report, tiny (and some not so tiny) aborted fetuses were being consumed in Shenzhen, China, by doctors, nurses or anyone who could get their hands on them for reasons of improved health, the halting of the aging process and the rejuvenation of the skin. After hearing rumors in Hong Kong about the consuming of fetuses in Shenzhen, the reporter had traveled to China. Through her investigation, she found the rumors to be true, and that the "medicine" was being smuggled out in thermoses and sold for a goodly profit in Hong Kong, which is where she had received her original lead. Her report discusses two related items mentioned by various people she interviewed.

One was the mention of the ancient Chinese custom of eating naturally aborted fetuses or stillborns in centuries past. The practice was believed to renew the mother's strength so that she could conceive and bear healthy, normal children in the future. All stated that it was well known and understood that the flesh of a fetus or newborn was the same as the mother's flesh, not a separate entity. And since the fetus or newborn was not yet a person, but an actual part of the mother, it was hers to re-absorb in order to create a new and healthier baby.

The second interesting item was that some of those interviewed rejected the eating of fetuses but spoke well of dining on placentas. One man said his mother fixed human placenta for him all through his childhood, but that since reaching adulthood and getting a degree he had removed the dish from his diet. As I read these words, my mind raced back to a BBC television program on cannibalism that concluded with the televised story of a British woman who had her doctors save the afterbirth when her child was born. The afterbirth was frozen and when Mum and Babe were both fit and well, the marvelous and magnanimous mum invited a few of her favorite friends over, roasted the afterbirth and served equal portions to her guests, all of whom knew the menu prior to accepting the mum's invite!

Back in China, of those interviewed concerning the eating of aborted fetuses, many said they had experienced an improvement in their health. An aged man from Hong Kong swore by them, saying he had recovered from a malady that had afflicted him for years, while a doctor said he could not believe that anyone could do such a thing, as nothing on Earth smells as horrid as an aborted fetus. My physician husband agreed fully with the

Chinese doctor's statement, but several people in the article mentioned the odor problem, then went on to tell how they got rid of it and gave instructions. All recipes called for great quantities of garlic and fresh ginger— which alone could improve one's health.

In 2003, Chinese researchers working for Mary Roach, author of *Stiff: The Curious Lives of Human Cadavers*, checked out the contents of the 1995 article. Following the footsteps of the original reporter, they were told that the practice of selling and consuming aborted fetuses had stopped some years back when the government began collecting all aborted fetuses and placentas for the manufacture of "Tai Bao Capsules." Those interviewed said the entire process was now under the control of the Board of Health, adding that the capsules were excellent for the skin and asthma . . . for starters. The researchers said that many clinicians held that fetal tissue offered real health benefits, their words fitting in with those of cannibals who held that human flesh, particularly certain organs, improved their health, stamina and vigor. European doctors in centuries past obviously believed the same when they prescribed cured human flesh to their patients.

There are writings from around the globe related to infant cannibalism—too many for it not to have validity—but it is probably the most difficult form of cannibalism to document with certainty. Perhaps the best available evidence comes from the Chinese openness on discussing the subject and Beth A. Conklin's personal interviews and research concerning the Wari tribes of central South America.

As described in a previous chapter, "The Lost Culture of the Wari," the Wari practiced endocannibalism, the consuming of tribal members on the occasion of their natural or accidental death. Within the context of Wari beliefs it was important that all close relatives be present at a funerary feast, making it impossible to roast and consume an older person until his or her relatives had arrived from other villages. But in the case of infants and children, the immediate family was already present and the funeral could commence without delay. In *Consuming Grief*, Conklin writes, "Children's corpses were roasted sooner and tended to have been consumed in their entirety."

Ms. Conklin states that fetuses and stillbirths were normally not eaten, except for one instance when a well-developed fetus was consumed after being extracted from its dead mother's womb.

To paraphrase the renowned philosopher and consul of Rome, Marcus Tullius Cicero (January 3, 106 BC–December 7, 43 BC), born at Arpinum:

If you wish to change that which you perceive,

All you have to do is change the way you perceive it.

CHAPTER THIRTEEN

SKELETONS IN OUR CLOSETS

"'Silly goose,' said the old woman. 'The door is big enough; just look, I can get in myself!' Then Grethel gave her a push that drove her into it, and shut the iron door, and fastened the bolt. Oh! Then she began to howl quite horribly, but Grethel ran away, and the godless witch was miserably burnt to death."[1]

Suni sat cross-legged in the center of a caribou skin. All eyes were upon her though she sat silently and still. Naked to the waist, Suni's cheeks glowed with seal oil in the dim light of soapstone oil lamps. Her hair, freshly washed in urine, was neatly plaited in two long braids tinged with gray. Carefully, she smoothed her braids to make sure they were hanging straight and even. Suni was the oldest member of her clan, having known more than 60 summers, yet despite her advanced years she took great care in her grooming.

It was a special night; Suni wore her favorite headband made of bleached and de-furred seal skin decorated with animal figures stained into the skin using a small willow twig brush and alder bark dye. A grandchild played with a variety of small ivory figurines representative of humans, sleds and animals. An infant whimpered, its mother offered her breast and silence once again fell within the small, dark, ice-and-skin dwelling situated inland from the frozen coastline of Baffin Island. The time was 4,500 BP in the season of ice and darkness. Within the entrance tunnel a small wind chime made of shells and sinew tinkled and clacked as it noted the wind whistling through a tiny rent in the hide that covered the opening. A storm from the northeast was in the process of covering the low-lying Dorset abode. The men sat listening, gauging the strength of the storm by the pitch and speed of the wind.

Oomi, Suni's son, broke the silence, offering thanks to the Ice God for bringing him a walrus, then he thanked the soul of the walrus for agreeing to die so that his people might live. Next, he asked that when the walrus was reincarnated, he be allowed the privilege of returning in the form of a man. Oomi sensed that the walrus's soul had not yet departed and felt sure the walrus would appreciate his wanting to see him again.

Suni sat in contemplation, her aged breasts hanging as empty sacks down to her waist. Of her nine children only three had survived to adulthood, and two of the three were now dead, one while giving birth to her first child, the other to the elements when the pack ice he was hunting on broke away and drifted him and two others to a slow and frightening death. The camp had heard their screams and run to the edge of the ice to wail their farewells; it had been a time of great sorrow.

Now, only Oomi remained. He looked at his mother from his place amongst the elders. Suni slowly opened her eyes and gazed into the flickering flame of the oil lamp that sat before her. She began:

"In the time of our ancestors life was rich with walrus, ivory, whale and seal. These gifts swam to the people. Whales sang their songs before leaving one of their young for the empty stomachs of our people. It was a time when the shell beds were full of mollusks and the women gathered great quantities to feed the people when the great animals were scarce. Babies grew strong and man challenged the bear with his long shaft. The wolf and the fox gave of themselves and there were parkas for all."

Suni looked at her people to see if they were paying attention to the verbal history she was imparting. Young Kaima leaned forward in full concentration. He was a strong boy of eight and if allowed to grow would become a fine hunter and take command of his people. Suni continued:

"It is said that many sleeping places had been made and the people were fat with food. Fine sealskin kayaks cut through the waters of summer after winter-ending storms worked to break up and melt the frozen seas, thus unlocking the land and water from the grip of the Ice God. Seldom did hunger plague the people and soon they forgot to thank the souls of the animals who had given their bodies so the people could eat. Their forgetfulness angered the Ice God and a never-ending winter covered the land so that people were forced to eat their dogs and then of their own kind. Man must never take an animal without giving thanks and praying for its soul; the gods are forever listening." By AD 1000, the Dorset people were extinct.

Today, in the northwest regions of North America, amongst many tribes of Eskimos, the Epic of Qayaq constitutes an ancient oral history told in mythic form; it is the oldest collection of stories known to the peoples of the north. Every tribe, from the Inupiat to the Tlingit, believes the story came from their river, from their people; that *qayaqtuagaqniqtuq* (forever-riding-a-kayak)—Qayaq's original name—was their own. In years recently past, the story cycle of Qayaq was told in the deepest depths of winter by the finest of storytellers. The mythological/historical cycle took a full month to tell, the narrator pausing only to eat and sleep. Qayaq is a legendary hero who leaves his parents to right the wrongs of the world. Through his travels he performs amazing and dangerous feats, always coming through by the skin of his teeth.

As the saga goes, Qayaq was the twelfth son born to his parents. Each of his brothers had grown and left in a kayak, promising to return; none had kept his promise. The thought of Qayaq following in the wake of his brothers was more than his father could bear, so he decided to kill the boy rather than watch him leave. Twice he tries to kill his son, once when Qayaq is an infant, and once again when he is near grown. With the last try the father comes to the realization that his son is unique, having powers beyond those of the average man.

As Qayaq prepares to leave, his mother makes Eskimo ice cream (*akutuq*) for him to take on the journeys that lie ahead. First she chews on caribou fat while her husband renders fat from a recently killed whale. Then she mixes the two liquid ingredients together and stirs for many hours as the *akutuq* becomes foamy, grows in volume and becomes white as snow. Then she gives herself a nosebleed and allows the fresh blood to drip into the *akutuq* while she continues to stir. When finished making the *akutuq*, Qayaq's mother pours the mixture into a sealskin leather bag; later Qayaq will carry it in the cured stomach of an animal. With her work finished, Qayaq's mother counsels him on many things, then explains that her blood will be his youth and his strength and that it is the only thing she has the power to give. And indeed, whenever Qayaq reaches a point of hopelessness, or gets into dire, life-threatening straits, he takes a bit of *akutuq* and is completely renewed and saved from imminent death.

Infanticide and murder dominate one of the Qayaq stories when the young wife of a shaman dies in childbirth; with no one to breast-feed the infant, he is sacrificed. The shaman remarries, and again his youthful wife dies in childbirth, but the child is a girl and dares to live through his ill treatment. While the shaman has great affection for his daughter, he is filled with rage over the deaths of his wives and infant son. As the girl grows and is courted, the shaman kills every man she dares to love. Qayaq enters the story and sets things right.

In another story, Qayaq comes upon a large village of cannibals who exist primarily on the flesh of humans. Qayaq admonishes them for their ways and suggests they eat the flesh of animals instead of humans, then asks how they would feel if their parent or child were killed and eaten by others. Unfortunately, Qayaq is called away from the cannibal village to fight a huge seagoing mole up at Point Barrow and we are left in the dark as to whether his words corrected the ways of the man-eaters.

The Qayaq stories instruct, as Qayaq passes on proper rules to live by, along with detailed instructions for making various tools, sleds and kayaks needed for survival in the frozen north. As with all strong and lasting myths, the Epic of Qayaq entertains as it teaches.

Through archaeological evidence we know our ancestors sat around night fires, no doubt watching as flickering flames cast shadows against cave walls or slanted rock-faces.[2] What we cannot know is when our ancestors first used their unique ability for speech to pass on information and create a process we know as storytelling. There are wonderful arguments within the field of paleoanthropology about when language first emerged from the mouths of Homo ("man"), who, it is believed, had previously communicated through grunts, cries, whistles, calls, tongue-clickings and whatever else his laryngeal apparatus could produce. But physical anthropologists have shown that Homo erectus, who inhabited the earth for more than 1.5 million years, their earliest bones showing dates bordering on two million years ago, could have spoken in modest form, as could the Neanderthals, whose oldest bones give a date of 300,000+ years. The Neanderthals possessed a brain larger than ours, with the same defined areas we possess for speech, plus a perfect hyoid bone, just like the one that is attached to your larynx (Adam's apple) by ligaments—a small wishbone-shaped piece of calcium that allows for modern speech. Still many insist that true language began much, much later even though Homo erectus was tootling around Java by 1.81 million years ago.

I sit on the side of those who think language—as we know it—emerged bit by bit over a very long period of time. I have trouble with the thought that after having the physical ability needed for speech for more than a million years, humans suddenly developed complex language over a relatively short span of time. The argument has little to do with cannibalism, but it is fun to think about our early ancestors huddled together around their night fires for warmth and protection, listening to the only entertainment available—the human voice.

Regardless of timing, with the capacity to vocalize thoughts through words, coupled with bodies primed for pantomime, stories would have been a logical outcome; stories of hunting, danger, birth, death, animals, volcanoes and all other moments of mental imprint. And with stories came the storyteller, a natural born teacher, full of generational wisdom and animated voice. As stories emerged, they became the library of the people they served. In time stories were memorized and passed from one storyteller to another, from one generation to another, and another, and another. Through story a child learned about his people, their codes of behavior and what they believed. He learned about courage, danger, the ways of animals and the making of tools. She learned where things grow, what to eat, when to eat it, what not to eat, as well as the husbanding of fire. She learned how to be a woman, the ways of babies, the ways of men, the ways of death. He learned how to hunt, track, kill and butcher. He learned cunning, deception and cruelty. He learned the sky, the weather and everything that existed within his patch of the world. They learned the ways of the snake, the cat and all life forms that offered death, and most importantly, they learned how to find water and how to remember the place of the water once found.

The Chinese tale of the Leaf Girl goes back a mere 1,200 years, but is the oldest written version of the story we know as Cinderella.

Leaf Girl was born to one of two wives. Her mother died when she was small, and a few years later her father died. That left Leaf Girl to live in a cave with an evil stepmother and a horrid half-sister. The stepmother gave Leaf Girl nothing, not even rags for her back, so Leaf Girl fashioned a dress of leaves in order to cover her nakedness.

Leaf Girl was forced to fetch wood from a tiger-infested forest and water from deep and dangerous pools. While fetching water one day, a small red fish swam into her bucket. Each day the red fish came to Leaf Girl, and as the fish grew they became friends. Thereafter, whenever Leaf Girl appeared at the pool, the red fish poked its head above the water, swam into her bucket and sang to Leaf Girl, who returned the favor.

One day the wicked stepmother followed Leaf Girl, observed her communication with the fish and decided then and there she wanted the red fish for dinner. The following day she gave Leaf Girl a dress and insisted on having water from an icy stream on the other side of the mountain. Then she dressed herself in Leaf Girl's botanical garb and went to the deep pool where the red fish lived. The red fish swam close thinking the stepmother to be Leaf Girl, but as soon as he poked his head up out of the water he was scooped up in a net the stepmother had hidden behind her back.

The stepmother killed, roasted and ate the delicious red fish, then threw the bones out in the garden. The following day Leaf Girl went to the pool and called for the fish. When he failed to appear she started to cry. Suddenly a mist swirled around her and an old man with long white hair appeared before her. This messenger from heaven wore the furs of many animals and carried a long staff. He told her what had happened and where her stepmother had thrown the bones. "Gather the bones and bury them under your sleeping mat. Whenever you need something, pray to the fish's spirit, and your desires will be met." In this way Leaf Girl provided herself with food and warm clothing.

At the time of the fall harvest, there was a feast to be held in the cave of the village's leader. Naturally, the evil stepmother left Leaf Girl to protect the orchards, but Leaf Girl prayed for a cloak made of beautiful kingfisher feathers and a pair of golden shoes. You know the rest of the story, but this oldest written version offers us a view into the past. It is not the clock that sends Leaf Girl running for the door but a glance of partial recognition from her half-sister, and it is the village leader who picks up the shoe and *sells* it! The shoe is then traded from hand to hand until it is offered as a gift to a powerful king. The king sets out to find Leaf Girl, and as her foot slips into the golden shoe, stones from heaven pelt the evil stepmother and her daughter until they are dead. The magnanimous king *accepts* Leaf Girl as one of his wives, takes the fish bones for himself, then wishes and prays and receives riches every day for a year, at which time the magic stops. Leaf Girl buries the bones on a sandy beach where they are swept out to sea . . . the storyteller making them safe from anyone who might wish to find them.

This ancient Chinese version of Cinderella offers polygamy, the stoning to death of two females, a king with a hundred wives and the right of a man to assume ownership over everything belonging to any wife he chooses and takes as his possession. The good part is that the old white-haired man-spirit cut the king off after a year of greed.

Some say the Cinderella story originated in China since the old-est known literary version comes from there. However, folklorists will tell you that the story could have originated anywhere, at any time, as nothing travels better than a story.

For thousands of years, traders crossed continents with trains of camels, mules and oxen, while others journeyed forth in floatable craft to cross relatively short expanses of water or skirt the shores of landmasses. At every stop people would turn out to meet the travelers and sit around evening fires or in the warmth of huts or wayside inns where stories were told and traded. Stories worth retelling traveled far and wide and may have been the most lasting and meaningful product ever transported.

Storyteller Ben Haggarty, in writing on the Leaf Girl and the history of stories, notes that in most Cinderella stories the mother's spirit appears in various ways: a calf (India, Scotland, Russia, Iraq); a snake (Portugal); a dove (Denmark, Italy, Scotland); a singing tree growing on the mother's grave, or a berry bush (Russia); a rose tree (England); or the old man with his long white hair (China). These variations present a small window that looks back to the travels of yesterday.

In 1697, Charles Perrault wrote a French version of Leaf Girl/Cinderella from which Walt Disney created the movie. Disney made many changes to Perrault's version, just as Perrault probably made changes to the "original" in his possession. Importantly, each version of Cinderella offers the same frame (truth?), only the incidentals are made to conform with the beliefs and customs of all who claim the story as one of their own.

In his landmark work, *Totem and Taboo*, Freud wrote:

> Primitive man is known to us by the stages of development through which he has passed . . . through our knowledge of his art, his religion and his attitudes towards life . . . [and] through the medium of legends, myths and fairy tales.[3]

A statement that holds true for all peoples regardless of sophistication.

When Charles Perrault tailored age-old stories for children, he put them in a book entitled *Les Contes de Fées*, hence the term "fairy tales."

Roger Sale, author of *Fairy Tales and After*, reminds us that the concept of childhood was invented during the seventeenth century. Prior to that, European children were considered "infants" until they were weaned from the breast, which was usually around the age of seven. Once weaned, a child was a person who could work, help with chores and was never sent into another room because of grown-up activities. So the stories we think of as child's fare are, in reality, ancient or medieval folk tales, many of which contained cannibalism, torture, the burning of witches and other niceties.

As for the Brothers Grimm, they never intended to write stories for children. Their books got their start when Jacob Grimm began gathering old folk tales solely in an effort to save and preserve the oral traditions of his native Germany. Napoleon had conquered much of Germany, and the French were doing all they could to suppress German culture. Jacob and his brother Wilhelm detested the French—you might say Napoleon gave us the Brothers Grimm.

Their first published volume, *Children's and Household Tales*, came out in 1812, and none too soon. Their mother had died, Wilhelm could not work due to poor health, and Jacob was trying to keep five siblings alive on a librarian's salary. The situation had reduced the family to one meal a day. Some believe their extreme hardships caused the brothers to select stories where the characters suffer from hunger, but Jacob was too much of a scholar for such plainness of thought. It is far more likely that the stories reflect the times in which they were created, as it is believed that many originated during medieval times and before. And what filled such times? Wars, plagues, starvation, the abandonment of children, packs of hungry dogs, wolves in every forest, cruelty beyond words and death in every form, including burnings, heads on spikes, the flaying and quartering of live bodies, and cannibalism.

The brothers' first volume hit the shelves as children all over Europe were learning to read; for the first time children's literature was sweeping the land. While some of the Grimm stories were well received and reproduced in high quality form, others were put down for their cruelty and frightening messages. The brothers listened to their publishers and changed cruel mothers into horrible stepmothers, incestuous fathers into devils, and sex- and position-seeking suitors into handsome young males as pure as the driven snow. What we think of today as fairy tales were now for sale.

While the brothers deleted stark sexuality and brutality, they left the majority of each original story intact, and so the complaints continued. In 1885, one American educator complained that the "folk tales" were much too loyal to the medieval worldview with its culture of heavy prejudice, extreme crudeness and barbarities. Others objected to the brutal punishments inflicted upon villains, i.e., Snow White's evil stepmother being forced to dance in red-hot iron shoes until dead; the treacherous servant in "The Goose Maiden" being stripped down, forced into a barrel studded with nails and then dragged and rolled through the streets; or the wicked old witch in Hansel and Grethel, who had planned on eating both children, but gets pushed into the baking oven by Grethel instead.

And then there is Snow White. What little girl does not love the story of Snow White? In an older version, her evil stepmother tries to kill Snow White—who is only seven years of age when the story begins—not once, but four times. Her first effort was to hire a huntsman to take Snow White deep into the woods, kill her and bring back her heart. The huntsman finds himself incapable of the deed, allows Snow White to run off, then kills a wild boar and takes its heart back to the evil stepmother, who eats the entire thing believing it to be that of her beauteous rival, Snow White. When the magic mirror spills the beans, more attempts on Snow White's life are made, but the seven dwarfs always manage to save our heroine until she takes a bite of the poisoned apple. And that is when things get better— or worse, depending on how you look at these things.

While Snow White lies comatose in the glass coffin in the middle of the woods, a prince finds her inert form and proceeds to rape her. Satisfied, he continues his hunt and returns home to his castle, wife and children. Months later he goes hunting and again finds Snow White, who is now wide awake and pregnant. As time passes, the prince and Ms. White have two children, and then the story gets really juicy. The prince's wife realizes her husband is hunting a bit too often and coming home with little to show for the time spent. She follows him into the woods and discovers his other family. After much plotting the wife has Snow White's children kidnapped and orders her cook to kill and cook them for her husband's dinner. We can tell by this version of the tale that at the time of writing, cannibalism was frowned upon, as the cook has not the heart to kill the children and serves forth pork in place of human flesh. The wife, not knowing the compassionate ways of the chef, announces to her husband, "I hope you are enjoying the flesh of your flesh."

As in all fairy tales, the story ends with the prince, Snow White and their beautiful children living happily ever after while the prince's wife and Snow White's evil stepmother are done away with.

As to accuracy of fact found within fairy tales, it should be noted that in an old version of Snow White it is said that the wild boar's heart had to be salted. The writer, or teller, of the story knew his culinary arts,

The soaking of wild game in saltwater removes its gaminess and tenderizes the meat. In another version, the evil stepmother demands the child's liver and lungs, which are provided by a deer as opposed to a boar. The liver of wild game is delicious. As to lungs? Never fixed them, but I am sure there is a way to make them edible.

In the oldest of fairy tales there is a recurring mention of "three drops of blood." The "drops" of blood represent the onset of menses and are always shed by, or found by, a very young, very beautiful girl who always ends up pregnant within the next page or paragraph. In times past (and in 49 countries of today), men took extremely young girls as brides—Pocahontas was twelve years of age when she met up with Captain John Smith—which is why many tales begin with a couple who are very much in love but distraught over their inability to have a child. Then three drops of blood are seen or spilt, and a child comes into the picture. Unfortunately, many of the "new" women, even those who live within the framework of fairy tales, are too young for the birthing of babies and die in childbirth, which conveniently makes way for an evil stepmother.

Perhaps the tale most relevant to our subject matter is "The Juniper Tree," also known as "The Almond Tree." It begins with "three drops of blood" shed by a much beloved, extremely young wife. A version by Grimm begins: "It is a long time ago now, as much as two thousand years maybe. . . ."

"The Juniper Tree" is replete with every misdeed of its day. After shedding three drops of blood the young wife bears a son, then dies. Her son survives, her husband remarries and a daughter is born to the second wife. The second wife so hates the son of the first wife that she kills him, blames the murder on her own beloved daughter and serves the flesh of the son to her husband in a stew. The daughter buries the boy's bones beneath a juniper tree, which transforms them into a bird that flits around correcting injustices in memory of his dear, departed mother. For being such a dutiful son, the boy is resurrected when the juniper tree goes up in flames. Amen.

The Big Bad Wolf represents the werewolf of medieval times, and the witch in "Hansel and Grethel" speaks to times when children were actually consumed. As cultures grow, diminish or are absorbed, their stories are painted anew by overriding circumstances. The stories we tell our children today have been swept clean of devastation, killing, torture and cannibalism, leaving us with stories that paint rosy pictures and always end "happily ever after."

As a child I was read stories that were more violent than what I find on bookshelves today. I thought they were wonderful. The evildoers who had threatened, or tried to kill—AND eat!—children such as myself, had been disposed of in horrid, gruesome ways. I was safe. Those monsters were not going to be lurking under my bed! Actually, it was a huge alligator that took up residency beneath my counterpane. . . .

CANNIBALISM:

PAST
AND
PRESENT

CHAPTER FOURTEEN

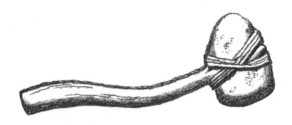

MAN THE WARRIOR

1933: The Japanese government begins indoctrinating its populace with thoughts of being surrounded by less-than-human foreign devils, specifically the Chinese, but also inhabitants of Siberia, India and the Pacific Islands, all of whom they plan to rule under their "New World Order." A Japanese military commentator writes: "It is well known that Japan's overpopulation grows more serious every year. Where should we find an outlet for these millions?"[1]

1937: Japan invades China, leaving their troops to provision themselves from available resources; genocide, torture and cannibalism follow. By 1945, an estimated 30 million Chinese had lost their lives.

n general, humans hold ardent desires for peace and times of prosperity. But peace is a fragile thing that is easily destroyed. Societal pressures, systems of belief, fanatical leaders, political zealots, overpopulation, natural disasters, drought, and greed breed destruction.

The Old Testament is a litany of wars that left un-tallied numbers dead. Similarly, Alexander the Great and Attila the Hun left wakes of human carnage as they crossed continents in their separate quests for land and power. In later centuries, the Crusades claimed an estimated one million lives, with the twentieth century witnessing more than 100 million war-related casualties.

Attila was of Mongol extraction. He was short, stocky, of swarthy complexion and sported a beard consisting of a few straggly hairs. He spent his seed from the eastern steppes of Eurasia to Turkey and around and down to Spain, his remnant genes showing up in scattered populations of today. But Attila is best known for leaving a wake of bodies and burned-out villages and cities spanning two continents. Aside from females gathered for himself and his men, Attila killed everything in his path. He demanded ransoms paid in gold, and some say he killed and ate two of his sons, but most references speak of a vengeful wife who killed two of his sons and served their flesh to Attila, telling him the meat was that of a young animal.

War, like cannibalism, has been observed in species ranging from insects to chimpanzees. Man did not invent war. But by the time humans were keeping detailed records of their confrontations, they had transformed war into a tactical art form.

The Assyrians have been noted as the first "military state," a nation that used mighty siege machines, some made of iron, to win their wars. So by 900 BC, methods of war had reached a high degree of technical sophistication. But the time and place of the first "war" between humans can never be known. Could the first intentional killing of a group by members of another group have occurred some two to three million years ago when rain failed to fall for months on end and an area's watering holes were reduced to one? Two groups of australopithecines, some of our really old ancestors, approach the last available water; there is very little, not enough for both groups. Did circumstances and dire necessity force the outcome?

Obviously, war demands warriors: individuals who strive to conquer their enemy through strength, cunning and tactics laced with survival instincts. In man, training, arms and group cooperation sway outcome.

But warriors come in all sizes.

I was sweeping out the kitchen in the old ranch house years ago and inadvertently swept a mouse into a corner that offered no way of escape. In an instant the mouse realized he was trapped and did what he could. He stood up on his hind legs, on his tippy-tippy toes, and spread his forelimbs out as far and wide as he could, then he stared up at me in a threatening way. He was a mouse of great courage. He had made himself look as large as he could in an effort to convince me that he was too large for my mouth. I looked down at him. He looked up at me, motionless in an impossible stance. I couldn't do it. The guy had guts. I swept him out the back door.

It all goes back to the four Fs: flee, fight, feed and fornicate. Fleeing was out of the question; there was no means of escape, so Mighty Mouse did what he could. Had I chosen to squash him I am sure the Mouse Times would have written him up as a hero. To this day I hold him in high esteem.

The Discovery Channel presented a program entitled *Warriors: From Civilian to Soldier*, in which veterans were interviewed concerning the first time they had killed another human being, an enemy in the heat of war. Most remembered the experience as being distinctively memorable, frightening and emotionally traumatic. Later in the program the same individuals were asked how they felt during subsequent kills. One gentleman summed up the bottom line. In essence he said that while the first time never leaves you, once experienced killing is easy.

Over the last 50 years, it has become increasingly popular to portray everyone's ancestors as being kind and peace loving. Following the dictates of political correctness, many have gone past its basic logic to the point of holding that warfare and violence were never a part of their heritage or the culture they study, or that people previously known for their warlike, sacrificial and/or cannibalistic past never participated in such activities. Such attitudes and thoughts have prevailed through books, writings, teaching, lectures, the media and popular accounts despite overwhelming evidence to the contrary.

An early example of a false portrayal of the past was put forth by Sir J. Eric S. Thompson (1898–1975). Thompson idolized the Maya and championed them through numerous scholarly writings as a peaceful, spiritual and high-minded people, a people he saw as the antithesis of the warring, cannibalistic Aztecs who followed them. But Thompson's take on the Maya began to crumble as precise decipherment of Mayan glyphs commenced in the 1950s. Ongoing discoveries of Mayan tombs and glyphs continue to substantiate the fact that the Maya were obsessed with power, blood and war. Mayan kings delighted in capturing rival rulers, publicly torturing and humiliating them for as long as a year, then decapitating them at the conclusion of a rigged ball game. And when Mayan rulers were not warring they indulged themselves with hallucinogenic or inebriating enemas using special syringes, punctured their penises with stingray spines and seemed to enjoy other acts of self-mutilation. And it was the Maya who perfected techniques for the extraction of beating hearts from live human beings, an operation that persisted to be employed throughout much of Central America until the arrival of Cortez who slaughtered people in different ways.

I remember reading Thompson's words, remember them filling my head with fantasies of a highly evolved, peaceful people well versed in astronomy, architecture, horticulture and myth. Still, I wondered what was going on with their magnificent art that illustrates acts of honoring rulers, warriors, the taking of hearts, decapitation, the piercing of penises, and so forth. If the Maya were peaceful, from where did their art emanate? Many answered the question for me by claiming the graphic pictorials were nothing more than demons of an imagined hell. Do tell?

Though war has shown itself to be an intermittent horror that has plagued mankind throughout and beyond the times of written history, it is well to remember that the more sophisticated a people, the more accomplished they are in war. The Maya of Central America produced high styles of art; magnificent architecture; precise calendars; a graphic, readable language; and were highly evolved in politics, religion, cosmology, agriculture and the list goes on and on. Two sides of the age-old coin—all over again.

Today, as I write, people are being tortured, killed, beheaded, blown-up and consumed for religious and political reasons as history continues to be rewritten. Political correctness has failed to save a single life.

Steven A. LeBlanc is the author of *Constant Battles: The Myth of the Peaceful, Noble Savage* and director of collections at Harvard University Peabody Museum of Archaeology and Ethnology. LeBlanc's book reflects decades of research and fieldwork that offer evidence of war reaching back to ancient archaeological sites. Through his writings he joins a select group of scientists who are trying to replace the rose-colored glasses of recent decades with historical specifics and archaeological evidence.

LeBlanc believes wars have been periodically waged throughout human history because of the scarcity of resources. Like reasoning leads to starvation as the impetus for primal acts of cannibalism.

History, in combination with research in the fields of paleoclimatology and archaeology, demonstrates that few wars were fought during times of good and stable weather conditions or when overpopulation was not crowding people out of long-held ranges. When good weather prevails, more food can be hunted, gathered or grown. And with better and more plentiful diets people produce more children, more of which survive the crucial first five years of life. As time passes, eras of plenty give way to periods of limited supply as overpopulation stresses all societal aspects and food-producing lands. Since the human lifespan is short—and was far shorter in times past—an individual would be hard-pressed to note an overpopulation problem, much less recognize that he or she was a part of the dilemma. When populations increase in number to the point where

the lands that feed them can no longer provide enough food, various actions are taken. A long-standing solution has been to invade and annihilate
those whose lands you need in order to feed yourself. To think that our
ancient ancestors were any different is folly. All organisms fight to survive.
The question is, when did man first wage war for the sole purpose of obtaining not only lands, but material goods held or owned by others. Today,
wars and genocide are being waged in Africa for possession of timber, gold
and, most precious of all, diamonds. Or, consider the killings in South
America and elsewhere, ordered by drug lords to maintain control of cash
crops worth millions.

Proof of war and invading enemies can be architecturally observed
through the millennia in man's constant effort to perfect the art of offense
and defense. Note the fortifications found at the oldest known settlements,
on through the ages to the hilltop castle-towns of Italy, some perched atop
such steep-sided pinnacles of land that from a distance they look like so
many morels pushing up between water-worn valley floors.

In the southwestern portion of the United States, there are Na-
tive-American cliff dwellings that were favored for the protection they offered, not for religious reasons or year-round air conditioning. Research
performed by Jonathan Hass of the Field Museum and Winifred Creamer
of Northern Illinois University has found demonstrable evidence for war
and defense amongst the ancient Amerindians of the American Southwest
during the thirteenth century. Concerning the Four Corners area of the
United States, LeBlanc lists three time periods that show various kinds of
fortifications, weaponry and art portraying both war and violence. In the
later periods, the threat of violence from others was such that huge walled
villages were built. Excavations of these large population centers produced
burnt-out buildings containing human remains, many of which exhibited
evidence of extreme brutality. At other sites bones, artifacts and human
feces have provided conclusive evidence of cannibalism. (See Chapter 16:
"Coming to the Americas.")

Recent books and scientific papers describe and document evidence of fortifications, violence and cannibalism in the Four Corners area of the United States, a region that has been championed over recent decades as a peaceful place. But while archaeology is proving times of extreme brutality, it also offers evidence of periods of peace—parcels of time when the best of humanity's many traits rise to the surface—until a society is threatened. It has yet to be proven if invaders destroyed the lives of a gentle people and/or whether drought drove the longtime inhabitants to last resorts. In dealing with the American Southwest, LeBlanc carefully skirts the issue of cannibalism, while furnishing all of the dots needed for the completion of a picture described by others.

Whether by mud-brick walls, or granite blocks, peoples of our past have worked to protect themselves. Large, magnificently designed defensive fortifications have been found around the globe. In South America, we find mountaintop battlements coupled with beautifully engineered and finely wrought walls of protection that have withstood both time and earthquakes. And every school child knows of the Great Wall of China, a thousand-mile barrier built some two thousand years ago to keep would-be invaders out—and indigenous populations in—and an architectural accomplishment so large that it can be seen from space. Moreover, evidence found in recent excavations in France is proving the words of ancient writers, as walls, ossuaries, bones and weapons are uncovered, further proof of times of violence.

Jean-Louis Brunaux,[2] speaking of warfare in northern Gaul (France) in the third and fourth centuries BC, notes a quote from Diodorus Siculus, *Bibliotheca historica* 5.29, part of which reads:

> When their enemies fall (the Gauls) cut off their heads
> and fasten them about the necks of their horses; turning
> over to their attendants the arms [weaponry] of their op-
> ponents, all covered with blood, they carry (the heads) off
> as booty, singing a paean over them and striking up a song
> of victory, and these first-fruits of battle they fasten by nails

upon their houses, just as men do, in certain kinds of hunting, with the heads of wild beasts they have mastered. The
heads of their most distinguished enemies they embalm in
cedar-oil and carefully preserve in a chest.

Caesar and others wrote that the Gauls proceeded with spontane-
ous rites at the end of battles, as opposed to the Greeks and Romans with
their well-planned cultic celebrations held some time following a battle.

Over the years historians and archaeologists have been hard-
pressed to prove the words of long ago. Now, at several sites in northern
France, the words of the ancient writers are being substantiated. Two sites
stand out, Gournay-sur-Aronde and Ribemont-sur-Ancre, where headless
skeletons and thousands of pieces of armor have been excavated. These
sites were permanent ritualistic centers that served two functions—martial
and cultic. The warrior tribes who built and used these sites are thought
to have been the Belgae, who are believed to have entered northern Gaul
from central Europe. Bodies of fallen enemies were triumphantly displayed
or sacrificed to the gods of the underworld, whom the Gauls believed to be
their ancestors. The cult's beliefs were similar to those held by the Greeks,
substantiated by a sunken altar found at one site that is reminiscent of
those found in Greece. Evidence shows that headless bodies were adorned
with armor and put on display, producing a horrific visual and olfactory
warning to any potential enemy. And at Ribemont-sur-Ancre the burned
bones of a thousand warriors have been uncovered in an open-topped os-
suary. Of interest is the fact that all of the long bones were crushed prior to
burning. Those working the site think priests crushed the bones in order
to expose the fatty marrow within to ensure a roaring blaze. But the same
priests believed the bone marrow of a human to be the most favored dish
upon which the gods of the underground feasted. And foods offered to
gods are commonly consumed by their believer-providers.

In the same vein, both the Greeks and the Gauls believed the soul of
a man resided within the marrow of his bone. Marrow is next in nutrition to

brain tissue and is known to have been sought after by humans and their ancestors from two million years ago into the present. Today, gourmets view
roasted marrow as one of the finest of delicacies. So, if a man's soul resides
within the marrow of his bones, and you commonly debase the bodies of
your enemies, *and* it takes a great deal of time and effort to de-flesh a body to
get at the bones in order to crack them, it would appear that if you devoured
the marrow of your enemy you would annihilate his soul while satisfying
your hunger. . . . Just massaging the neurons.

At Gournay-sur-Aronde, 2,000 iron weapons and pieces of armor
were found, including swords, scabbards, war girdles, shields, and lances,
which, due to placement of deposition, are believed to have been arrayed
on headless corpses or hung in groupings on poles. The weaponry constitutes enough to outfit 500 warriors. The excavators believe the weaponry
was collected through many decades and many wars, but fail to state the
why of their claim. Certainly, wars of old slew thousands at a time, but it
is quite possible that the victors choose only elite victims for their celebra-
tory rituals.

Another possibility presents itself. At the time, metal was a precious
commodity, and it is entirely possible that metal implements were gathered,
melted down and forged into new armaments by winning armies.

The two French sites offer verification of the words of Julius Caesar, who wrote concerning the Gallic War that the Belgae constituted the
bravest of the Gauls, and agreed with other writers that those of northern
Gaul spared no enemy, glorified their victories and completely abused the
bodies of their victims.

Brunaux makes no mention of cannibalism in connection with the
Gallic sites, but they offer sparkling proof of the northern Gaul's tendency
towards war and the inhumane treatment of their enemies.

Weather, war and unsupplied battalions can work together as
prompters of cannibalism, and we need not look to ancient times to find
examples.

In John J. Stephan's book, *The Russian Far East: A History*, he

comments on prisoners being sent to the *kolyma*, forced labor gold min-
ing camps in the far reaches of northeast Siberia: "In late 1933 the [ship]
Dzhurma lodged in ice after passing through the Bering Strait. Over a thousand prisoners froze; the guards survived by eating them."

During World War II, more than a million lives were lost in the
battle of Stalingrad. When the fighting ended, starvation set in upon the
living and the number of dead continued to increase. Food supplies took
weeks, then months to arrive. Corpses lay everywhere, and if one went up
certain back stairs of certain buildings on streets with whispered names,
meat—human meat—could be purchased. The local police and Soviet
army did all they could to stop the consumption of human flesh by publicly executing known cannibals, but times were beyond tragic, starvation
took new victims on a daily basis, and many things happened. By the time
enough food supplies were brought in to curb the rampant hunger, the
situation had reached the point where a person could be arrested simply for
looking well fed. It was one of history's sad moments. While many were
executed for practicing cannibalism, many more followed the will to live
and managed to survive by eating the only food available.

In 1937, Japan invaded China. In 1940, a young, educated Japanese
youth, Shozo Tominaga, was drafted into the army, made a lieutenant and
sent to join forces in China. The first time Tominaga looked into the eyes
of his 20-man platoon, he was frightened and appalled. He saw their eyes
as being evil, inhuman; like the eyes of tigers or leopards. (See Chapters
15 and 18: "Keep the River on Your Right" and "Africa: Then and Now.")
However, after being forced to learn the art of beheading a person with his
samurai sword, Tominaga became a true "spirit warrior." Though sickened
and frightened at first, once he had successfully decapitated his first Chinese he "felt something change inside me. I don't know how to put it, but
I gained strength somewhere in my gut."[3] The eyes of his men no longer
frightened him.

In the war known as the "Rape of China," cannibalism was sometimes practiced in prison camps as well as in the field. Masayo Enomoto,

a farm boy who had cried while dissecting a frog in science class, became a Japanese officer who served in China. When he and his men ran out of food, he went out on his own. Upon entering the abandoned remains of a village, he found one woman who had stayed behind. She spoke Japanese and viewed the Japanese as reasonable people. Enomoto raped her, killed her and butchered her remains to take back to his men. Decades after the event he commented that the experience had held little emotion other than sexual desire and the physical sense of extreme hunger, then went on to explain that there was little blood and that what you see in movies or on television has nothing to do with the real thing.

Enomoto procured large chunks of meat from the thighs, buttocks and other fleshy areas of his victim using a Chinese kitchen knife; it took him about 10 minutes and he never cut to the bone or disarticulated the body in any way. The camp cook did not ask where the meat came from, and once it was sliced, it looked like any other meat. The sliced meat was barbecued and served to Enomoto's hungry men. The meat was received enthusiastically and many commented on its fine taste.

During WWII, on various islands of the Pacific, the Japanese cannibalized several of our downed pilots, Australians, and U.S. Marines, in addition to their own. War and total commitment to following orders in combination with extreme hunger prompted horrific behaviors. The above information concerning the cannibalism in the Pacific was classified for more than 50 years so as not to perpetuate hatred towards the Japanese or cause excessive anguish within the families of victims. Since the declassification of the files, surviving U.S. pilots, including President George Bush I, have met with surviving Japanese, many of whom had eaten of human flesh. The results of these meetings were forgiveness, understanding and unlikely friendships felt and expressed by both sides.

Who said war is hell?

The war stories told above provide a glimpse of the kind of circumstances that can lead to cannibalism. Proof of the cannibalism that took place in China and the Pacific consists of documents, witnesses and confes-

sions made under oath in courts of law by those who killed victims and/
or ate of their flesh, plus statements from eyewitness prisoners who were
rescued prior to becoming victims. When WWII ended in the Pacific, the
U.S. military quickly and quietly executed five top-ranking Japanese military personnel known to have cannibalized U.S. servicemen. The deed was
performed on the island where the cannibalism had taken place.

In reviewing these cases, it is extremely doubtful that future archaeologists will ever find evidence adequate for the suspicion or detection
of the horrors that took place within the arena of WWII, a war fought
between "civilized" populations.

Situations, ideas and beliefs can cloak any behavior in a shimmer-
ing shell of righteousness. Those who brought about the disasters of 9/11
viewed airline passengers and building occupants as sacrifices to Allah and
firmly believed they would be rewarded in heaven for their offerings.

Cannibalism does not occur solely on snowbound passes or high
mountain peaks. It can rear its ugly head whenever people are schooled
to think of others as less than human, during wars, or when a lack of resources bring forth survival tactics inherent within the form.

CHAPTER FIFTEEN

KEEP THE RIVER ON YOUR RIGHT

> *Throughout history there have been individuals who have managed to uncover a wealth of information concerning other people by the simple act of following their own desires.*

From your local library you can take out a 1995 video entitled *Keep the River on Your Right*, directed by David and Laurie Shapiro. (Not recommended for those who find homosexuality objectionable.)

The direction and photography of this film did not prompt its numerous prizes; the man who is the focus of the film won the many awards it received. Tobias Schneebaum was a New York artist, an avowed homosexual, a sometime anthropologist and a self-absorbed philosopher. Tobias also ate of human flesh. The film is intriguing, but Schneebaum's 1969 book of the same name offers more information and detail.

Tobias's odyssey began in the early '50s in response to a photographic exhibit of Machu Picchu, Peru, on exhibit at the New York Museum of Modern Art. As soon as Tobias saw the photographs, he knew he had to walk among the ruins perched high upon an Andean mountain top. Within a year he had managed to round up enough money and was standing where the Incas had stood; everything about the place enthralled him. When he left Machu Picchu, he started walking and traveling through remote areas of Peru. In time, he met an anthropologist who told him of a Dominican missionary stationed in the middle of nowhere, which is exactly where Tobias wanted to go. Tobias had no idea as to why, but he wanted to go where no one like him had ever gone before, and to get there he had to find the edge of all things known to the outside world. Tobias asked directions for finding the mission. The anthropologist told him, "Keep the river on your right."

Tobias had been at the mission a week or so when a thin old man with long hair and bangs down to his eyelashes entered the compound. Six long red and yellow feathers seemed to sprout from around his mouth. Red and black seeds, animal teeth, monkey bones, snail shells, jaguar fur and such were threaded or tied onto various necklaces. His tattooed penis was tied up against his abdomen with a fiber string that wrapped round his waist. The old man was obviously weak and in pain; Manolo, a lay missionary, set about giving him a shot of penicillin. In the process he touched one of the feathers framing the old man's mouth. The old man took the feather out of its holder, which was a crosscut piece of limb bone from a small animal. The space where marrow had once existed provided a hole of perfect size for the shaft of the feather. Little of the implanted bone could be seen as skin had grown to encase it. When the feather was replaced, it fit snuggly into its ingenious socket.

The old man's name was Wassen, and he spoke a dialect known to some at the mission. He told of the massacre of his tribe, saying that his village was far away, that it was no longer his place, that he could not go back as the Akaramas had attacked his people. He said they had taken some of his women, leaving all others dead on the ground with holes in their bellies. He claimed that many of his "fathers" (men) had been decapitated and that "my children were broken. My brothers were gone, and they are now inside the bellies of the Akaramas."

In desolate despair, Wassen explained how he had spent the day in the jungle collecting herbs and medicines. Not until evening was approaching did he start for home. Smoke filled his lungs as he neared his village; he ran as fast as he could to find nothing more than remnants of his former world.

Tobias trembled as the old man told his story. From deep within he knew he had to meet the people who had raided Wassen's village. A few days later Tobias asked the young lay priest Manolo to help him. Together they went to the old man and asked if he knew the whereabouts of the village of warriors who had destroyed his village and killed his people, the tribe Wassen had called the Akaramas.

Wassen drew a map in the dirt as he spoke. He said the Akaramas lived three sleepings away, "maybe another sleeping." That their place was known as Hitapo, which was by the river and that they only left their village to hunt, raid and kill. Wassen told of his people living in fear, and how other people of the forest knew this fear, as it was never known during which full moon the Akaramas would attack.

Tobias accepted the fact that he might never return as he left the mission compound and walked into the jungles wearing nothing but trousers, a shirt and tennis shoes. He carried a small backpack containing drawing materials, a few medicines and a ball of cooked farina. Two and a half days later he encountered a group of handsome, naked men with coppery-brown skin. They were away from their village, and when Tobias first spotted them they appeared as part of the forest as each man in turn remained motionless—Tobias could not even tell if they were breathing. Their faces were painted a deep red and around their necks they, like Wassen, wore necklaces strung with various and wondrous things: fish scales, spines and fins; the tails, heads and wings of birds; the teeth, toenails and paws of monkeys; crocodile teeth; jaguar claws; the shed skin of a snake; and little furred legs and feet of creatures unknown to Tobias. The natives stared at Tobias, but no one moved or changed expression. Ever so slowly Tobias walked over to a young man, smiled and touched his shoulder. The native smiled, touched Tobias, then put his arms around him and hugged him. Suddenly, all the natives were jumping up and down as they hugged Tobias and one another. Then they were undressing him and laughing to the point of tears over the whiteness of his skin. Meanwhile, Tobias, the artist, was in awe of the thin-line, geometric designs painted upon the bodies of his newfound friends.

The natives took Tobias to their village where a half-cooked monkey was simmering in a pot that sat upon an open fire. The smell of burnt monkey hair turned Tobias's stomach, but he continued to smile. The men removed the monkey from its pot and dismembered it, handing various parts and pieces to members of the tribe. A man came and sat up close behind Tobias, placing a leg on either side of him. The man was masticating a piece of monkey meat, but he never seemed to swallow. To Tobias's amazement, the man opened his mouth and let the chewed meat fall into the palm of his hand and offered it to Tobias. Startled, but extremely hungry, Tobias took it, put it in his mouth, chewed and swallowed. The native laughed with delight, craned his neck to look at Tobias, then gave him the charred arm from which he had been eating. The arm of the monkey was covered with singed hairs, like little thorns, and as he bit into the flesh, warm blood and juices ran. Though tough and stringy and boiled without salt, Tobias was hungry enough to label it delicious.

Tobias stayed with the Akaramas. The men took him everywhere and taught him the ways of their life. Tobias imitated everything as best he could, but he wasn't much of a hunter. It took countless hunting trips before he was able to bring down a few birds with his bow and arrow. His lack of hunting skills did not bother Tobias; he was in his element, in love with the primitive, open society and the childlike playfulness and enthusiasm of the people. He came to understand some of their language. He slept, ate, hunted, bathed and lived in all respects as they did. From the moment of contact, Tobias followed their lead no matter where it led him. The men slept in spoon-like formation in cubicles that ringed the large thatched hut in which the tribe lived. Each cubicle held four to six men. The first man Tobias had walked up to and touched claimed him for his cubicle. Women and children slept around multiple fires in the middle of the structure.

Months passed. Early one morning the men made ready for a hunting trip. Every hunter's face was freshly painted in red, their bodies fine-lined with the juice of the huito fruit. Many of the men carried not only their bow and arrows, but also stone axes. Tobias carried his bow and arrows. The group numbered 23 in all.

Rain fell; they crossed swollen rivers. The waters caused their scarlet face paint to drip down their bodies in diluted form. In a small forest opening, the men formed a circle, hip to hip to hip, arms on one another's shoulders. In the center were all of their weapons. They swayed, whispering "Ooooo-ooooo" in a low growl. One man entered the circle, rubbed his penis hard then walked around the circle touching the tip of his penis to that of each man in turn, then he rejoined the circle. "Ooooo-ooooo" was growled again in a low whisper.

The rain stopped, the sun went down, they marched on in silence. Then the smell of smoke reached their nostrils and the noise of a village could be detected through the trees. Silently the men split into groups, then all were running, each group to a different hut. Tobias ran with his group into a fire-lit hut where arrows normally used for the killing of animals were used as spears, while stone axes split open the skulls of men.

In a matter of minutes seven men lay dead in front of Tobias, with bellies and chests pouring blood from gaping wounds. Brains oozed from crushed skulls as women huddled in corners, wrapping themselves around their children as they chanted a deep moaning lament. Then Tobias's friends were laughing and throwing their arms around him. Michii, his close friend, the one he first touched, the man who had been in the center of the circle, put an arrow in Tobias's hand and plunged it into the chest of a man already dead; it was an act that would haunt Tobias for the rest of his life.

Not one Akaramas was harmed. The entire raid was over in minutes. One body from each hut was chosen, brought out and butchered. Entrails and organs were washed in a nearby stream, wrapped in leaves and tied in bundles. Torsos and limbs were tied to poles. They chose some of the healthiest and fattest women and children who came along in silence, without protest.

The following evening found them back at their own river. Young Akaramas boys who had recently gone through their sexual initiation into manhood had built many fires, and over these they helped to roast the flesh of humans. No women were present. The men brought out elaborately feathered maces and danced around the fires, eventually forming a large ribbon of individual dancers that encompassed all of the fires. They chanted in low, hoarse voices as they bounced up and down going from one foot to the other. The song-chant went on and on until it became an intolerable roar that would disturb Tobias's nightmares throughout all the years that followed.

The words of the song spoke of roaring jaguars that were there with them, teaching the warriors their ways, looped around into a constant, macabre noise that worked its way into the soul. The dance went on through the night and the song continued even as men took turns to sit and lie around the fires eating and swaying back and forth—feasting jaguars all. Tobias and two friends stood by a fire. A friend handed him a piece of meat, he ate, then had some more. Minutes later they returned to the dance. Prior to dawn silence fell. Select pieces of meat were chosen and the men reformed back into their raiding groups. Tobias lay shoulder to shoulder upon the ground with his group. Michii had chosen a roasted heart. Holding it high in his hand he looked up at the moon and showed the heart to it, then he took a huge bite, bit down several times, then placed a portion into the mouth of each man. Tobias and his shoulder mates chewed and swallowed. After the eating of the heart, Michii had sex with one of the men, then they all ran through the forest into the mist of morning.

During his sojourn in Peru, Tobias found that homosexuality was common among many tribes, including the one that lived back at the mission. The head priest turned his back and prayed; there was a natural limit as to how much he could change. And while the priest read his Bible, the young lay priest, Manolo, confessed to Tobias his lustfulness and shame, then went on to complain that while he was always looking for something real and lasting, the natives attached no emotional value on sex; they enjoyed it, but it was something that was always there, a fleeting pleasure, nothing more.

A few days after the raid, after the fires of the cannibalistic feast were cold, after all traces of human butchery were gone, while the new women and children were adapting to the ways of the Akaramas, three of the tribe fell ill. Tobias took those sick, plus two others back down along the river to the mission. One of his dearest friends, a lad of 16 or 17, died of amoebic dysentery while Tobias cradled him in his arms; the other two were easily cured. After a few weeks at the mission, where the Akaramas had observed, played with and laughed over the magical material goods of the modern world, Tobias and the four remaining Akaramas returned to their village. Tobias could not help but notice that the death of their young friend seemed to have no emotional impact on them—as with sex, death was a common thing, an ever-present reality they accepted without emotion.

Once back at the Akaramas village, life continued as it had been before, but in Tobias's heart everything seemed wrong and different. One day he took a walk alone and simply slipped away. With him he carried all the food his backpack could manage. He skirted the mission area and followed his footsteps of the year before, this time keeping the river on his left. In time he reached the white man's village of Pasniquti from where he had begun his journey. Opening a door, a closure that had hinges, a doorknob and a lock, Tobias walked into a room where people he had met a year before stared at him in disbelief. He stood silently, a strange wild man, stark naked with painted designs fading from his skin.

Tobias returned to his native New York, where everyone wanted to know of his adventures. In the 2003 film, Tobias is asked how human flesh tasted. First he says he thinks it tasted somewhat like pork, then admits that he cannot remember what it tasted like: "It wasn't bad, just a piece of meat."

Tobias was out of step and New York struck him as being more foreign than the jungle had when he first entered it. He packed his bags and took off again. By the late '60s, Tobias found himself in New Guinea, where he lived for four years with an Asmat tribe whose members still hunted heads and practiced cannibalism, though both activities had been outlawed.

The Asmat are bisexual, the men living much of their lives in a separate "men's" structure. Tobias took a lover, was adopted into the man's tribe and given a mother and father. He learned their language and continued to sing many of their songs until his death. The only thing he did not do while in New Guinea was attend a cannibal feast. He knew of them, and his friends spoke openly to him about them, but he had made it plain that he had no desire to participate, and since the government had forbidden the practice, his wishes were honored.

As Tobias fell back into step with native life, he discovered the art of the Asmat: large wooden carvings of fantastic design epitomizing gods, demons, plants, animals, men, women, lovers and sexual organs—anything that was a part of their lives and belief systems. Tobias put together a catalog of Asmat art for the Asmat cultural center in New Guinea and made many friends, but in time he recognized the half-truth of his existence, and once again, as he had done with the Akarama, he left a life he was comfortable with—a life that included his lover and adoptive family.

In the film Tobias expresses his belief that the Asmats of pre-contact days, with all the killing, cannibalizing and warring bound up within the framework of their mythology, represented a true part of nature whose natural forces pushed and pulled them to many extremes.

After a 40-year absence, the film's producers take Tobias back to New Guinea where he inadvertently finds his old lover, whom he had thought to be dead—after all it had been 40 years. The two of them sit in a dugout canoe and speak of being partners. The old man tells Tobias of his current male lovers, who live up and down the river, and also of the women he visits.

Being among the Asmat again, Tobias comments on how outside influences have greatly diminished the Asmats' cultural, spiritual and emotional strength. A film from 1973 is shown; the difference is obvious. A man from Tobias's adoptive tribe looks at the camera and says, "We blame the foreigners for changing our old ways. I remember my family talking about our people eating people. That is in the past, I do not want to talk about it anymore." No one wants to talk about it anymore.

The film shows a clip of the Otsjanep tribe that claims to have found Michael Rockefeller's body at the edge of a river in 1961. They claim to have consumed his remains. "Sometimes they lie, we may never know," says Tobias.

A favored scene is 78-year-old Tobias in one of a dozen war canoes, each full of natives in full regalia. All stand and sing as they paddle. Tobias sings, too, and translates:

> The shit is in the river,
> The piss is in the river,
> The shrimp are in the river,
> The shrimp eat the shit,
> The shrimp eat the piss,
> We eat the shrimp.

The Asmat headhunters of New Guinea comprise many tribes and villages, one of which Tobias Schneebaum joined and lived with. For thousands of years, the Asmat practiced many and various forms of extreme violence, yet are best known through literature for their times of headhunting and cannibalism.

The beliefs of any given people differentiate or bind them to others.

Tribes of Asmat were bound by common beliefs, which also worked to pit them one against the other. For an Asmat male to obtain a soul, he had to take a human head. A married man who had never taken a head could not hold a position of power or authority within his village. Such a man was often abused by his wife with the words "*nas minu*"(piece of meat), since if a man be nothing but a piece of meat, he has neither soul nor courage. Headhunting proved a man's courage and cunning, and the procurement of a skull was integral to his initiation. Professor Kerry M. Zubrinich writes: "By virtue of a relationship to the victim, the initiate became a member of the victim's group."[1]

Conversely, the consuming of the victim's body incorporated the deceased into the victorious group. Head taking and the accompanying cannibalism figured into the mythical life of the Asmat by defining boundaries, expanding victorious villages and depleting, or totally destroying, a losing group. At all times, every village was potentially at war with every other village.

Even today the Asmat, as a nation or individual village, have no high priests or despots reigning over them. Such titles and positions were never achieved by any one individual because of the continual threat and proximity of other competing, raiding, headhunting groups within their area. Anyone, at any time, was a possible target.

Most killings were motivated by revenge, but people could be purposefully chosen or killed for nothing more than being on the wrong trail at the wrong time. An example of purposeful revenge took place in 1967, when a woman was killed while visiting her relatives. She had married outside her village, and someone from her husband's village had killed a man from hers. The victim's female relatives observed the killing with calm, but stopped the men from decapitating the body and preparing it for a ritual feast. Most of the village's men objected, but the elders overrode them and sided with the women. Because of the killing of a man from the woman's natal group by members of her husband's village, coupled with her choice of marrying outside of her family group, the woman became an obvious target.

The case is interesting, as all bodies of all victims regardless of age or sex were traditionally decapitated, butchered and consumed—including the brains. This particular incident illustrates changing attitudes within a cannibalistic culture, prompted by laws set forth by outsiders who forbade the practice of anthropophagy.

The Asmat differed from many cannibalistic tribes from other areas of the world in that they took revenge on both men and women. People of both sexes and all ages were killed during large-scale raids or herded back to the victor's village to be held until a head was needed, either for revenge or for an initiate. During the march, captives were often beaten or abused with great brutality, while some females were chosen as wives. If a woman was raped on the journey to the victor's camp, it constituted marriage. Since both men and women were killed in revenge, Asmat women became active participants in headhunting by organizing raids and verbally and emotionally encouraging their men to take heads. Heads equaled wealth and status—nothing more need be said.

Traditionally, the Asmat connected cannibalism with headhunting, but the procurement of human flesh was never the primary reason for the taking of a life, unlike the headhunters of French Guinea where the consuming of human flesh was not ancillary, but central to the taking of heads. It is a point well taken, as cannibalism on a global scale varies from one people to the next, each society holding fast to its own unique beliefs and customs.

Aside from taking revenge, headhunting constituted the acting out of a constant battle for equilibrium between the living and the dead. The Asmat believed their connection with their ancestors to be uncertain, and much of their time was spent trying to drive ancestral spirits from areas where they wished to live or through which they wanted to travel. A great Asmat warrior would declare his ability to take heads and defeat all enemies before taking up a task or during rituals in order to keep the spirits of the dead at bay. These boastful speeches were meant to appease the spirits while driving them from the warrior's presence.

With spirits ruling the day, ambush and the development of deceit and cunning were part of Asmat training. Males were schooled to lie, to be devious in nature and to take an enemy by surprise in order to become warriors and overcome the "spirit world." Another form of schooling was musical. Songs were a part of everything the Asmat did. Songs told stories and provided instruction while instilling courage.

The Asmat consumed sago beetle grubs, which look like large maggots, but taste somewhat like bacon. While the beetles provided need-ed protein, the soft tissue of the sago palm tree itself offered necessary fiber when eaten in combination with human flesh. In connection with cannibalism, the Asmat have a myth relating sago to rebirth, regeneration and the teaching of songs of decapitation. The myth tells of Mom, Pop and their young son going to the river to pound sago. The boy's head is decorated; it is a special day. Once at the river they parents kill the son with their sago pounders. The boy's decorated head flies into a tree, where its blood drips onto the trunk of a cut sago palm where the parents are pounding the boy's body, sago and blood together. The merging of ingredi-ents changes the composition of the sago. At that moment, the son's head begins to talk, and he teaches his father the songs that must be sung at all decapitation festivals, songs to be sung on the way home from a raid, songs for arriving victoriously back home and many others—including songs for when the brains are shaken out of the skull.[2]

The skull of a victim is identified with the fallen sago fruit, which in turn represents reproduction and sustenance. All hunter-agrarians have, or had, myths concerning reproduction and sustenance, things essential for the continuance of life. The vast majority of these myths contain a sacrifice believed to be the agent for rebirth and revelation, as in the child's head speaking to his father and training him in the ways of ritual and song.

When a head was taken for a young Asmat's initiation, it was smoked for a few days and then placed between the legs of the initiate and pushed up hard against his genitals to ensure fertility from his loins. The initiate then had to sit on the floor of the men's hut with the newly smoked head snuggled up against his maleness for several days without crying or whining. When people live in hostile and difficult places with nothing but stone, bone, shell and bamboo tools, they will perish if not schooled in the ways of the wild and how to be strong and courageous. And, should a person live in a society where everyone around them views their head as a possible trophy, they had better learn their lessons well.

Writer and professor Kerry M. Zubinich studied every historical and anthropological writing available concerning the Asmat, beginning with texts dating back into the sixteenth century. She found something others have found in other places around the world: the Asmat practiced cannibalism on and off through the centuries. Periods of persistent cannibalism would fade out of fashion only to be taken up again decades or centuries later. There are stories and myths from cannibalistic societies that offer allegorical wisdom concerning cannibalism, warning against over-consumption lest you run out of food, family, friends or enemies. Did practices of habitual cannibalism stop periodically because of decreases in population, or did a period of more favorable climate provide more to eat? Did beliefs change in connection with new leaders, or did disease decimate populations, making cannibalism unwise lest tribes dine themselves into extinction? Did a prion disease diminish numbers as with the Fore, who came close to extinction from kuru, or did natural catastrophes such as killer typhoons cut populations, thus forcing changes in behavior?

Starvation is the obvious impetus for a return to cannibalism, which in turn could be sustained by the revival of myths or the sense of power so many claim to experience from the practice. Raids and war, coupled with the vicious emotional fever that often infects marauding warriors, might also have encouraged the return to the consuming of one's enemies.

Now back to Tobias, who had enjoyed returning to New Guinea, but had no desire to return to Peru. In the film he states outright that he is afraid, citing his age, health problems, his nightmares, the hardship of the trip, and that it has been 45 years since he walked out of the jungle, but the film's producers encourage him, and once back at Machu Picchu he is once again thrilled and enchanted.

The process of finding his tribe was another story.[3] There was a new bridge over the river in a new place, the old one now gone and replaced, and the tribe had moved. The way was difficult and things appeared as familiar and unfamiliar at the same time. Tobias became confused and complained that he wanted to go home. The movie crew urged him onwards, and after a stormy boat trip across a wide river and a steep climb, Tobias's tribe is found. To his delight and amazement many people remember him.

Old photographs from the mission are passed around, and one person after another says, "That's me." "That's my brother." Tobias reminds them that they used to call him "*Habe*," a word he always thought meant "Ignorant one."

"No," says a native, "it means, 'Come here.'"

Another man, who looks into the camera with anger, says, "Our name is not Amarekaire, that is a name given us by outsiders, it means traitor, criminal and bad things like that. We are the Harakambut. Yes, we ate our enemies, but we don't want to talk about that anymore."

Sounds familiar.

The re-found Harakambut go on to tell how shortly after Tobias's departure they were given machetes and clothes from the mission, but that prior to that they wore no clothes and used stone tools. Tobias speaks again of the freedom and compassion he had found within truly primitive tribes, adding that while they may have killed and eaten those they viewed as enemies, within their small enclaves there was profound bonding and gentleness.

An old man remembers the song that had been the stimulus for Tobias's nightmares; he sings the song for Tobias and the camera.

> Roaring Jaguar, roaring Jaguar
> You who wander over the banks of the river Eyori
> Roaring Jaguar, roaring Jaguar
> Here you are saying, this is how you growl,
> this is how you growl

Roaring Jaguar, roaring Jaguar
Here I am, here I am
Roaring Jaguar, roaring Jaguar
Give me your strength
Roaring Jaguar, roaring Jaguar

In the mid-'50s, Tobias had been a participant in a chant-song that had imbued his friends with the spirit and strength of the jaguar much as the Leopard Society of Sierra Leone, whose members danced and chanted around fires or wandered through the jungles repeatedly imitating the roar of the leopard. For Tobias, the raid and following cannibalism, complete with hours of song-chant and dancing had been so emotionally charged that it produced a lifetime of disturbed sleep. With tired eyes and a bit of pathos, Tobias speaks to his episode of cannibalism. He says that the flesh he ate may have been a part of the heart, but he is not completely sure. Then he complains that the cannibalism, of which he was a part of, was nothing compared to the rest of his odyssey in the jungles of Peru, but that his one act of cannibalism seems to be the only thing people remember.

Remember Conklin's saying that most people hold to emotions of fascination and revulsion whenever cannibalism is mentioned? Tobias would have agreed with her.

Remember the old man, Wassen, who entered the mission compound and told of the killing and cannibalizing of his tribe? The man whose words propelled Tobias into the deepest parts of the Peruvian jungles?

"He'll get sick and die here," Manolo said. "He's the oldest Indian I've ever seen and he may be as old as the padre. You can see that he already misses his village and his people. He'll probably sit here by himself all the time. He'll have no one to talk to or laugh with, and he can't go out hunting any longer. Besides, the people here will always be frightened of him. So he'll tell himself it is time to die, and he will."[4]

And so he did.

CHAPTER SIXTEEN

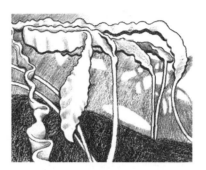

COMING TO THE AMERICAS

"In 1725 four savages were brought from the Mississippi to Fontainebleau. I had the honor of conversing with them. Among them was a young woman whom I asked if she had eaten men. 'Of course,' she answered with great simplicity. I appeared to be a little scandalized, whereupon she continued, 'Is it not better to eat one's dead enemy than to leave him to be devoured by wild beasts? And surely victors deserve the spoils.'

We kill our neighbors in fights or skirmishes, and for the most trifling reasons, then leave them to the crows and worms. In killing is the horror and the crime; what does it matter when a man is dead whether he be eaten by a soldier or by a vulture?"   —Voltaire, A Philosophical Dictionary (1843)

In times long past, the Eskimos of the frozen north, when faced with imminent starvation, killed and consumed their dogs. Only after all of their precious canines had been devoured did they kill and consume their old women. The Eskimos felt great shame over such occurrences and went to great lengths to keep such events secret from others. Older women were chosen for sacrifice to ensure the survival of breeding age adults. If a breeding population is not maintained, a group, or species, will cease to exist. During times of starvation, most animals set upon the young, the reason being that they are incapable of defending or feeding themselves and are too young to conceive and bear young. Humans have tended to follow the same pattern, but Eskimo children were rarely taken, as conceiving is difficult in climates of extreme cold. In the frigid, high altitude deserts of northern Mongolia, successful pregnancies are so few and far between that large celebrations are held whenever a healthy baby is born. In such settings fertile women and growing children are promises of the continuation of life, so the most salient course of action for people living in extreme cold is to sacrifice the elderly. Why old women instead of old men? That is another book, but regardless of who is chosen, dire times demand that people make the decision to live or die.

In the 1800s, at the other end of the western hemisphere, the Fuegians of Tierra del Fuego also set upon their oldest females, whom they killed and roasted, when all buried whale blubber had been consumed and starvation was a reality.

In his book, *The Voyage of the Beagle*, Charles Darwin tells of Captain Fitz Roy having taken several Fuegians back to England on his former voyage (1826–1830): two men, an adolescent boy and a girl. One of the men died of smallpox while in England, but York Minster, Jemmy Button and Fuegia Basket were returned on the second voyage that began on December 27, 1831. Aboard that second voyage, Mr. Low, a sealing master who had dealt extensively with the Fuegians, told Darwin that when starvation hit, they ate old women instead of their dogs. When Mr. Low asked a Fuegian man why old women, the man replied, "Doggies catch otter, old woman no." Jemmy Button confirmed the statement and explained how the old women were always strangled over a smoking fire, but gave no reason as to why.

After watching the tall Fuegians dive into frigid waters to gather shellfish and go around half-naked in freezing temperatures, Darwin made note in his journal that they had to have some sort of antifreeze coursing through their veins, as despite freezing temperatures and howling winds, the Fuegians showed no signs of hypothermia or disease.

For more than a century, scientists felt Darwin had missed the boat on the antifreeze and dismissed his words until a few decades ago when modern scientists, with the aid of better technology, took blood samples from remaining Fuegians and found that their blood contains a glycoprotein, a protein molecule that protects against freezing. Further studies showed metabolic adaptation, higher skin temperatures and above-normal rectal temperatures among peoples of Tierra del Fuego and peoples of the northern Arctic areas. Such findings prove Darwin's prescient thought and nature's adaptability; her incomparable capacity to evolve protective devices so that life might continue.

Survival cannibalism is comprehensible, but gaining strength, protection, wisdom, sexual prowess or courage from an enemy by the eating of his heart, liver, brain, or the entirety of his body, opens other doors. The belief that human flesh offers the diner positive benefits are rife within so many cannibalistic societies that it begs the question as to when such ideas entered into the human mind. Could they have been conceived millennia prior to the agrarian age, which began some 12,000 to 15,000 years ago? Were such beliefs already a part of our luggage when our forebears first began trekking around the globe close to two million years ago? While the myths of practicing cannibals are unique to each and every group, all show similarities concerning what is gained by the consuming of human flesh. Modern technology allows us to analyze foodstuffs individually to reveal their specific nutrients, vitamins and minerals. For example, the heart of any animal offers iron and protein as well as vitamins and minerals, whereas the liver has even more to offer. As for the brain, it contains the maximum number of calories per gram; pure oils and fat are its partners. Did cannibals claim that eating the heart, liver or brain of their enemies gave them strength, courage, and virility as a mere boast, or had it been noticed over time that a good dose of vitamin A from a liver, plus iron and vitamins B, D, E and K, were revitalizing and surmise a connection? Had they failed to notice that the same thing occurred after eating the organs of other mammals? Or did the adrenaline rush that coursed through their veins during the killing of one of their own kind sway the mind more than the body?

Today, on city streets of Peru, Uruguay, Argentina and other South American countries, you will find vendors selling skewers of cubed, dark red meat hot off their portable barbecues. The meat? Beef heart, chewy and delicious. But in December 1999, it was human hearts and livers that were being grilled on city streets when machete-wielding Dyaks (Christian and pagan by religion) of the Kalimantan province of Borneo, slew hundreds of Madurese Muslims in retaliation for the taking of jobs, lands, fisheries and hunting grounds, and, most important, the mass killing of Christian Dyaks. Previously, the Dyaks had lost lands and hunting grounds to government-run loggers and corporate farms, but they had lost more to the Madurese, complete strangers who had been relocated onto Dyak lands by the Indonesian government. Without an army or political clout, the Dyaks returned to the ways of their fathers, whose practice of headhunting and cannibalism had been steeped in religious tradition and ritual. In time the Indonesian government relocated many of the "strangers."

Contemporary thought holds that man entered the western hemisphere by walking through an un-glaciated land corridor that ran from northeastern Siberia, over and down through Alaska and Canada, crossing over the Bering Strait by way of a land bridge that existed during times of lower sea levels. But when did humans first enter the Americas? In 1930, at a New Mexico site known as Blackwater Draw, near the town of Clovis, bones of extinct mammoths were found. In the rib of one of the beasts was a Clovis point, a unique stone point fashioned by a previously unknown people. The point and the people who fashioned it were given the name Clovis. Clovis-lovers continue to hold firmly to radiocarbon dates that hover between 11,200 and 10,800 years ago and believe the Clovis people to have been the first to enter the Americas.

But there is other evidence and newer finds. Over the last decades, arrival arguments have become boisterous, as new Paleo-Indian sites have been discovered. One found in Virginia dates to 18,000 or so, the excavators say, while others in Pennsylvania, Brazil and Chile show dates from 13,000 years and beyond into a past yet to be proven. Such sites offer a wealth of artifacts that suggest that others made their way into the Americas earlier than the Clovis people.

I suggest the reading of Thomas D. Dillehay's book *The Settlement of the Americas* and *The Early Settlement of North America* by Gary Haynes for contrary sides of the argument.

A recent study of the Y chromosome found an inherent gene specific to all native peoples of the Americas, causing the gene's finder to suggest that only one small band of people made it into the western hemisphere and were therefore ancestral to all tribes from Alaska to Tierra del Fuego. But other Y chromosome and DNA studies have strongly suggested two or three waves of migration. Add to that decades of study on dental morphology, blood chemistry, linguistics, archaeology and ethnography of the peoples of the western hemisphere, which, when put together, strongly suggest two or three different migrations arriving at various times.

Dentition, a subject that could bring on the ZZZZs, turns out to be paramount in the verification of different hominids and humans, past and present. Teeth evolve slowly and by looking at your teeth a scholar can tell a lot about your ancestry. The australopithecine "Lucy" and her ilk are known by their teeth, as are Asians, Africans, Caucasians and three groupings of Americans, from Alaska to Tierra del Fuego: the oldest, Amerind (from Canada to Tierra del Fuego), to Eskimo-Aleut (most of Alaska, the Northern Territory and most of Greenland), to the last arrival, Na-Dene (farthest reaches of Northern Territory, the eastern islands of same, and the western edge of Greenland). Adding to these dental studies, researched by Professor Christy G. Turner II, are genetic evidence and valuable findings from linguists. Though many tribes of Native Americans are no longer extant, linguists claim that a minimum of 1,000 languages were spoken by the Amerinds at the time of the "white man's" arrival. In 1891, explorer, geologist and anthropologist John Wesley Powell sorted the languages of North American Indians into 58 families. He never got to South America. Most interesting is that Amerind languages do not mesh with any old world languages. In combination, such data are highly suggestive of early migrations from the "old world."

Aside from who and when, is the question of how. There is now good reason to believe that people may have arrived by rafting or boating along the Pacific Rim. For me, this is an obvious possibility. I grew up along the Pacific coast and for decades surfed, sat before, or drove along that greatest of oceans when its waters could have easily been managed by anything that floats. Of archaeological importance is that sea levels were 300 to 400 feet lower during the last ice age. Unfortunately, thousands of miles of ancient coastlines that could offer evidence of prehistoric migrations have been covered by higher seas for the last 10,000 years, making archaeological exploration difficult at best.

Out from the coast of the Queen Charlotte Islands, off the shoreline of British Columbia, lies an underwater archaeological site that affirms the possibility of a water route. Canadian researchers Daryl W. Fedje and Heiner Josenhans used new sonar technology to prove the existence of iceage pine forests, river valleys and ancient lakes that now lie beneath 160 feet of seawater. Also found are what appear to be shell middens, plus one flaked tool brought up from the muck; all highly suggestive of human habitation during times of peak glaciation. Yes, people could have been walking along the coast when they stopped for clams, seals and land life, but *only* if they had climbed out of the inland corridor, over mountains and across frozen lands.

A coastal route works easily when we remember that the Australian Aborigines crossed either the Timor Sea or the Torres Strait some 60,000 years ago in order to reach Australia.

By going along the coasts of continents during calm weather, and going ashore during foul—or when fresh supplies were needed—a water route would have been far faster and easier. Try to imagine walking women and children thousands of miles—many of them impassable—all the way south to Chile where the site of Monte Verde has produced butchered mammoth bones, remnants of dwellings, fire pits and artifacts that date to a minimum of 12,500 years.

As this manuscript was being readied for publication, new evidence supporting a water route was published. Through years of research, an interdisciplinary group of scientists uncovered various bits of information that relate to the coastal migration theory. Coming from numerous fields of science, the group collected data that suggest man reached the Americas 35,000 to 15,000 years ago by a coastal route. Their findings speak of kelp beds, nicknamed the "kelp highway," that ran from Japan and the Ryukyu Islands, curved north, then east, along the southern coasts of the Aleutian Islands, down the western coast of North America to Baja California, then picked up again along the coast of South America. Kelp beds harbor an abundance of sea life and kelp forests hold down wave action, creating a glassine strip of water that produces calmer waters from kelp to shoreline. Any boat without a keel could swiftly navigate the kelp highway in relative safety.

Three points sway the argument for a water route: (1) The Chilean site of Monte Verde has been verified at a minimum date of 12,500 years in age; (2) the ice-free land corridor championed by the land-routers did not open until 12,500 years ago; (3) the discovery of remnant kelp forests growing off the shores of the Pacific Rim at ice-age sea levels. Add to that new finds of ever-older coastal settlements such as an island on the southern rim of the Aleutians that was never ice-bound or glaciated during the course of the last ice age. On that island researchers have found the bones of a bear that lived 30,000 years ago. It is not known if humans killed the bear, but it is known that the bear was butchered and eaten by humans.

With extremely suggestive evidence for a water route, there is a possibility that peoples from north of Lake Baikal, located in southern Siberia near the Mongolian border, from whence the blood profiles and genetics of many Amerindians stem, traveled eastward along the edges of existing glaciers to the Asian coast, jumped on the "Kelp Highway" and tootled north, around and down into our current neighborhood. (Yes, I am trying to make trouble.)

Science is not a static idea, but a constant search for the truth. To stand still in the quest for knowledge is unconscionable. If we were to return to the year 1960, there would be no bypass surgery, no transplants, no hip or knee replacements, millions would die of breast and testicular cancer, DNA would be an unknown, the existence of other planets within our universe would still be in question, and you would not have a computer, cell phone or a Palm Pilot, etc.

As to the earliest inhabitants of the Americas, there are things to consider. The people who first entered the human-free continents found a virtual meat market of animals, in concert with edible plants, many of which had never been encountered before. Conversely, the animals had never seen bipedal, tool-bearing, bright-minded organisms that were skilled killers. The western hemisphere was a hunter's paradise.

Today, only the Galapagos Islands and a small area of the Congo have animals that fail to recognize man as a threat.

As time passed the weather changed, and the ice sheets retreated. While some believe a change in the weather brought forth faunal extinctions, others hold that a highly communicable disease brought in by humans killed them. But a majority holds to the most plausible—*man* brought about the extinctions through indiscriminate killing. Today, human behavior is causing the extinction of 1,000 species per day. Most are forest- or jungle-dwelling microorganisms, insects and plants, many of which might have saved you from a disease, or increased your longevity.

Above the raucous arguments over the extinction of North Ameri-

can fauna, there is general agreement concerning the demise of one animal: the horse. Paleontology tells us that the evolutionary birthplace of the
horse was North America. Archaeology tells us that the first Americans
ate *Equus caballus* to extinction. Earlier species of horses had migrated from
North America into Asia, Europe and the Near East during prehistoric
times, so the first Americans may have been familiar with the horse and
how to harvest him for food. And that is an important point. Prior to the
Spaniards' landing on the gulf shores of Mexico, no horse had been seen
in the western hemisphere for 10,000 years. When you think of Native
Americans astride their trusty steeds, remember that it was a mere 500
years ago that the horse was returned to his native land, but upon his return the human inhabitants of North America embraced him as a soulmate
and rarely served him for dinner.

Prior to the return of the horse, America was a place where women
carried all possessions when moving from camp to camp. For northern
tribes the winters were long and cold, and their belongings were heavy and
bulky. With human ingenuity came the invention of the travois, a hauling
mechanism fashioned of two long, trailing poles, crossed and attached in
front with a makeshift collar. The poles were connected behind the pul-
ler with a large hide or fiber-netting on which possessions were placed.
Women, children and dogs pulled travois of variable size. The word "travois" comes from the French "travail," the shaft of a cart, but obviously the
inventors had other names for the device.

The travois was probably the invention of a woman, as the men
were always out front on constant guard against predatory beasts and hostile humans, and not being the carriers, they would not have felt the need
for invention. Prior to the return of the horse, the only animals husbanded
in the western hemisphere were dogs that may have arrived with their human partners. Aside from pulling travois, sleds, carrying packs, and aiding
in the hunt, dogs were often eaten and consumed for medicinal purposes.
Many Native Americans considered dog meat to be the most medicinal of
all animal protein.

A wonderful old painted buffalo hide shows a scene of moving camp with every woman, child and dog sporting a travois; the men are on horseback.

As to the canoe, I would credit a man. Was the canoe a new design or a takeoff of earlier known means of traveling by water? With canoes, rivers could be used as highways. But those who lived in areas without watery roads, or those with winter sites away from big bodies of water, used the travois, which, in time, was hitched to a horse.

The first Americans were hunter-gatherers; they needed water, prey animals and natural forage in order to live. The Americas provided all in abundance, and as the millennia rolled by, populations grew and groups of people were forced to break away to search for adequate food resources. Very possibly, more groups arrived; we may never know, but eventually, all sustainable niches of this rich and varied land were settled upon. Specific tribes and cultures developed; time passed, and still populations grew. Tribal feuds and fighting increased; *enemies* were defined, and warfare became endemic. In concert with all other parts of the world, wars, raids, torture, and cannibalism followed.

Many tribes of North America were still practicing cannibalism when foreign boats landed on eastern shores. In the 1600s, it was noted by a Dutch clergyman that the Mohawks held religious cannibal feasts where commoners were given the limbs and trunks to eat, while the chiefs dined upon brains and hearts. The same was reported in regard to the Huron and the Miamis. The Iroquois were known for running prisoners down gauntlets of attackers, pulling out their fingernails and hacking off their limbs before decapitating them or roasting them alive; either way, an awaiting throng came for dinner. Various histories and documents cite many tribes, but a listing would be superfluous. Once again, it was revenge and sacrifice to the powers that be, and within some tribes everyone was a participating executioner, and everyone had a bowl.

There is an abundance of written material, and firsthand accounts are impressive and worthy of note, but the strongest, most scientific evi-

dence of cannibalism in North America has been found among the ruins of
the Four Corners area of the American Southwest: Utah, Colorado, New
Mexico and Arizona.

An anthropologist and a specialist in dentition, Christy G. Turner
II, together with his late wife Jacqueline Turner, worked for decades to
produce the most complete, detailed and scientific analyses of bone assemblages that imply cannibalism in the Four Corners area. The Turners
performed hands-on field research by butchering and de-fleshing animals
using stone tools so as to compare the marks with those left on human
bones many hundreds of year ago. In so doing, they established what had
been proposed more than a century before when the same archaeological
sites were first explored.

Then, in the late '80s, Professor Tim White and associates journeyed to the Four Corners area to investigate the cannibal site of Mancos
5MTUMR-2346. They were puzzled by scrape marks on the insides of the
large clay pots in which human flesh had been cooked. Besides the shallow
grooves on pot shards, there were small pieces of bone, usually pieces of a
femur, that showed frayed, rounded and slanted edges on one end. After
examining the evidence, White killed a deer and replicated what had occurred at the site. After cooking and eating the deer, the group broke open
the deer's femurs for extraction of the marrow, then broke off small pieces
of bone. After drinking the broth, they used the femur pieces to scrape the
fat residue from the inside of their large clay cooking pot. Back at their lab
they put the ancient frayed bone pieces, the newly frayed bone pieces, pieces of old pot shards and new pot pieces under an electron microscope—a
perfect match. The term pot-polishing was born.

The efforts of the Turners and White enhanced criteria for distin-
guishing evidence that infers cannibalism among bone assemblages. Such
criteria are now used as guidelines around the world. Over the last century
many others formulated such criteria, but the in-depth studies performed
in the Four Corners area helped to establish standard guidelines supported
by modern technologies.

Over the years, the Turners meticulously examined 76 bone assemblages showing gross signs of cannibalism—evidence distinct from all
other bone modifications—in combination with moderate to extreme perimortem (prior to death) violence. The dates of these sites run from AD
900 to 1300.

In the same geologic area are archaeological sites showing evidence
of cannibalism dating to another time period: AD 400—another era of
drought.

Archaeological evidence paints the following scenario:

It's AD 1150. A tiny village of pit houses is home to a minimum of
35 people. The houses are partially dug into the ground. They are thatch-
roofed with a hole that serves both as an entrance and a chimney. There
are storage chambers and benches recessed into the walls. Small ventila-
tion tunnels bring in fresh air to feed the fire, while stone deflectors kept
the draft from scattering ash, embers and smoke. Grinding palettes slant
in permanent positions, their grinding-stone mates near by. Tools, orna-
ments, armaments, baskets, ceramic cooking pots, hides, clothing and
cooking utensils complete the bulk of household treasures.

Drought has plagued the area on and off for many years; there is
little to eat and the people are often hungry. Silently a marauding group of
foreign warriors enters the village, divides into teams and bursts through
the roofs of the houses. Few escape; the slaughter is horrible and complete.
Thirty-five people die, their bodies butchered and boiled in clay pots, then
eaten, their long bones cracked for the extraction of marrow. The maraud-
ers leave a stone knife covered with blood. Centuries later a scientist will
run tests proving the blood to be human.

As time passes, other villages are attacked; at one site more than
1,000 small human bone fragments are left scattered across a floor to be
discovered in the distant future. At the Mancos site, more than 2,000 bone
pieces are found.

Hundreds of years after the actual events, some claim that the
1,000 fragments speak of a ritualistic annihilation of witches. But one site

after another paints a picture of cannibalism, and then an artifact is found at the Cowboy Wash site that puts a cap on decades of quarrels. One of the cannibals left his calling card, a coprolite (well-preserved feces), when he relieved himself over a cool hearth. Richard A. Marlar, a biochemist at the University of Colorado Medical School, analyzed the coprolite and found myoglobin, a protein unique to human muscle. The coprolite could only contain myoglobin if the person who left it had eaten of human flesh—witchy enough for me.

Drought is known to have plagued the Four Corners area during the same centuries when evidence of cannibalism was laid down at site after site. Many researchers believe the cannibalizing of men, women and children was prompted by drought and starvation. Turner agrees in general, but has examined many sites that offer evidence of warrior tribes traveling north from Mexico, their arrival coinciding with periods of drought. At the time, Mexico was rife with civil unrest, and a combination of drought and marauding gangs would have produced the large number of cannibalistic sites that show signs of violence. Amongst the rubble of human remains many artifacts were found. For example, a Mimbres bowl of Aztec design (AD 1000–1300) depicting a man in horned serpent garb holding a decapitated head; the victim's headless body graces the bottom of the bowl as a thin red line (blood) connects the body with the dismembered head. Also, ball courts, Aztec-style ruins (AD 1110–1275), and pottery lend credence to the idea of people coming into the American Southwest from Mesoamerica.

Turner sees evidence of northbound tribes fleeing civil unrest, bringing with them sacrifice and cannibalism. While cannibalism in the Four Corners area has now been accepted (the evidence is exceptional), few are ready to join Turner in his southern invaders theory. However, architecture, pottery and artifacts offer evidence. Some pieces of pottery depict ancient Teotihuacán gods that date back 2,000 years; gods later borrowed by the Aztecs. These archaeological finds coincide with the reappearance of cannibalism in the American Southwest. Such data are bringing more researchers on board. Turner's argument, coupled with artifacts, is strong, and many sites fit his theory, while other sites offer clear inference of survival cannibalism.

Among the individual tribes of North America that existed prior to the white man's arrival, were hundreds of prescribed methods of warfare, torture and the capture and treatment of prisoners. It was not uncommon for a Native American who killed an enemy in dangerous territory to eat his enemy's heart on the spot or take some part of the body back as proof of the kill. In cases where a group of prisoners was taken, most were absorbed into the victor's camp and made slaves or tribal members complete with marriage privileges. But the strongest and highest-ranking prisoners were set aside for torture, death, and within some tribes, cannibalism. Prior to torture and death, the selected captive(s) was treated as royalty in sharp contrast to his prearranged end. The accounts are not pretty, but reflect like practices found around the globe. Is it possible that methods of torture originated elsewhere prior to migration into the Americas? Global archaeological evidence for cannibalism and brutality dates back hundreds of thousands of years, so there is no reason to assume that such behaviors developed independently among those who entered the western hemisphere so recently.

The histories of the Native Americans are so rife with detailed methods of torture that when I first began to research the subject of cannibalism, I had a difficult time understanding why, or how, peoples from around the world could do such things to others.

Marvin Harris, in his book *Cannibals and Kings*, addresses the fact, commenting that torture has been practiced over the eons for the sake of entertainment, and that the torturing of one individual is emotionally equal to a thousand deaths. Thus, the torturing of a single foe simulates the slaughter of a thousand enemies.

Historical descriptions of places and methods of torture present images akin to spectator sports; think of the Romans and the Coliseum—case closed.

Torture was so rampant among the tribes of North America that warriors were trained to be immune to pain. To show courage and sto-icism while being tortured proved the ultimate strength and courage of a warrior, a trait sought by males on a global scale, but best perfected by the natives of North America. Males were not only trained to be stoic in the face of excruciating pain, but were taught songs to sing while being tortured. The stories of braves who bore up under incomprehensible pain can be found in eyewitness accounts and within the myths of all American tribes. Many times the courage of a torture victim is portrayed as being far more significant than the methods of torture or cannibalism. Systems of belief supported the perpetuity of rules of war, slavery, torture, and can-nibalism. Elaborate rituals determined every event, filling each individual with a sense of fulfillment during peaceful times and justification for the destruction of an enemy when times were difficult, something all belief systems seek to do.

While the torture of an enemy cited for cannibalism was impor-tant to some, others leaned towards more epicurean thoughts and deeds. During the 1800s, the Kwakiutl Indians of coastal British Columbia prac-ticed an extremely odd and ritualistic kind of cannibalism. The Kwakiutl were divided into three classes: nobles, commoners and slaves. Among the nobles were the "Hamatsa"—cannibals. As young initiates they would run out of the woods and take bites out of villagers, usually on the chest or leg. Several observers left ethnological writings, and later, as the practice dwindled, personal reports from old Hamatsa were taken.

In 1859, one Mr. Hunt, a Dutch/Inuit ethnologist, watched as a slave was bound to a post and disemboweled. Then high-ranking tribes-men rushed forward to fill their hands with the victim's blood and drink it. Before feasting on the victim, the Hamatsa forced Hunt to leave. Years later an aged Hamatsa mourned the loss of the good old days when they could kill and eat slaves and prisoners without hindrance from the white man, then added facts on how they had devised other ways of gaining human flesh by soaking the bodies of victims in salt and curing them before hiding them in trees to be consumed a year or two later. For the Hamatsa, the eating of human flesh was an extreme privilege that greatly strengthened the diner; a common person was never allowed that honor.

For new Hamatsa members, elaborate initiation feasts were performed in long houses. Naked female shamans danced while men shook skull rattles about the heads of the initiates. Victim slaves were killed by their owners, after which the eating of the body commenced with frenetic initiates biting off chunks of flesh. Following "hors d'oeuvres," the body was cut up and devoured. As a finale, the "Kyimkalatla" broke open the skull and bones for the brains and marrow. Both men and women were victimized.

Following a cannibalistic feast, a Hamatsu initiate had to follow strict regulations for four months. He had to speak in whispers, have limited contact with the rest of the tribe, enter and exit his domicile from a separate door made for the occasion, upon rising turn around four times to the left and make four false steps forward before actually taking a step, and the litany goes on and on. The bones of the corpse were kept with the initiate during the four months; alternately, four days under his sleeping pallet, then four days beneath rocks by the sea. At the end of the fourth month they were thrown into the sea . . . again, no evidence.

When all regulations had been observed, the new Hamatsa would go around his village and pay those he had taken a bite out of.

In 1895, anthropologist Frans Boaz claimed the highly ritualistic cannibalism of the Hamatsa was confined to a small area and had been introduced by the Heiltsuk tribe. In Kwakiutl legends, cannibals are *baxbakwalanuxsiwae*—"man who is first to eat man at the mouth of the river" or "man-eater at the north end of the world" or "man-eating-man-beside-high-prowed-boat."

On another river, at another time, French lieutenant Étienne Brûlé became the first known Caucasian to set foot in what is now the state of Wisconsin. For years Brûlé canoed the waters of the northern most Great Lakes and rivers, living and trading with friendly Chippewa and Huron Indians.

"In 1633, however, his adopted Huron clubbed him to death and ate him."[1]

The work of the Turners and White, along with many others, has broken down much of the resistance to the idea of cannibalism that grew out of revisionist writings. And current research is continuing to document cannibalism on a global scale, including the homelands of my European ancestors:

On a glass shelf, in a neatly designed modern Danish cabinet in the Museum of Natural History, Copenhagen, Denmark, lay two piles. One pile consists of baked clamshells while the other pile is made up of bone fragments from a cannibalized human. A thousand years ago, my Viking ancestors had a two-course meal: stone-baked clams and roasted "Sigvaard." Who Sigvaard was, or why he was consumed is not known, but the remains of that long ago meal offer clear evidence of cannibalism . . . Oh, for a time machine.

CHAPTER SEVENTEEN

POLITICS AND THE COLOR RED

> "As late as the nineteenth century it was not unusual for Chinese executioners to eat the heart and brains of the criminals they dispatched . . . extra meat was sold for profit."[1]

I n 1996, Zheng Yi authored *Scarlet Memorial: Tales of Cannibalism in Modern China*, in which he detailed his government-sanctioned investigations into occurrences of cannibalism during the darkest days of Mao's regime. China's most southwestern province, Guangxi, was the area most implicated

During the '60s, Mao's Cultural Revolution stormed across China. Orders came down for the persecution (killing) of all who showed any opposition to Mao's totalitarian government, along with "death lists" nam·

ing those to be "subjected to dictatorship" (beaten to death). Guilty and innocent alike suffered public humiliation, followed by cruel deaths at the hands of the public.

In the midst of the torment, Mao, along with the Gang of Four, further decreed that "dictatorship is dictatorship by the masses," thus giving a thin slice of anarchy to the *masses* in order to rid the country of all persons who did not hold to or obey the rules and beliefs of Mao. As "trials" began in every city, town and village, the government opened the doors of sanitariums where persons diagnosed as being deranged, retarded or mentally deficient had been incarcerated.

When orders to exterminate all "enemies of the state" through "dictatorship by the masses" first reached Guangxi Province, perfunctory trials were played out. Most of the accused were found guilty and given an immediate death sentence. After sentencing, the "enemy" was thrown into the street where they were beaten and stabbed to death by the locals. In one case the heads of two men were severed and hung in trees within minutes of their conviction. Observers said that in the beginning most of the killings were performed by young bachelors, but that men and women alike soon took up the club and knife.

As the killings increased, the general populace quickly made a distinction between those "convicted" and themselves. In the eyes of the Guangxi masses, no innocent people were ever hurt or beaten. Those killed were viewed as being guilty of crimes against the state, making the murderers guiltless by way of governmental edict coupled with the belief that they, the killers, had helped to purge the country of vermin. In Luxu, a town famous for its roasted dog dishes, not one person publicly, or in written form, opposed the indiscriminate slaughter that had taken place around them. At the same time an unspoken panic swept the surrounding countryside, and within months things got so out of hand that people took care not to show mourning, empathy or even a desire to bury their dead, as those who did quickly became victims themselves. As a result, many corpses were left to rot.

All too soon, formal trials ended in Guangxi. People suspected of crimes were publicly criticized anywhere they were found, or told to appear, and then thrown to awaiting crowds. As time passed, a program ordered and condoned by the government led to impromptu killings, often resulting in executions meted out of vengeance, greed and jealousy. As things went from bad to worse, ad-hoc killings became acts of cannibalism. Former inmates of emptied sanitariums were accused of performing the initial acts of cannibalism.

An early case of cannibalism tells of a man who attacked and killed an older woman, cut out her liver and ran home to cook it. When he got home to the light of his kitchen, he found that he had cut out the lung, so he went back into the night and extracted the liver. Not long after that incident several mutilated bodies were found with hearts and/or livers missing. Though most organ-seeking murders occurred at night, there were many witnesses. And as more and more bodies with missing organs were found, others joined in the feeding frenzy as a sick, fevered type of crowd psychology took hold of the area. From torture and brutal killings, to organ taking for the sake of consumption, came wanton cannibalism that eventually escalated into the cannibalizing of entire bodies. People became adept at removing preferred organs, while some seemed to relish the flesh. The director of a local bureau of commerce was seen walking home with a human leg slung over his shoulder.

A well-documented case details an instance where teenage students killed a teacher and roasted him in the large school ovens, then served him forth on long cafeteria tables. In Zheng's book, there is a picture of the school, its white walls reflecting the sunlight.

In an effort to place meaning and worth onto their actions, those who had taken the first livers and hearts kept reiterating beliefs from times gone by, that in eating the liver of a human one gained courage, health and power, some stating that the liver from a young, unmarried male provided the most benefits. Similar beliefs were held for other organs, including the lungs. Words echoing from other places and other times reassured the offenders that cannibalism was not only natural, but also a way of completely eliminating the enemy. It was reasoned that in the killing and eating of those "subjected to dictatorship," the murderers were helping to rid their country of evil by obliterating the enemy.

One government official interviewed by the author stated, "Wrongly killing one hundred is better than letting one guilty person escape." He would not comment on acts of cannibalism though documentation of them sat behind him in file drawers. (Zheng was eventually allowed to comb the files.)

During his investigation, Zheng dined in the home of Wei Kequan, Director of the Shanglin County Party Committee (Shanglin County is in the province of Guangxi) and a Zhuang by birth. The Zhuang comprise the largest minority in China. After telling his hosts about his research, they immediately told him of many incidences of cannibalism, emphasizing cases where the victim's liver was consumed. Over a lovely dinner, Zheng learned that the Zhuang people still believe that the consuming of human liver acts as a tonic. When asked if cannibalism was, or ever had been, a tradition in the area, his hosts, without hesitation or irritation, cited numerous historical writings that clearly state the facts and said that their verbal histories, as well as their myths, speak freely of and to the practice of cannibalism.

Another photograph: a young man stands calmly facing the camera; there is a visible sadness about his eyes—five members of his family were killed and eaten.

Though many cases of murder and cannibalism were investigated by the authorities and filed in governmental archives, it was Zheng's tracking down and interviewing of government officials, survivors, witnesses and participants that filled in the gruesome details of the story. One witness told of three people being chopped to death with knives and spears by a mob of people, adding that the entire scene was beyond imagination. Others told of young girls being encouraged to kill; later they were referred to as "sister nine" or "sister ten," commensurate with the number of people they had killed. In one case, investigators found victims whose stomachs had been sliced open and their livers extracted, and who had then been left to die . . . the murderers had cut open the victims when they were still alive."

According to Zheng's research, the most blatant incidents of cannibalism occurred in the county of Wuxuan, Guangxi Province. Witnesses told him that when a victim was forced to walk through the streets while being "subjected to criticism," a crowd would join in the procession, including old women clutching their knives and vegetable baskets. As soon as the victim was killed, people would run forward to butcher the corpse. The first to get at the body got the best pieces, while those at the back, or those who came later, had to divide up the bones.

Over and over again, during his government-sanctioned investigations, Zheng found more than he wanted to, including something he had assumed for a long time. For years, cover-ups and distortions had become standard procedure when the Communist Central Committee insisted time and again that "historical" issues should be handled in a lax manner, ignoring all pertinent details. Historians employed by the government glossed over, or completely ignored, immense crimes perpetrated against, or within, the masses. Letters complaining about acts of cannibalism were secreted out of Guangxi and sent north to Beijing; they too were ignored. Eventually, Zheng ferreted out the fact that Mao and the Group of Four were fully aware of what was happening in the southern province but did nothing to stop the cannibalistic fever that had befallen the area.

When the killing and the cannibalism stopped, people who had led the way into ghoulishness not only went free, but, in some cases, were promoted. Others, upon arrest, demanded fairer treatment and received it, some serving no real jail time. Only 56 people were ever convicted of any crime connected with cannibalism. One person was executed. Years of research brought both disgust and dismay; author Zheng Yi writes:

> The theft of a bag of rice led to a sentence of seven years
> in prison, and the victim [thief], was later killed and can-
> nibalized, whereas the murderer Wang Chunrong, who

had engaged in frenzied killing and feasted on human flesh while enjoying his liquor, was sentenced to only thirteen years in prison.

In the end, of all he had uncovered and learned, what hit Zheng the hardest was a total lack of remorse within those who had killed and cannibalized or by those who had been observers to such atrocities. In their view, Mao had said it was "dictatorship by the masses" and had ordered all enemies of the state to be "persecuted," and once the dreaded enemy was dead, there was no law against eating the body.

The occurrences of cannibalism that took place during Mao's reign offer testimony to the capacity of humans to believe and do anything and everything within the realm of possibility, especially when the leaders of their society sanction their behavior. Official dictatorial mandates gave rise to a crowd psychology that was fed by fear, hatred, greed, revenge and jealousy, which led to unbridled anarchy that was psychologically exonerated through beliefs scraped up from pits of the past. It was a time of great sadness.

Another factor figured into the cannibalizing of the nation's "enemies"; episodes of cannibalism had littered thousands of years of Chinese history, including times when human flesh had been looked upon as a culinary delicacy.

During his investigative work, Zheng made many friends with members of the Zhuang minority. Those friendships made it difficult for him to accept the words of several professors who told him that the recent episodes of cannibalism were simply throwbacks to customs of not so very long ago. Unsettled by all he had learned, he left the area and spent months studying the histories of the peoples of Guangxi. A year later, he returned to cement his findings and confront his emotions.

The Zhuang are China's most populous minority. In 1990, they numbered 15 million and comprised one half of the population in Guangxi Province. They speak a Sino-Thai language and have lived under Chinese rule since the thirteenth century. The other minority in the area is the Yao, who numbered two million in 1990. The majority population in China is the Han, many of whom began migrating into Guangxi at the time of the communist takeover in 1949. Prior to the influx of Han, the province was principally made up of the Zhuang and Yao peoples.

Historical records clearly indicate that the Zhuang and Yao practiced cannibalism. One of the earliest written records of cannibalism among the peoples of southern China was penned by Qu Yuan in the second century AD. His poem "Summons to the Soul" is found in *The Elegies of Chu*.[2]

> O soul, come back!
> In the south you cannot stay.
> There the people have tattooed faces
> and blackened teeth;
> They sacrifice flesh of men and pound
> their bones for meat paste.

And from Fan Ye of the Song dynasty (AD 960–1279) can be read:

> In the west lies a kingdom of cannibalism where the firstborn son is consumed, a practice known there as "discharging duties toward the younger brother." . . . South of Canton, human hands and feet are consumed as delicacies. The old folks are also cannibalized.[3]

By the end of his research, Zheng had a better understanding of his new friends, but had to face the truth. Everything from written histories to fascinating myths, beliefs and legends of the Zhuang and Yao told the same story. From the times of their most ancient ancestors, the two tribes had been militant peoples who fought endless tribal wars and practiced cannibalism as a custom. Their detailed and complicated myths tell of how they flayed the flesh of victims and how they came to cannibalize their firstborn sons, their elderly and others.

When the Zhuang and Yao went from roving bands of hunter-gatherers to community-based agrarians, they settled on soil of low productivity in an area of unreliable rainfall. In time, episodes of drought and starvation, aggravated by growing populations, drove them back to their old ways of cannibalism. And when the usual offerings failed to do the trick, they offered more through sacrifice in increasingly brutal ways in order to appease the gods and thwart annihilation through starvation.

The increased practice of consuming human flesh mandated an expansion of their myths so as to make peace with themselves and their gods. Over time, intricate beliefs wrapped around the practices of sacrifice and cannibalism. Though more elaborate than most, their myths mirror those of others that demanded sacrifice and cannibalism in order to bring forth a good crop, fertility among their animals, as well as productive weather patterns.

Today, the Zhuang no longer flay, sacrifice and consume humans; cattle are used in their stead, followed by a feast.

Currently, both the Zhuang and the Yao peoples are known to be of great honesty and passion, with a gift for hospitality. One scholar told Zheng, "If they love you they will offer you everything; if, however, they happen to resent you they will feel like eating your liver."

Another noted that when they become angry with someone they still use the ancient phrase, "I feel like eating his liver."

In time Zheng Yi became a leader of the 1989 Tiananmen Square protests. For the next three years, he was a fugitive within his own country, during which time he wrote *Scarlet Memorial*. He and his wife now reside in the United States. At the back of the book, Zheng admits that he used an alias, then writes heartfelt words against communism and the reign of Mao. He equates the deaths of 10,000 cannibalized victims to those who lost their lives in Nazi gas chambers and hopes that one day there will be a Scarlet Memorial erected in their honor with the words, "No, Never Again!"

Zheng's book is a dark and bilious read, but worthy of attention because of its consideration to detail and historical exactness. His review of the myths of the Zhuang and the Yao is of critical importance; though more convoluted than most, they reflect and join others from around the globe. When trying to understand and acknowledge the practice of cannibalism, the myths and beliefs formulated during more primitive times need to be studied, as they open doors to times beyond our imaginations and uncover the foundations upon which cultural practices are performed.

Scarlet Memorial opened China's unknown doors to me, but further research proved its contents to be but a small packet of Asian spice in a crowded cupboard. China has a 4,000-year written history of cannibalism. Through the ages and into the twentieth century, various forms of cannibalism were practiced. When criminals of Imperial China were publicly executed, their bodies were often put on display and offered for consumption. Written reports tell of the flesh of Chang'an rebels being sold by government troops during a time of hunger and wild inflation in the year 882. From 1876 to 1879, horrendous drought and famine racked the provinces of China. A Roman Catholic bishop wrote of husbands killing and eating their wives, parents preparing the bodies of their children, and children surviving by consuming the corpses of their parents. A Chinese district magistrate confirmed the bishop's reports by detailing a more horrendous litany of tragic occurrences. And during the Sino-Japanese War of 1894–1895 the flesh of Aborigines was sold openly in the marketplace and eaten in lieu of pork.

My interest in the culinary side of cannibalism was peaked by author Key Ray Chong, whose writings offer a list of the most favored Chinese methods of preparing human flesh: in order, they were broiling (most cannibals agree that the barbie's the way to go), roasting, boiling and steaming. A method of pickling in salt, wine and herbs was also found worthy, done much as human cadavers were pickled or cured in Europe in the making of "mummy," prescribed by physicians to cure the ill. And since the Chinese dine for health as much as for pleasure, it should come as no surprise that they used, and still use, human flesh and fluids in medicinal ways. (See Chapter 8: "Murder and Medicine.")

In recent years, several authors of Chinese descent have written on the cannibalism that has peppered Chinese history, including episodes of revenge cannibalism during times of war, survival cannibalism in times of drought and war, medicinal cannibalism throughout the millennia and culinary cannibalism for the pleasure of dining. There is nothing unknown within the most ancient culture of China.

> Beijing (AP), April 16, 1998:
> Cannibalism reported in famine stricken North Korea.
> French aid workers, along with representatives from Doctors Without Borders compiled a report concerning cannibalism after interviewing Korean refugees and people living near the Chinese/North Korean border. All accounts cited children as victims. Drought was seen as the stimulus for this age-old survival technique.

In the same article, Catherine Bertini, an executive director of the World Food Program, spent four days in North Korea and said she saw no evidence of cannibalism. Since her tour was under the tight control of the North Korean government, it would have been impossible for her to have seen, or obtain, any evidence of cannibalism.

Again, in 2003, other news reports rumored of cannibalism in the northern sections of North Korea due to a six-year drought, a fallen economy and brutal dictatorship. As yet there is no hard proof of the alleged cannibalism. But at the present time, it is hard, if not impossible, to get the truth regarding any subject out of North Korea. Perhaps, at some future date, there will be a Korean "Zheng" who will describe the circumstances that led to episodes of cannibalism.

CHAPTER EIGHTEEN

AFRICA: THEN AND NOW

Niger River basin—words of anthropologist C. H. Meek, 1930:
"... normally only enemy captives were eaten; their skulls were carefully preserved
and when young men went to war they drank medicine out of these trophies."[1]

Chicago Tribune, Wednesday May 21, 2003:
"The Congo Aid workers said they had found 231 bodies of people killed since
May 4 on the streets of Bunia, including women and children, some decapitated,
others with hearts, livers and lungs missing."

I n the lush forests of northeastern Congo, small branch and thatch huts sit empty among tall trees. It is an abandoned village of Ituri Pygmies who have fled from marauding bands of Congolese rebel soldiers. As monkeys cry from on high, an Ituri Pygmy tells his story of Memba troops coming in waves, pushing through the forests looking for valuables, money and beautiful women. As people fled, many were caught and tortured. "They even stole people's hunting nets out of sheer wickedness."[2]

A hundred kilometers away, a man watched from a hiding place on a hill above his village as soldiers killed, cut up, roasted and consumed his mother, brother, sister and a child. The man said the soldiers drank the warm blood of their victims as they slaughtered them. After feasting, the raucous soldiers packed up the leftovers and left.

At yet another site, a man who had been away gathering wood with two friends returned to find a group known as the "Blackboards" inhabiting his village. The man was held captive and forced to share in a cannibalistic feast that included meat from members of his family.

While high-ranking UN officials in Kinshasa sought to investigate dozens of similar reports, other UN officials in both Kinshasa and the eastern city of Goma confirmed that widespread cannibalism had already been established.

Events of carnage are the latest in an all-fall-down killing spree that began in 1998 when civil war broke out in the Congo. Six nations have entered the war at various intervals; between 2.5 and 3 million people have lost their lives. There are two major Congolese factions, the Movement for the Liberation of Congo (MLC) and the allied troops of the Congolese Rally for Democracy-National (RCD-N). Ugandan troops are also major players, having joined the fracas in hopes of procuring domination over borderlands rich in timber, gold and diamonds—borderlands the musical, mystical pygmies have inhabited for thousands of years, far longer than all other inhabitants of the area.

In times past, both the Ugandans and the Congolese enslaved pygmies as hunters of game and prospectors of minerals. When war broke out, the Pygmies got a slight reprieve. Then in 2002, Congolese troops, hardened by four years of brutal fighting, swarmed the northeastern area and forced the Pygmies to provide them with fresh supplies of meat. Deforestation, along with the torching of select areas leveled for war maneuvers, worked towards the annihilation of wildlife. Commensurate with a depletion of bush meat, cannibalism began. As the story goes, it all began when a Pygmy hunter returned from a long day in the forest and announced that there was no meat left in the forest. A rebel soldier grabbed the hunter and said, "Yes, there is."

The slaughter had begun, and soon a pattern was set, as increasing numbers of cannibals took to raiding villages and gathering human flesh proportionate with their needs. As news spread, villagers took to hiding their children and often themselves.

New York Times, July 17, 2003:
New International Criminal Courts is likely to open its first case by investigating leaders most responsible for flagrant abuses against civilians in eastern Congo . . . extensive atrocities in region including massacre of unarmed civilians, mass rape, torture, kidnappings, mutilations and ritual cannibalism. . . . [The trials] will focus on Ituri in eastern Congo. . . .

Events of cannibalism were followed by a violent blood lust and desire for victory exhibited by the Congolese rebels as they sought to debase and annihilate all in their path. As troops pushed forward, they wreaked havoc. Towns were demolished; women gang-raped; young children raped, trampled or killed, throats slit and bodies defiled. Graveyards were dug up in search of valuable items. Soldiers marched into towns with the heads of Pygmy victims hanging about their necks and "penis bracelets" encircling their wrists. Some danced around town squares singing songs about their cannibalistic exploits. One man was shown a bag full of male sex organs that was being taken back to the soldier's chief, while others gave reports of cannibals cutting and ripping out sexual and other organs from bodies of both sexes for consumption. Other stories told of hearts being ripped from the bodies of infants and small children, the devourers believing the meal would provide them with strength, sexual prowess and good health.

An Italian priest in one town ran to hide amongst a herd of cattle. The rebels mowed down the cattle with automatic weapons, then captured the priest from amidst the bellowing bovines and demanded money. He threatened them with exposure to which they laughed, saying they had done things a thousand times worse in other places, then had several townspeople brought forward and slit their throats. When the rebels left, the priest reported the atrocities. Three weeks later, international forces arrived to investigate. UN investigators said attacks occurred at Mombasa and Mangina, 30 and 45 miles respectively from the northeastern city of Beni. Articles and news clippings listed some of the horrors. Victims and witnesses told of cannibalism where people were forced by rebels to eat flesh from members of their own family. Investigators cited acts of cutting hearts from infants to be devoured on the spot; little girls raped, killed and sexually mutilated; and of people being forced to watch as friends and family were slaughtered. Most reports proposed beliefs in magic as the instigator behind acts of cannibalism, stating the many soldiers and locals held that the consuming of selected parts of human flesh offered special powers including physical strength and sexual prowess.

A front-page headline from the Monday, July 28, 2003 issue of the *Wall Street Journal*: "Peace and Justice: A Prosecutor Vows No Deals for Thugs in Sierra Leone War—Freetown, Sierra Leone."

The article tells how American prosecutor David Crane assembled the staff of his United Nations-backed court after seven months of investigation into atrocities practiced during the civil war in Sierra Leone, a country situated on the western bulge of the African continent. Mr. Crane's efforts found incidents that mirror all that has been reported in the Congo. Even the various factions admit to being similar. Troops sent by President Taylor of Liberia got into the action so as to enslave the locals and work the area's diamond mines in order to finance his wars and lifestyle. As the war progressed, each new takeover faction became more ruthless towards their victims than those who had come before. In the end, those most responsible denied all allegations; Mr. Crane's investigations proved otherwise. He comments:

> I thought I'd seen it all, but I hadn't. The intentional depravity, the ritualistic deaths, the mass graves, the cannibalism. Now I have actually touched, felt, smelled and seen the horror with my own eyes.

Mr. Crane's observations were not well received. In the article he complains of "very little moral or political support" from state department officials, who appeared to be agitated by Mr. Crane's report, as it was believed the prosecution "would be a quiet little effort indicting a few people and then disappearing." According to later news accounts, and lack thereof, it would seem the higher ups won the day.

Two newspapers, *Le Monde* and the *Wall Street Journal*, offered the best coverage detailing the incidents of recent cannibalism in the Congo and Sierra Leone. Reports from other publications were overtly politically correct, gave minimal coverage and were usually hidden on back pages; most being no more than a paragraph or two in length. The word "cannibalism" was avoided.

Though distant and distinct unto themselves, the recent episodes of cannibalism reflect the cannibalistic practices of centuries past. From the seventeenth century to the end of the nineteenth century, explorers trekked into remote areas of Africa and claimed lands for colonization. The British, Dutch, French, Italians, Belgians and Germans colonized the bulk of the continent. Across the belly of Africa, they found many peoples who indulged in cannibalism. The practice of consuming human flesh varied from one tribe to another, the differences defined by ritual, mythology, and sometimes, diabolical planning.

Early travelers, explorers and anthropologists wrote that the man-eaters of Africa were concentrated in the Congo and Niger River basin, and that human flesh was looked upon for what it was—meat, a favored protein that was readily available. But as anthropologists of the last century learned more about African societies, they found that most acts of canni-balism were steeped in ritual, the eating of human flesh being an integral part of local religions awash with beliefs in magic.

Centuries ago, in Sierra Leone, a group of highly stylized cannibal-warriors was discovered. Existing amongst many tribes, the members-only group was known as the Leopard Society, which was first noted by early explorers in 1607.

The British colonized the country in 1807, but did not become fully aware of the Society's actions until 1891. The time lapse is understandable since the Leopard Society acted in extreme secrecy and performed their rites in the deepest depths of the forests. To no white man would anyone dare speak of this powerful and dangerous group that lived and functioned far from the Western-styled compounds of the British. So secret was the Leopard Society that many native Africans knew little of them, thus mak-ing investigations difficult for the British.

The Leopard Society made potent medicines from the blood, liv-er and entrails of their victims to enhance their health and increase their stamina and courage. The rest of the body was roasted and consumed.

In centuries past, when leopards were more plentiful, and humans far fewer, a man had to single-handedly kill a leopard, then carefully skin it while maintaining the head in connection with the pelt in order to join the Leopard Society. After scraping and curing the hide, it was worn only in the presence of other society members. By the time the British were hold-ing court, members possessing a full skin were few, but no member was without a leopard knife.

The Leopard Society's cannibalistic sacrifices were planned well in advance. First and foremost, a freeborn girl over the age of 14 had to be selected; neither slave nor captive was acceptable. In some cases a family would be told they had been chosen to offer one of their teenage daughters for sacrifice. Out of fear of reprisal or by way of a belief system that accepted the ultimate gift as a befitting offering to the gods, the chosen family would choose a daughter in submission.

Men wishing to join the Society had to choose a young female from their family group for sacrifice. Many chose girls who, according to the initiates, "had a devil in her." Regardless of how a girl was chosen, she was instructed to take a specific path deep into the forest at a certain time, on a set date. Among the sound-smothering trees of the forest the men of the Leopard Society waited, each with the skull of his leopard skin tied to his head, the beautifully marked skin covering the majority of his body.

As the girl ran down the path, the leopard-men would come out from behind trees and chase her into the hands of the chief who would rush out, grab her and drag her to a clearing far from the eyes and ears of the village. According to accounts gathered over the years, the girl would either be killed immediately or tied to a stake before a fire and tortured as members of the Leopard Society danced around the flames snarling, hissing and growling savagely so as to take on the identity of the leopard, an animal well known for devouring its victims.

In other chapters, from other villages, men of the Leopard Society prowled through the forest from the time a girl was selected until her death. This ritual could go on continuously for more than a day with the sound of snarling and growling forever reverberating through the forest.

Different methods of killing were followed; anything from a quick death by the slitting of the throat, to rape and torture lay in wait for the victim. But whether the men danced around a fire, or roared through the forest for hours on end, they all worked to maintain their identity with the spirit of the leopard.

Stories of the Leopard Society found on recent, as well as aged, pages offer a clear view of transposition. By the wearing of their leopard garb, by dancing and/or roaring in imitation of the leopard, by their every act, each man convinced himself that he had become a leopard, a wild animal known for its killing ways, an animal that stalks and chases down its prey, an animal that devours the still warm flesh of its kill with relish and hunger.

Through numerous writings, court records and interrogations of members from different tribes it becomes clear that each chapter of the Society performed the prescribed rituals in different ways. Some took pieces of the victim's flesh back to her mother and father. Some never chased the girl, but walked her to the place of torture, death and slaughter. Some danced, while others did not, but all feasted on the remains after capturing the blood, liver and intestines in order to make powerful potions and medicines.

Did the making of medicines and potions bring on events of cannibalism, or did cannibalism lead to the making of medicines? Did our ancient ancestors feel strengthened and renewed after an event of cannibalism? Did they attach the adrenaline high of ceremony and murder with the consuming of human flesh? And did such occurrences lead to beliefs that are still held by many, beliefs of human flesh providing unusual, health-promoting and/or magical benefits?

In the early 1800s, the British outlawed cannibalism. Only later did they lay down laws specifically targeted at the Leopard Society. Every member that could be found was placed behind bars, but few could be found, so the British took to arresting any man known to own a full leopard skin. In retaliation the members of the Society chose another beast as their emblem. Over the decades they switched from one animal to another. By 1901, they had become the Human Alligator Society.

In 1903, it was proven that the highest-ranking chiefs were deeply involved and always had been. More laws were written. By 1912, 17 cases had been tried before the courts under the new laws. It took the British more than a hundred years to prove the existence of and stop the activities of the Leopard Society. All the while, as the British searched, jailed and strengthened their laws, the Leopard Society not only switched totem animals but also continually moved their places of cannibalistic sacrifice and medicine making ever deeper into the forests of their wild lands. Towards the end men and boys were sometimes offered for sacrifice so that no young girl's disappearance could be reported to the British, but young girls never lost their place as being the most favored for sacrifice and consumption.

It should be noted that during the Leopard Society trials, the prosecutors did not always act in general recognition of normal court proceedings, and it is also true that many "witnesses" obviously made up wild lies while giving testimony, but overall the evidence for the longtime existence and customs of the Leopard Society is profound.

A headline from the Thursday, February 27, 2003 edition of *Le Monde*, Paris, France, translates to: "In the Congo Pygmies Victims of Cannibalism."

The article speaks of torture, murder, cannibalism and a deepseated belief that human flesh can strengthen a man and give him special powers.

On March 27, 2004, the newspaper *The Independent* (UK) ran an article by Eliza Griswold, who went into the Ituri Rainforest to re-investigate acts of cannibalism. She spoke with Amuzati Nzoli, the man who was returning home when he heard unusual noises coming from his village. Halting his approach and taking care not to be seen, he watched as DRC (Democratic Republic of Congo) soldiers butchered his mother, younger sister, his older brother and his nephew. "They were cutting them the way they cut meat."

Amuzati has become somewhat of a celebrity and has even been to the capital, Kinshasa, to meet with President Joseph Kabila. He traded his story for T-shirts and shoes; Eliza offered nothing. They talked about clothes, of how the Pygmies are covering their bodies with Western clothing. Amuzati said his people want to be like everyone else. "By the next generation, the pygmies who don't wear clothes will be gone."

A Catholic bishop talked of "Bemba's men," who often cut off fingers and ears—". . . that was normal." But, when they started feeding them to prisoners, "that was something new."

Two tribes, the Lendu and Hema, have been added to a growing list of practicing cannibals. When colonists left in the '60s, the Hema moved into lands formerly farmed by the Lendu; sporadic fighting ensued, but when oil reserves were discovered under the disputed lands, war broke out. (The Lendu outnumber the Hema 750,000 to 150,000.) Petronille Vaweka, president of the Special Assembly of Ituri: ". . . the Lendu kill. So do the Hema, but they kill in secret. Now in this war, with drugs, they cook people and eat them. No one can lie—both sides have eaten each other."

While a prisoner of the Lendu, Vivienne Nyamutale was witness to five episodes of cannibalism when Lendu fighters brought Hema men into camp, cooked them and fed them to the troops. Vivienne escaped the "rape camp" after one such episode when most of the fighters had left on a raid.

Then Eliza met Chantal Tsesi who told her about the early morning of August 27, 2002. She was alone with her six-year-old son when Lendu fighters, armed with machetes, entered her home. They told her they were going to cut off her arm so she could no longer make "mandro," a favored beer. The men not only cut off Chantal's arm, but drank her mandro as they cooked her arm, which they ate with rice and beans as she looked on. Her son escaped.

Chantal spent three months in the Drodo Hospital. Following her release, rebels stormed the hospital and went from bed to bed killing every patient.

The Lendu fighters who had cut off Chantal's arm told her they were going to find her husband and eat his heart; instead her husband left her because she could no longer work or make beer.

Chantal returned to her natal village where her mother, Eliza Dz'da, lived with her sister Georgette and her four children. In another raid, prior to Chantal's return, the Lendu killed Georgette and her children, tore down a family-owned shed, used the wood to build a fire, and according to Chantal's mother, "Took our food and cooked pieces of

Georgette and the children."

Chantal and Eliza are both devout Christians and have known and worked with the Lendu for most of their lives; both are trying to forgive them.

Reporter Eliza Griswold writes: "At a distance, their desire to forgive seems inexplicable. Up close, amid the fatigue of war, it's easier to understand. . . . In the past five years, more than 50,000 people have been killed in Ituri."

No one knows how many people of the Ituri Rainforest have been cannibalized; there is not even a reasonable estimation. But stories such as Chantal's open another dimension on cannibalism. The Lendu fighters did not kill her, but they did cannibalize her. The arm bones of Chantal, if they should fossilize or be preserved in a dry desert sand, then found some time in the future, would speak of amputation, and possibly of cooking, cut marks or gnawing, whereas the taking of livers, hearts and other morsels often leave future scientists without a clue. Even now, all we have are victims, eye-witnesses and people minus ears, noses, fingers, breasts, buttocks and arms, plus an approximation of numbers dead, plus thousands unaccounted for.

From an 1890 volume entitled *Nature's Wonderland, or Short Talks on Natural History for Young and Old*, by J. Sterling Kingsley and Edward Breck, M.A. Ph.D., concerning the inhabitants of the Marquesas Islands:

> According to Wood, they are fierce in war, and are never satisfied until they have gained a trophy of victory. When a Marquesan kills an enemy, he cuts off the head of his fallen antagonist, tears open the skull, and eats the brain. He then cleans the skull very carefully, adorns it with tufts of bristles, and slings it by a cord to his girdle. When he goes to battle again he always carries this trophy with him, partly on account of the respect in which it is held by his comrades, and partly to strike awe into the enemy by the sight of so redoubtable a warrior.[3]

And from the March 17, 2005, *Chicago Tribune*:
Kinshasa—Militiamen grilled bodies on a spit and boiled
two girls alive as their mother watched, UN peacekeepers
charged Wednesday, adding cannibalism to a list of atrocities allegedly carried out by one of the tribal groups fighting
in northeast Congo . . . the site of the world's worst hu-
manitarian crisis. . . . Peacekeepers have begun working to
cut off weapons supplies to the group.

We seem to have been playing the same games for a very long
time.

FINALE:

LOOKING
BACK
TO
THE
PRESENT

CHAPTER NINETEEN

IT'S A WRAP—
FILM AT ELEVEN

From the time Japan invaded Manchuria (China) in 1937, to the end of World War II in 1945, the samurai sword claimed more lives than the atomic bombs dropped on Hiroshima and Nagasaki. During the years 1937 and 1938, 300,000 Chinese were slaughtered. Many were cannibalized. Later, in the Pacific theater, American and allied troops were treated in kind.

n 1981, my late husband and I journeyed first to New Zealand and then to Fiji where he had previously made friends with Meli, a Fijian chief. Upon meeting Meli, I was instantly enthralled. The man was at least 6′ 8″, his gigantic feet had never known a pair of shoes and his eyes spoke volumes of strength, history and beliefs; we became fast friends. One evening Meli came over and the three of us spoke into the black hours of the night. He told of his ancestors, proudly telling tales of his paternal great-grandfather, who was one of the last major cannibals of the Fijian Islands. As with my Maori friend, he saw no shame in his family's cannibalistic past and indicated that if the British had been dissuaded from settling on Fiji, things would have remained the same as they had been for centuries. He then suggested that within the interior mountains of the Fijian Island chain (there are 329 islands), should "So and so" fall from a tree, the body might be disposed of in ways other than burial, as human flesh was still spoken of as being a great delicacy.

> *AP Newsflash*, November 14, 2003:
> Nabutautau, Fiji—Villagers from the high hills of Viti Levu Island staged an elaborate ceremonial apology Thursday, put on for the relatives of Reverend Thomas Baker and eight Fijian followers who were killed and eaten in 1867.

The killing and cannibalism occurred when Reverend Baker lent the chief of Nabutautau a comb, and then touched the chieftain's head as he tried to extricate it from the headman's curly hair. This may have been the case, but others say Baker lent the chief his hat, which he then retrieved from the chief's head unaware that to touch the head of a chief was taboo and punishable by death. (See Chapter 6: "Dinner with a Cannibal.")

The current villagers believe Baker's spirit has kept their community from receiving the modern developments that have been given to other communities over the last 136 years. In an effort to appease Baker's ghost and his family, a month-long ritualistic apology was made of gifts and the return of items held since 1867. Along with gifts of cows, specially woven mats and 30 *tabua* (carved sperm whale teeth), they returned Baker's boot—which they had cooked and tried to eat—to the Methodist Church of Fiji. Ratu Filimoni Nawawabalavu, great-grandson of the chief and chef who roasted Baker and his followers in an earthen oven, told reporters: "This is our third apology but, unlike the first two, this one is being offered physically to the family of Mr. Baker."

Doing the right thing works. The prime minister of Fiji, Laisenia Qarase, flew into Nabutautau for the ceremony by helicopter with promises to improve life in remote areas. And, two weeks prior, a logging company cut a track into the village. . . . The people of Nabutautau may live to regret their apology.

On the same island, at a place called Rakiraki, is the burial place of Ratu Udre Udre, who was a renowned chief of the nineteenth century. Ratu Udre Udre was famous for his love of human flesh and his practice of finding and keeping a special stone for every person he consumed. Prior to his death he ordered his collection of stones to be set around his gravesite. Today, people argue about the number, some claiming that many stones have been stolen, but all agree that Ratu Udre Udre dined upon 872 to 999 people over the course of his long and healthy lifetime.

Fossil and archaeological evidence confirm that cannibalism has been practiced by the species *Homo sapiens* from the times of our evolutionary beginnings, with the Spanish site of Gran Dolina setting a prominent example. Closer in time we find both Neanderthal and modern human cave sites that span two-thirds of the globe and offer the same telltale signatures that imply the butchering and eating of humans.

At Baume Moula-Guercy, a cave overlooking the Rhône river near Soyons, France (dated occupation from 80,000 to 120,000 years ago), teams of paleoanthropologists have secured firm evidence for the cannibalizing of six Neanderthal individuals by other Neanderthals. Professor Tim White pieced together hundreds of bone fragments to expose and determine the method of butchery, de-fleshing, and the crushing and pounding of bones for the extraction of marrow, as well as craniums for the removal of the brain. Moula-Guercy is the first site excavated using tools and methods that allow for a consensus on the systematic practice of cannibalism. An amazing component of the find is that the group of six cannibalized individuals is represented by a male and a female from three age groups: adults; adolescents between 16 and 17 years of age; and children, ages six or seven. The careful pairing of sexes and age groups speaks to ceremony.

which would be hard to believe—considering a dating of 100,000 years—were it not for gross evidence of an accompaniment of faunal remains that remove the possibility of starvation as a motivator for the cannibalism that took place.

Aside from Moula-Guercy, there are Neanderthal sites that prove medical knowledge and caring for injured or disabled individuals, while many sites offer proof of violence through the examination of skulls fractured by stone axes. Still others reveal purposeful burials complete with flowers, red ochre and artifacts. The multifaceted evidence prompts the question, who were our cousins the Neanderthals?

The shattered skulls and cannibalized bones, in comparison with compassion and formal burials, appear to be in conflict with one another until we look at ourselves. Violence and compassion can be found within all societies. It appears the devils and angels have been at odds with one another from the beginning.

Did ancient peoples practice endocannibalism? Habitually, or only when hungry? Did they consume their enemies? Was it a common or uncommon practice? The reasons for practicing cannibalism in the far distant past can never be known, but the evidence strongly suggests that our ancestors were aggressive and in no way adverse to dining upon those of their own kind.

Over the course of human history, cannibalism has been a recurrent, sometime custom practiced out of hunger, hatred, love or revenge; in observance of a religion or system of belief; as a funerary rite; for the production of medicine; or to please the palate. Those with deranged minds have killed and consumed innocents in ways so vile that cannibalism is currently seen as the most grotesque and uncivilized of human actions. But there are litanies of things man has done to others of his own kind that outweigh the act of ingesting the flesh of another human being. One might start with heinous methods of killing or horrendous tortures perfected and practiced by many peoples of the world over the course of thousands of years. History books are full of incidents of entire villages being annihilated by invaders—every man, woman and child, their bodies gutted, torn and left to rot to be scavenged by animals. When set up against the mass slaughters of countless wars perpetrated by *civilized* leaders, primitive tribes that raided and swiftly killed an enemy out of revenge and then dined upon his flesh appear as less violent. While a tribal conflict may take a handful of lives, the great and small wars of history have cut short the lives of billions.

In war, the aim is to annihilate or overcome an enemy in order to gain or maintain that which you desire while upholding the beliefs of your society, whereas cannibalism is performed for reasons of survival, revenge, ritual mourning, religious realization or culinary satisfaction. An editor asked, "So: what's the difference?"

A salient question whose answer is slim to none.

History in no way absolves the practice of cannibalism, but it does demand a review of this multifaceted subject. Once again, it is back to the four Fs: flee, fight, feed and fornicate—instincts that function within all living organisms, including humans, in a natural and continual quest for self-preservation. Fear and aggression are built into the system, part of the flee or fight response, but with our highly evolved, complex brains we have the capacity to hold the first two Fs in check, thus allowing instinctual reactions to surface only in times of real peril. Unfortunately, the Hitlers of yesteryear and today are masters at manipulating the first and second Fs of their followers, bending natural instincts into weapons against those they perceive or claim as enemies.

We refer to the curbing of the first two Fs as "being civilized," but civilizations expect individuals to obey the laws of the state while standing ready to defend their civilization with their lives. The process makes perfect sense. If a people should refuse to band together to protect their society by fighting those who would annihilate it, then they will become a people that no longer exist. Fight or die. There have always been those who want what others possess, be it land, riches or eligible women. Today the main quest is for power, i.e., control of resources, land and, to a lesser degree, women—things are still pretty much the same.

Books call out from crowded shelves attesting to human intelligence, a thing called a conscience—a Houdini that can disappear in a nanosecond—and most profound, a soul; spirit, essence, psyche. The ubiquitous nature of the cannibal's concept of a person's soul being destroyed, or assisted into the next world, opens volumes of thought. Can a person's conscience be molded by societal memes? Do "souls" survive death?

Remember the vicious "ants" that drove the Australian Aborigines out onto the open oceans, away from their original home? Today, if you set sail in search of new lands all you would find would be more ants. Dr. Paul R. Ehrlich, in his book *The Population Bomb*, claimed the "optimal population size" of the world to be two billion. His estimate may be low, but one need not be a genius to realize that there are too many of us. At present, we stand at 6.4 billion and growing.

Still, we are a unique species. No other animal survives pole to pole, and no other animal eats as wide an array of foodstuffs as humans. As omnivorous creatures we have gathered protein for millions of years, risking our lives (until recently) in order to feed our bodies. With the nutrients found in protein, coupled with the thought-provoking dexterity of our upper limbs and our upright stance, our brains expanded greatly in size and function; in that we also stand unique. We are amazing creatures with brains that can outthink all others . . . on this planet at least. We think and love, dance and compute, and most can finagle themselves into and out of the most difficult of situations. Add to that our natural curiosity, which surpasses that of any feline. We build skyscrapers and tenements, land computer-driven workhorses onto the surface of Mars, and gas millions in chambers built for the task. We transplant hearts and grow poppies that will destroy the lives of millions. We love music, art and any form that stirs our emotions, of which we have more than any other species on Earth. We cry from an abundance of joy; we cry in recognition of someone else's accomplishment; we cry in pain over our own doings; and we cry most when we lose someone to the inevitable—death. We kill each other, enslave one another and practice genocide. Within our ranks exist minds that navigate the universe while others peer into atoms and particles in an effort to find the source: What is? What isn't? There are gangs of youths for which life has no meaning and others for whom every moment of life is precious. At the moment there are too many of us on this little blue-mottled planet we call Earth; she is struggling beneath our weight and our killing ways. There are still wars—many of them—people who wish to overwhelm and destroy others, people who would kill any and all in order to rule, to gain the treasure of a land, or simply to be top dog and rule the minds of the masses. Ever-expanding populations facilitate all such endeavors.

If you place cannibalism, murder, genocide, burning people at the stake, pulling live victims limb from limb with the strength of horses, serial killers and other niceties into a bin marked "bad," then cannibalism comes out standing on the "dark" side of the human condition.

But if you offer your body, or the bodies of others, for ritual sacrifice and consumption to honor your god so the sun will continue to rise and sustain life on planet Earth, and you believe with all your heart and mind that through acts of sacrifice and cannibalism you, along with all those sacrificed, will not only save life on Earth but be at one with your god—do your actions fall into the "bad" bin? A bin marked religion? How about societal memes?

If you and others survive a plane crash high on an Andean mountaintop and the only way of surviving is to eat of the dead, should your actions be relegated to the "bad" bin? You killed no one, you asked your god for guidance and proceeded to do that which you did not want to do. And after doing that which you did not want to do, you gave thanks to your god for providing you with the means of survival. "Good"? "Bad"? Or simple necessity?

If your mother, grandmother and all your other grandmothers going back thousands of years, cooked and ate the placenta following the birth of every child so as to replenish their tired bodies and insure future fecundity, would you grow up to do the same? "Good" or "bad"?

If a warrior kills an enemy and the custom of his people is to cut out the heart of the fallen enemy and eat it—into which bin will you throw the remains?

And when hunger strikes and you take to eating your dead as a way to honor the deceased while gaining much needed protein, fat, vitamins and minerals, does the practice make you a horrid, bad people? Or if your people process their grief over the death of a loved one through ritual cannibalism where no part of the body is wasted, do your actions emanate from basic survival instincts or the need for societal acceptance? Or, do you simply belong to the world's most ingenious species? None? Or all of the above?

Cannibalism is not a simple matter, but a complex and multifaceted subject that can tip either end of the moral scale, a sometime custom or singular event that has been with us from the beginning. And while cannibalism continues to be practiced throughout the animal kingdom, it has—for the most part—been tossed out of the human closet.

History, in concert with cultural studies, shows that non-survival cannibalism has been encapsulated within the protective covering of belief systems that are expressed through customs that often change enough through time to obscure the original circumstances that first prompted the practice.

Again, it is all about belief. Belief systems bind people to the group in which they live and few have the nerve to step away from home plate. Some 30 years ago, I read a sterling article written by a doctoral student who journeyed into the Deep South to obtain firsthand information for his dissertation. His quest was to understand how a group of human beings could lynch a man without someone yelling, "Stop!" I will never forget his frankness as he described his utter horror when he found himself being helplessly bound up and manipulated by the mood and emotions of the crowd. His astonishment as some part of his brain watched in complete disgust as he joined the jeering throng and began to shout, "Lynch him. Lynch him. Lynch him." Today, we have a better understanding of crowd mentality, of emotional states that can be manipulated by a knowing leader when large numbers of people are massed together. Marauding, warring, egotistical rulers of the past understood crowd psychology, as do evangelical preachers, rock stars and leaders—good and maniacal—of today.

With all the knowledge humans have amassed, few have the mental and emotional wherewithal to resist the customs of their society, family or religion. The student who failed himself in the midst of a lynch mob had a brave heart; he had the courage to confess his experience, which changed his life as it imbued him with knowledge about people and himself. Understanding the power of crowd psychology allows for an understanding as to how an individual can lose his uniqueness and why ostracism, or expulsion from a group, is so powerful. To be ejected from your group is to die an emotional, and sometimes physical, death. Gang leaders know this fact and work with it. When the world was younger, and we with it, total rejection, as opposed to outright killing, probably did more to hold a group fast to its leader's rules than anything else. Where would you go? Hyenas or saber-toothed cats would make quick work of a person alone; the group was everything, the individual, nothing. To a lesser degree this psychological reality remains a part of the human condition, thus is the individual linked to their society.

Individuals are taught according to the beliefs of those who raise them. If you are taught to be a warrior, to have courage and gain your manhood through slaughter, you will strive towards those ends. Today, children around the world are being taught to hate Americans or Jews or those across the border or in the next valley or alley. Hatred emanates from fear, and hatred provokes aggression. It is an age-old problem that will not go away in a crowded world.

It is time we take stock, count our numbers and begin to plan and sacrifice; not others of our own kind, or animals in lieu of, but sacrifice in the form of wise choices that will benefit humankind and the world at large by bringing our numbers into balance with the health and holding capacity of our planet. Wouldn't it be nice if people didn't have to go to bed hungry, or live in desert lands that recently sported thick rain forests full of biota that once offered cures for multiple diseases—cures that have been lost forever?

Once more, it all goes back to programming. If you had been born in a jungle so deep that the only other people you ever came in contact with were those of your group, and your parents taught you to hunt and forage and how to be a woman or a warrior, that is all you would know. And if the men of your tribe raided the village across the mountain and killed a man and brought his body home to roast and devour, you would be in complete acceptance of the practice. And should you be a young boy, you would dream of your first kill and the taking of the prize.

It can be read that my Viking ancestors were dirty, mean-spirited cannibals who raped, pillaged and plundered. The judgments, for the most part, are true. I do not know just how dirty they were, but I know they built the town of York in Northern England and put the latrine right in the heart of town—nice town, lousy decision.

To go "a-Viking" was to go pirating, but when those independent vagabonds were not pirating, they were trading goods in faraway places, sitting upon thrones across the channel, building seafaring vessels of astonishing design and beauty, and giving us the word "law," which came about from their fine administrative skills as they set up, or took over, one town after another by establishing Danelaw.

Aside from dining on their own people, or on enemies once in awhile, the Vikings traveled the seas with impunity and courage, reaching the North American continent hundreds of years before Christopher Columbus was born. They also bore generations whose genes led to minds such as that of Niels Bohr (1885–1962; Danish Nobel Prize winner in 1922 for his discovery of the hydrogen atom), and to societies that today are among the most educated, gentle and peaceful on Earth.

What our ancestors did or did not do has little to do with what is possible for us at present.

As a species we have disgraced ourselves in every conceivable way, but we have also reached for the stars and performed feats unimaginable a mere hundred years ago. We are artists, choreographers and musicians.

We are good at mothering and achieving; we conceive ideas and give them birth; we pass on knowledge from one generation to the next. We are prodigious warriors. As survivors we are supreme. We are many things, and we all carry genes from ancient ancestors that indicate that they practiced some form of cannibalism.

We no longer burn people at the stake and, for the most part, we do not consume one another, but cannibalism does happen, even today, even in this "modern" world of ours.

The fact that we possess an unimaginable capacity for inflicting pain and death upon those of our own kind attests to the fact that our ancestors survived some very rough times during our long walk into the present. Only an existence that constantly threatened life could have molded minds ever ready to respond to danger, be it a hungry cat or crocodile or a pack of huge hyenas, a lurking snake or one of our own kind. Only repeated violence put upon an individual, a group, a band or a people could elicit the same in return, and with survival of the fittest ruling the day, it had to be the most vicious and devious of our ancestors who stayed the course— or did some manage to run away and hide from those more treacherous than they?

The ancient flee-or-fight response still produces fear and rage as our adrenals pump chemicals to fuel a reaction that may be violent, yet only creatures who lived in closely bound groups could come away with emotions and abilities such as long-term parenting, pride, leadership, sadness, grief, caring, laughing, dancing, altruism, friendship and the relatively new acquisition, love.

Where does the angelic side of us come from? Do the beautiful qualities of humankind confirm the true nature of *Homo sapiens*? The human ability to laugh, play, love, imagine, dream, create, persevere, smile through our tears and do for others are but a sampling of what makes us special. Look at us! We climb mountains, visit the bottoms of oceans, walk the surface of the moon and paint pictures and compose music that touch the hearts of all who see and hear. How can an organism be so loathsome on one hand and so magnificent on the other? That is the question. Those who study us say we need the beautiful side so as to ingratiate others of our own kind. Without emotional bonds, there would be no cohesion within groups; each person would be an individual, alone and vulnerable. Individuals need their family, band or society; they need to belong, as belonging equates with safety—as in the old safety in numbers bit. But what served us well in times past may work to undo us today. Without means of preventing pregnancy, females of the past produced more children than they could feed and care for during their years of fecundity. But few of their issue reached the age of maturity, and in cases where a child was born deformed or a mother was overburdened, newborns were let go so that others could survive, including the mother. Today, the accepted of yesterday is deemed unlawful and unthinkable, but nature, being a continuum, knows not.

The times of our common past life must have been dangerous enough to demand that our bodies produce an excess of offspring so that a stabilizing number would mature to continue our line. In all of Nature's organisms we see fecundity geared to the number of infants who will be taken by predators or disease. The crocodile lays up to 50 eggs, but only 1 in 10 hatchlings makes it through the first weeks, with a majority of survivors losing out prior to maturity. We, in our more primitive forms, also would have conformed naturally to nature's ways. Nature always has survival in mind. If an organism bears 50 young and all 50 are devoured by predators, nature will allow for the bearing of 54 and on up until a balance in population is achieved. But we are not crocodiles, and over time we learned how to outsmart the predators—most of the time—be they wild animals, other humans, microbes or diseases. Such dangers still take their toll, but we have developed advanced strategies for survival, allowing our numbers to grow exponentially. That leaves us with bodies performing in ancient ways, living in a world where we have tipped nature's scales and spilled the beans. Six billion plus people are too many for planet Earth. Her resources, both flora and fauna, are being depleted, and we have even devised ways to worsen the weather. Many will soon be without enough potable water, uncontrollable diseases are a real threat and changing weather patterns will defeat farmers. I know, we always have each other, but if the other guy dies of a communicable disease, the handling of his body could be lethal and now you are really in a fix! Cannibalism is rarely the right answer. If we do not learn from our past, if we fail to understand the possibilities, both good and bad, we will follow the words of a thousand historians, philosophers and poets and repeat ourselves over and over again until we are gone. . . . How sad it would be if we loved ourselves to death.

The challenges can be met and the results could be magnificent, but it will not be easy—seems we are still living in rough times.

Sounds pretty scary, and some may scoff at the picture, especially those living in safe and peaceful places. Nevertheless, the road humans have walked in order to get us to where we are today has been littered with wars, plagues and repression—and yes, cannibalism. Such times have strength-ened our species, making us the most adaptable and resilient of all. Over the course of many millions of years we have grown and prospered as op-posed to withering and falling from the tree of life. We should stand proud of our ingenuity, creativeness and forethought. Which roads we choose to follow into the future will set our fate. How we rule ourselves, how we treat our environment and each other will write our future. Our minds have the ability to imagine and execute myriad outcomes. Will greed and fear-filled hatred bring forth an undesired end? Will peoples of the earth work from a place of comprehension and subject themselves to rules that will allow for a more balanced, peaceful world? It is up to us, each of us, all of us—the reptilian survivor within will not allow one group to succeed over the rest. But we two-legged-featherless ones, the ones with the big brains—and that thing we call a conscience—could do it. Everything is possible.

So, here we are, all dressed up in our dirty underwear, eyes set on the horizon (or the refrigerator), our minds composed of the past, present and dreams of a future that is ours to write.

I am going to end this gustatorial examination of the human spe-cies with the words of another. I had not intended such, but that is how it is. There are moments in life that present you with gifts of recognition, when someone else presents your thoughts in a nutshell.

After reading about an exhibit of Lee Bontecou's art and sculpture, I could hardly wait to get to the Museum of Contemporary Art in Chicago. Bontecou is an exceptional artist who made her mark in the 1960s, then, in the mid-'70s, wrote off New York, agents, critics and gallery owners and moved to Pennsylvania where she set up a studio, enjoyed her family and taught art. Through it all she never stopped producing magical and meaningful masterpieces, and like a fine wine she matured, her most recent pieces taking hold of one's soul as they mesmerize the mind with their haunting appeal. I see some of her new hanging sculptures as phantasmagorical galaxies, some with white "holes," as opposed to black, at their centers. My favorite has taut, muslin sails that hasten it on its course through the universe. Much of Bontecou's art speaks to me viscerally; the taut, muslin sails will live with me the rest of my days.

As my husband and I moved from one work of Bontecou's to the next, we took note that every piece, regardless of medium, was listed "untitled." Art—and life—is as the viewer sees it, and each viewer brings with him a lifetime of experiences. We all see, hear and feel in unique ways. Biologically we are much the same, but as individuals we are unique unto ourselves. And while groups of us live in accordance with the societal memes of our surroundings, the collective *we* is capable of all possibilities inherent within the form. Emotional experiences mark our individual lives—the more meaningful, the bigger the stain. I have lost many of my closest family to death. During and following periods of grief, I began to see and hear on a seemingly different level. Art and music now mean more to me, seeing the bright eyes of a child fills me with joy, and the horrors of life reflect differently upon my visual screen.

Each of us views all things in accordance with the experiences we have known, thus we are changed daily and are constantly in the act of becoming. So too were our ancestors. All of us come from a long background full of danger and beauty, times of hardship and ease, eras of brutality and times of peace. We are complex and versatile, and our will to live is so intense that humans have survived all odds and somehow, some way, made it into the present.

For years I researched the brutal, the wicked, the proud, the greedy, the mean and the awful. In amongst the wretchedness I found courage, honor, fear, failures, beliefs and customs; people wise in the ways of their environment and people pushed to extremes by the presence of death and/or starvation. We come in many sizes, shapes and colors. We believe many things and live our lives accordingly, often times in opposition to others.

In Lee Bontecou I found a kindred spirit. Her words allow us to see the place from which her magnificent art emanates.

> The natural world and its visual wonders and horrors—
> man-made devices with their mind-boggling engineering
> feats and destructive abominations, elusive human nature
> and its multiple ramifications—from the sublime to unbe-
> lievable abhorrences—to me are all one.
>
> Lee Bontecou 2003

What *is*, is. What *was*, was. What *will be* is up to us.
It is time we tame the beast.

NOTES

Foreword
1. *Star Food* (Jackson, WY: Teton Publishing House, 1981).

Introduction
1. April 11, 2003: Collinge and Mead of University College, London, announced in the journal *Science* their findings regarding genetic markers that protect against prion diseases and speak to a long history of cannibalism within the human species. (See Chapter 5: "Cannibalism, Disease and Genetics")

Chapter One
1. Some accounts of the Donner Party state that when first marooned, much of the livestock that had been shepherded into the Sierras ran off prior to the onset of starvation.
2. Of the Andean plane crash survivors, one woman refused to eat of the dead. She was nearing death from starvation when the avalanche that killed nine crashed through the open back of the torn fuselage and ended her life.

Chapter Two
1. Tim D. White, *Prehistoric Cannibalism at Mancos 5MTUMR-2346* (New Jersey: Princeton Press, 1992).

Chapter Three
1. H. G. Wells, *The Outline of History: Being a Plain History of Life and Mankind*, 4th ed., vol. 2 (New York: P.F.Collier & Son Company, 1922), 385–386.

Chapter Five

1. Auguste Escoffier, *The Escoffier Cookbook* (New York: Crown Publishers, 1969).
2. In 1961, Australian doctor Michael Alpers joined Dr. Daniel Carlton Gajdusek, the first doctor of modern medicine to work with the Fore. Together, they worked to understand the deadly disease known as "kuru."

Chapter Six

1. T. Athol Joyce and N. W. Thomas, *Women of All Nations*.

Chapter Seven

1. 2 Kings 6:25–30 (King James Version).
2. Lamentations 4:3–5, 9–10 (Masoretic Text).
3. Deuteronomy 28: 53, 56–57 (KJV).
4. For further reading see: Lev. 26:29, Jer. 19:9, Ezek. 5:10, Mic. 3:3, Deut. 28:47 and 53–59
5. Molech is a version of the ancient word *melech*, "king," who was one of three sun gods: "The worship of Molech involved the sacrifice of children. Primitive men felt that the dearer and more loved the object sacrificed to a god, the more impressed the god would be and the more apt to answer the prayer. In times of dire distress, then, children would be sacrificed, even perhaps the child of the king." *Asimov's Guide to the Bible*, Isaac Asimov (2 vols., New York: Doubleday, 1968–1969; New York: Wings Books, 1981). Citations are to the Wings Books edition.
6. John 6:47–59 (KJV).

Chapter Eight

1. Various books, articles and writings on the Inquisition offer different dates for its beginning, each set forth in accordance with the historical occurrence that is referenced.

    If many volumes are perused on the subject the reader will find that many events coalesced over time into a groundswell of reprehensible actions that formed the basis for the Inquisition.

2. Adriaan J. Barnouw, *The Fantasy of Pieter Brueghel* (New York: Lear, 1947).

Chapter Nine

1. K. Schmidt, "Cultural Traces of a Vital Fluid." Review of *Blood: Perspectives on Art, Power, Politics and Pathology*, ed. J. P. Bradburne.
2. Terrazas, *National Geographic* (October 2003): 91
3. Durán, *Book of the Gods and Rites and the Ancient Calendar*, trans. Doris Heyden and Fernando Horcasitas (Norman: University of Oklahoma Press, 1971), 191.

Chapter Eleven

1. T. Athol Joyce and N. W. Thomas, *Women of All Nations*.

Chapter Twelve

1. Alexandra Fuller, *Don't Let's Go to the Dogs Tonight: An African Childhood* (New York: Random House, 2003), 35.
2. "Special Tribune Report: The Bride Was 7," *Chicago Tribune*, December 12–13, 2004.

Chapter Thirteen

1. *Grimm's Tales* as printed in the 1937 edition of the Harvard Classics copyrighted by P.F. Collier and Son, 1906
2. Two hearths dated to 1.5 million years have been confirmed in Africa by paleoanthropologist Jack Harris.
3. Sigmund Freud, *Totem and Taboo* (New York: Random House, 1946).

Chapter Fourteen

1. James Bradley, *Flyboys: A True Story of Courage* (New York: Little, Brown & Co., 2003).

2. Jean-Luis Brunaux, "Gallic Blood-Excavations of Sanctuaries in Northern France Support Ancient Literary Accounts of Violent Gallic Rituals," *Archaeology* (March/April 2001).
3. James Bradley, *Flyboys*.

Chapter Fifteen

1. Kerry M. Zubrinich, "Asmat Cosmology and the Practice of Cannibalism," in *The Anthropology of Cannibalism*, ed. Laurence R. Goldman (Westport, CT: Bergin and Garvey, 1999).
2. Tobias Schneebaum knew the song of decapitation, and on film shows a thin, oval, teardrop-shaped stone tool sharply pointed at one end. It is given as a bride price and was used to open a hole in the base of the skull of a victim so as to shake out the brains for consumption while maintaining the overall integrity of the skull so it could be retained as a trophy.
3. The film *Keep the River on Your Right* refers to Tobias's adopted tribe as the Amarekaire as opposed to the book's Akaramas.
4. Tobias Schneebaum, *Keep the River on Your Right* (New York: Grove Press, 1969), 49.

Chapter Sixteen

1. Nels Akerlund and Joe Glickman, *Our Wisconsin River* (Rockford, IL: Pamacheyon Publishing, 1997), 21.

Chapter Seventeen

1. Key Ray Chong, *Cannibalism in China*.
2. *The Elegies of Chu*, 200 A.D. anthology of southern poets. Quoted from *The Songs of the South: An Anthology of Ancient Chinese Poems by Qu Yuan and Other Poets*, translated by David Hawkes (New York: Penguin Books, 1985), 224.
3. Zheng Yi, *Scarlet Memorial: Tales of Cannibalism in Modern China*, trans. and ed. T. P. Sym (Boulder, CO: Westview Press, 1996), 131.

Chapter Eighteen

1. Nigel Davies, *Human Sacrifice* (New York: William Morrow & Co., 1981).
2. *Le Monde*, Paris, France, February 27, 2003.
3. J. Sterling Kingsley and Edward Breck, *Nature's Wonderland, or Short Talks on Natural History for Young and Old*, vol. 4 (New York: F. R. Niglutsch, 1890), 151.

BIBLIOGRAPHY

Adovasio, J. M., and J. Page. *The First Americans*. New York: The Modern Library, 2003.

Afro News. "Pygmies of Central Africa Still 'Seen as Sub-Human.'" June 22, 2003.

Akerlund, N., and J. Glickman. *Our Wisconsin River: Border to Border*. Rockford, IL: Pamacheyon Publishing, 1997.

Alcock, J. *Animal Behavior*. Sunderland, MA: Sinauer Associates, 1998.

Allman, J. M. *Evolving Brains*. New York: Scientific American Library, 1999.

Appenzeller, T., and D. R. Dimick. "Global Warming: Signs of Earth." *National Geographic*, September 2004.

Arens, W. *The Man-Eating Myth*. New York: Oxford University Press, 1979.

Arsuaga, J. L. *The Neanderthal's Necklace*. New York. Four Walls, Eight Windows, 2002.

Arsuaga, J. L., B. de Castro, and E. Carbonell. *Atapuerca: Un Millón de Años de Historia*. Spain: Plot Ediciones/Editorial Complutense, 1998.

Asimov, I. *Asimov's Guide to the Bible*. New York: Wings Books, 1969.

Askenasy, H. *Cannibalism: From Sacrifice to Survival*. New York: Prometheus Books, 1994.

Associated Press. "U.N.: Congolese Rebels Practicing Cannibalism." FoxNews. com. January 8, 2003. http://www.foxnews.com/story/0, 2933,74950,00.html.

Associated Press. "U.N. Investigators Report on Congolese Acts of Cannibalism." UN Wire, January 8, 2003.

Associated Press. "Congo Kinshasa." *Afro News*, June 22, 2003.

Associated Press. " Congo." *Chicago Tribune*, March 17, 2005.

Barnouw, A. J. *The Fantasy of Pieter Brueghel*. New York: Lear, 1947.

Bates, D. *The Passing of the Aborigines*. Melbourne, Australia: Oxford University Press, 1944.

Begg, A. C., and N. C. Begg. *James Cook and New Zealand*. Wellington, New Zealand: A. R. Shearer, 1970.

Bergner, D. "The Most Unconventional Weapon." *New York Times Magazine*, October 26, 2003.

Berthoff, A. E. "Susanne K. Langer and 'the Odyssey of the Mind.'" *Semiotica* 128, no. 1–2 (2000): 1–34.

Billard, J. B., ed. *The World of the American Indian*. Washington DC: National Geographic, 1974.

Bjerre, J. *The Last Cannibals*. New York: William Morrow & Co., 1957.

Bloom, S. *In Praise of Primates*. Germany: Konemann, 1999.

Bocquet-Appel, J. P., and J. L. Arsuaga. "Probable Catastrophic Mortality of the Atapuerca (SH) and Krapina Hominid Samples." In *Humanity from African Naissance to Coming Millennia*, ed. P. V. Tobias, M. A. Raath, J. Moggi-Cecchi, and G. A. Doyle. Florence, Italy: Firenze University Press, 2001.

Bollingen Foundation. *African Folktales and Sculpture*. New York: Bollingen Foundation Inc., 1964.

Bradley, J. *Flyboys*. New York: Little, Brown & Co., 2003.

Brandon, W. *The American Heritage Book of Indians*. New York: Simon & Schuster, 1961.

Breeden, S. "The First Australians." *National Geographic*, February 1988.

Breuil, H., and R. Lantier. *The Men of the Old Stone Age*. London, England: George G. Harrap & Co., 1965. First published 1959.

Britton, M. *Jungle Journey*. New York: Pantheon, 1959.

Brongersma, L. D., and G. F. Venema. *To the Mountains of the Stars*. New York: Doubleday, 1963.

Brown, H. E., P. S. Brown, K. Best, and K. Hillyer. *The Virginia City Cook Book*. Los Angeles: Ward Ritchie Press, 1953.

Burns, E. *The Sex Lives of Wild Animals: A North American Study*. New York: Rinehart & Co., 1953.

Campbell, J. *The Flight of the Wild Gander*. Chicago: Regnery Gateway, 1951.

———. *The Masks of God*. Vol. 1, *Primitive Mythology*. New York: Viking Press, 1959.

———. *The Masks of God*. Vol. 2, *Oriental Mythology*. New York: Viking Press, 1962.

———. *Mythos*. Hosted by Susan Sarandon. First aired in 1997.

———. *Joseph Campbell and the Power of Myth*. VHS. With Bill Moyers. Mystic Fire Video, 2001.

Capps, B. *The Indians: The Old West*. New York: Time-Life Books, 1973.

Carrasco, D. *City of Sacrifice: The Aztec Empire and the Role of Violence in Civilization*. Boston: Beacon Press, 1999.

Cartwright, F. F. *Disease and History*. New York: Barnes and Noble Books, 1972.

Catlin, G. *North American Indians*. 2 vols. New York: Dover Publications, 1973.

Ceram, C. W. *Gods, Graves and Scholars*. New York: Bantam, 1980. Originally printed in 1949.

Chagnon, N. A. *Yanomamo*. New York: HBJ Publishers, 1992.

Chicago Tribune. "Haggis Fans Glad Health Officials' Gut Feeling Proves False." November 21, 2002.

Chicago Tribune. "231 Mutilated bodies found in town." May 21, 2003.

Chicago Tribune. "SARS Link Found in 3 Mammals." May 24, 2003.

Chicago Tribune. "SARS Alert Hasn't Dulled Exotic Tastes." June 1, 2003.

Chinese Academy of Sciences. *Atlas of Primative Man in China*. China: Institute of Vertebrate Paleontology and Paleoanthropology, Science Press, 1980.

Chong, K. R. *Cannibalism in China*. Wakefield, NH: Longwood Academic, 1990.

Collinge, J., S. Mead, M. P. H. Stumpf, J. Whitfield, J. A. Beck, M. Poulter, T. Campbell, J. B. Uphill, D. Goldstein, M. Alpers, and E. M. C. Fisher. "Balancing Selection at the Prion Protein Gene Consistent with Prehistoric Kurulike Epidemics." *Science* 300, no. 5619 (April 25, 2003), 640–3.

Conklin, B. A. *Consuming Grief: Compassionate Cannibalism in an Amazonian Society*. Austin, TX: University of Texas Press, 2001.

Cooke, J. *Cannibals, Cows & the CJD Catastrophe*. Australia: Random House, 1998.

Damasio, A. R. *Descartes' Error*. New York: Grosset/Putnam, 1994.

Darwin, C. R. *The Voyage of the Beagle*. New York: Bantam, 1958.

———. *The Origin of Species*. New York: Gramercy Books, 1979.

Davies, N. *Human Sacrifice*. New York: William Morrow & Co., 1981.

Deacon, T. W. *The Symbolic Species*. New York: W.W. Norton & Co., 1997.

Dempsey, H. A. *History in Their Blood: The Indian Portraits of Nicholas de Grandmaison*. Vancouver/Toronto: Douglas & McIntyre, 1982.

Denham, T. P., S. G. Haberle, C. Lentfer, R. Fullagar, J. Field, M. Therin, N. Porch, and B. Winsborough. "Origins of Agriculture at Kuk Swamp in the Highlands of New Guinea." *Science* 301, no. 5630 (July 11, 2003): 189.

Dening, S. *The Mythology of Sex*. England and New York: Labyrinth Publishing Ltd. and Simon & Schuster, 1996.

De Waal, F. *Chimpanzee Politics*. New York: Harper & Row, 1989.

De Waal, F. B. M., and F. Lanting. *Bonobo: The Forgotten Ape*. Berkeley and Los Angeles: University of California Press, 1997.

Dickeman, M. "Concepts and Classification in the Study of Human Infanticide: Sectional Introduction and Some Cautionary Notes." In *Infanticide: Comparative and Evolutionary Perspectives*, ed. G. Hausfater and S. Hrdy, 440. New York: Aldine, 1984.

Dillehay, T. D. *The Settlement of the Americas*. New York: Basic Books, 2000.

Dolmach, T., ed. *Information Please Almanac*. New York: Simon & Schuster, 1981.

Ebbutt, M. I. *The British Myths and Legends*. London: Senate, 1994. First published 1910 by George G. Harrap & Co.

Edwards, M. "Marco Polo Part III Journey Home." *National Geographic*, July 2001.

Ehrman, B. D. *Lost Christianities: The Battles for Scripture and the Faiths We Never Knew*. New York: Oxford University Press, 2003.

Encyclopedia Americana. 30 vols. New York: Grolier, 1999.

Escoffier, A. *The Escoffier Cookbook*. New York: Crown, 1969.

Fagan, B. M. *The Rape of the Nile*. New York: Scribner's Sons, 1975.

———. *World Prehistory*. New York: Little, Brown & Co., 1977.

———. *People of the Earth*. New York: Little, Brown & Co., 1989.

———. *Floods, Famines and Emperors*. New York: Basic Books, 1999.

Fernandez-Armesto, F. *Near a Thousand Tables*. New York: Free Press, 2002.

———. *Humankind*. Oxford, New York: Oxford University Press, 2004.

Figuier, L. *The Human Race*. New York: Appleton & Co., 1872.

Fontanel, B., and C. Harcourt. *Babies Celebrated*. New York: Harry N. Abrams, 1998.

Fuller, A., *Don't Let's Go to the Dogs Tonight: An African Childhood*. New York: Random House, 2003.

Galdikas, B. M. F. *Reflections of Eden*. New York: Little, Brown & Co., 1995.

Geertz, C. *The Interpretation of Cultures: Selected Essays*. New York: Basic Books, 1973.

Goodall, J. *My Friends the Wild Chimpanzees*. Washington DC: National Geographic Society, 1967.

——. *The Chimpanzees of Gombe*. Boston: Harvard University Press, 1986.

Gravell, K. *Fiji's Times: A History of Fiji*. 3 vols. Fiji: Fiji Times Print, 1979.

Gregor, R. A., and D. Tuzin. *Gender in Amazonia and Melanesia*. Berkeley and Los Angeles: University of California Press, 2001.

Grimm, J., and W. Grimm. *Folk-Lore and Fable*. Vol. 17. New York: Harvard Classics, 1937.

Griswold, E. "The Truth Behind the Cannibals of Congo." *The Independent* (UK), March 26, 2004.

Gruzinski, S. *The Aztecs: Rise and Fall of an Empire*. New York: Harry N. Abrams, 1992.

Guardian Unlimited. "Congolese Rebels in Cannibal Atrocities." Special Reports, January 16, 2003.

Harris, M. *Cannibal Kings*. New York: Random House, 1991.

Hausfater, G., and S. Hrdy, eds. *Infanticide: Comparative and Evolutionary Perspectives*. New York: Aldine, 1984.

Haviland, W. A. *Anthropology*. 8th ed. Fort Worth: Harcourt Brace College Publishers, 1996.

Hesselt van Dinter, M. *Tribal Tattoo Designs*. Boston: Shambhala, 2000.

Hessler, P. "The New Story of China's Ancient Past." *National Geographic*, July 2003.

Holloway, R., D. Broadfield, and M. Yuan. *The Human Fossil Record*. Vol. 3, *Brain Endocasts*. Hoboken, NJ: Wiley-Liss, 2004.

Itzkoff, S. W. *The Form of Man*. Asheville, MA: Paideia, 1983.

Jahn, R. G., and B.J. Dunne. *Margins of Reality*. New York: HBJ Publishers, 1987.

Johanson, D., and B. Edgar. *From Lucy to Language*. New York: Simon & Schuster, 1996.

Johnson, M. *Cannibal Land*. Boston and New York: Riverside Press, 1921.

Jones, S., and B. M. Eagle. *Simply Living*. Novato, CA: New World Library, 1999.

Joyce, T. A., and N. W. Thomas, eds. *Women of All Nations*. New York: Metro Publications, 1942.

Kahn, A. R. *Mind Shapes: Understanding the Differences in Thinking and Communication*. St. Paul, MN: Paragon House, 2005.

Kahn, A. R., and K. A. Radcliffe. "The Masters We Serve: The Gene and the Meme in Human Affairs." *International Journal on World Peace* 21, no. 1 (March 2004): 61–88.

Kane, J. *Savages*. New York: Knopf, 1995.

Katz, F. *Ancient American Civilizations*. London: Weidenfeld and Nicolson, 1969.

Keep the River on Your Right: A Modern Cannibal Tale. DVD. New Video Group, 2002.

Kingsley, J. S., and E. Breck. *Nature's Wonderland, or Short Talks on Natural History for Young and Old*. Vol. 4. New York: F. R. Niglutsch, 1890.

Klein, R. G. *The Human Career*. Chicago: University of Chicago Press, 1989.

Konrad, G., and U. Konrad, eds. *Asmat: Myth and Ritual*. Venice, Italy: Erizzo Editrice, 1996.

Krieger, M. *Conversations with the Cannibals*. New Jersey: Ecco Press, 1994.

Kroeber, T. *Ishi in Two Worlds*. Berkeley: University of California Press, 1961.

Langer, S. K. *Mind: An Essay on Human Feelings*. New York: John Hopkins University Press, 1967.

Leahy, M. J. *Exploration into Highland New Guinea*. Tuscaloosa and London: University of Alabama Press, 1991. Originally published 1937.

Leakey, R., and R. Lewin. *Origins*. New York: E. P. Dutton, 1977.

LeBlanc, S. A., and K. E. Regester. *Constant Battles: The Myth of the Peaceful, Noble Savage*. New York: St. Martin's Press, 2003.

Le Monde. "Congo Pygmies Victims of Cannibalism." February 27, 2003.

Leroi-Gourhan, A. *The Hunters of Prehistory*. New York: Atheneum, 1989.

Levi-Strauss, C. *Tristes Tropiques*. Translated by John and Doreen Weightman. New York: Penguin Books, 1992. First published 1974.

Lewin, R. *In the Age of Mankind*. Washington DC: Smithsonian Books, 1988.

———. *Patterns in Evolution*. New York: Scientific American Library, 1996.

Lindsay, C., and R. Schefold. *Mentawai Shaman: Keeper of the Rain Forest*. New York: Aperture Book, 1988.

Livingston, A. D., and H. Livingston. *Edible Plants and Animals*. New York: Facts On File, 1993.

Lundberg, F. *The Natural Depravity of Mankind*. New York: Barricade Books Inc., 1994.

Markham, C. *The Incas of Peru*. London: Smith, Elder & Co., 1910.

Marriner, B. *Cannibalism: The Last Taboo*. London: Senate/Random House UK Ltd., 1997.

Marriott, E. *The Lost Tribe*. New York: Henry Holt & Co., 1996.

McPhee, J. *Annals of the Former World*. New York: Farrar, Straus and Giroux, 1981.

Menzel, P., and F. D'Aluisio. *Man Eating Bugs*. Napa, CA: World Book NAPA California, 1998.

Meyer, A. J. P. *Oceanic Art; Ozeanische Kunst; Art Oceanien*. Germany: Konemann, Koln, 1995.

Milanich, J. T. *The Timucua*. Malden, MA: Blackwell Publishers, 1996.

Morris, D. *The Human Sexes*. New York: St. Martin's Press, 1997.

Moser, S. *Ancestral Images: The Iconography of Human Origins*. Ithaca, NY: Cornell University Press, 1998.

Mudrooroo, N. *Aboriginal Mythology*. New York: Aquarian, 1994.

Mytinger, C. *Head Hunting in the Solomon Islands*. New York: McMillan, 1942.

National Geographic Atlas of the World. 5th ed. Washington DC: National Geographic, 1981.

New York Times. "Court Likely to Take Up Congo First." July 17, 2003.

Nitecki, M. H., and D. V. Nitecki. *Origins of Anatomically Modern Humans*. New York: Plenum Press, 1994.

Noble, L. "The Ingestible Corpse: Practices in Cannibalim." Lecture, England, 2003.

Oliver, W. H. *The Story of New Zealand*. London: Faber & Faber, 1960.

Oman, K. K. *The Epic of Qayaq*. Ottawa: Carleton University Press, 1995.

Ornstein, R., and R. Thompson. *The Amazing Brain*. Boston: Houghton & Mifflin, 1984.

Ortiz de Montellano, R. "Aztec Cannibalism." *Science* 200, no. 4342 (May 1978): 611–617.

Parker, K. L. *Australian Legendary Tales*. FLS Books, 2001. Originally published in 1896.

Peoples and Places of the Past: The National Geographic Illustrated Cultural Atlas of the Ancient World. Washington DC: National Geographic, 1983.

Pert, C. B. *Molecules of Emotion*. New York: Scribner, 1997.

Pinker, S. *The Language Instinct*. New York: William Morrow & Co., 1994.

Radin, P., ed. *African Folktales & Sculpture*. New York: Pantheon Books, 1952.

Ratzan, S. G. *The Mad Cow Crisis*. New York: New York University Press, 1998.

Read, C. *Man and His Superstitions*. London: Senate, 1995. First published 1925.

Read, P. P. *Alive*. Philadelphia and New York: J. B. Lippencott, 1974.

Reed, A. W., and A. E. Brougham. *The Concise Maori Handbook*. Wellington, New Zealand: Redd LTD, 1978.

Rees, L. *Horrors in the East: Japan and the Atrocities of World War II*. Cambridge, MA: Da Capo Press, 2001.

Ressler, R. K., and T. Shachtman. *Whoever Fights Monsters*. New York: St. Martin's Press, 1992.

Reynolds, C. R. *American Indian Portraits: From the Wanamaker Expedition of 1913*. Brattleboro, VT: Stephan Greene Press, 1971.

Rhodes, R. *Deadly Feasts*. New York: Simon & Schuster, 1997.

Roach, M. *Stiff: The Curious Lives of Human Cadavers*. New York: W.W. Norton & Co., 2003.

Root, W. *Food*. New York: Simon & Schuster, 1980.

Sale, R. *Fairy Tales and After*. Cambridge: Harvard University Press, 1979.

Sanday, P. R. *Divine Hunger*. New York: Cambridge University Press, 1986.

Sargent, W. *People of the Valley*. New York: Random House, 1974.

Sarno, L. *Song from the Forest*. New York: Houghton Mifflin Co., 1993.

Sempowski, M. L., and M. W. Spence. *Mortuary Practices and Skeletal Remains at Teotihuacan*. Salt Lake: University of Utah Press, 1994.

Schmidt, K. "Cultural Traces of a Vital Fluid." Review of *Blood: Perspectives on Art, Power, Politics and Pathology*, ed. J. P. Bradburne. *Science* 295, no. 5552 (January 2002): 49–50.

Schneebaum, T. *Keep the River on Your Right*. New York: Grove Press, 1969.

Science News. "Troubling Treat, Guam Mystery Disease From Bat Entrée?" May 17, 2003.

Secret Museum of Mankind. New York: Manhattan House, 1941.

Severin, T. *Vanishing Primitive Man*. New York: American Heritage, 1973.

Shreeve, J. *The Neandertal Enigma*. New York: William Morrow & Co., 1995.

Smith, R. W. *Aborigine: Myths and Legends*. London: Senate, 1996. First printed 1930 by George G. Harrap & Co.

Sollas, W. J. *Ancient Hunters and Their Modern Representatives*. London: MacMillan and Co., 1911.

Sprague de Camp, L. *The Ape-Man Within*. New York: Prometheus, 1995.

Stephan, J. J. *The Russian Far East: A History*. Palo Alto, CA: Stanford University Press, 1994.

Stoor, A. *Human Aggression*. New York: Atheneum, 1968.

Suleri, S. *Meatless Days*. Chicago: University of Chicago Press, 1989.

Swisher, C. C., G. H. Curtis, and R. Lewin. *Java Man*. New York: Scribner, 2000.

Talbot, M. *The Holographic Universe*. New York: Harper Collins, 1991.

Tannahill, R. *Flesh and Blood*. New York: Dorset Press, 1975.

Tanner, J. *The Falcon*. New York: Penguin Books, 1994.

Tattersall, I. *The Last Neanderthal*. New York: MacMillan, 1995.

———. *Becoming Human*. New York: Harcourt and Brace, 1998.

Thomas, H. *Human Origins*. New York: Harry N. Abrams, 1994.

Tierney, P. *The Highest Altar*. New York: Penguin Books, 1989.

Tolnay, C. *Hieronymus Bosch*. New York: Morrow, 1966.

Tomkins, S. S. "Script Theory." In *Personality Structure in the Life Course: Essays on Personology in the Murray Tradition*, ed. R. A. Zucker, A. I. Rabin, J. Aronoff, and S. Frank. New York: Springer Publishing, 1992.

Townsend, R. F. *Ancient West Mexico*. Chicago: The Art Institute of Chicago, Thames and Hudson, 1999.

Turner, C., II, and J. Turner. *Man Corn: Cannibalism and Violence in the Prehistoric American Southwest.* Salt Lake: University of Utah Press, 1998.

Vesilind, P. J. "Watery Graves of the Maya." *National Geographic*, October 2003.

Voltaire. *Voltaire's Alphabet of Wit.* Mount Vernon, NY: Peter Pauper Press, 1955.

Vrba, E. S., G. H. Denton, T. C. Partridge, and L. H. Burckle, eds. *Paleoclimate and Evolution.* New Haven: Yale University Press, 1995.

Walker, A., and R. Leakey. *The Nariokotome Homo Erectus Skeleton.* Cambridge, MA: Harvard University Press, 1993.

Walker, B. *The Woman's Encyclopedia of Myths and Secrets.* San Francisco: Harper, 1983.

Wall Street Journal. "Sierra Leone." July 28, 2003.

Webster's New International Dictionary. 2nd ed., unabridged. Springfield, MA: G & C Merriam Co., 1948.

Weisman, A. *The World Without Us.* New York: Thomas Dunne Books/St. Martin's Press, 2007.

Wells, H. G. *The Outline of History: Being a Plain History of Life and Mankind.* 4th ed. Vol 2. New York: P. F. Collier & Son Company, 1922.

Weyer, E., Jr. *Primitive Peoples Today.* Garden City, NY: Doubleday, 1958.

Wheeler, W. F. *Efe Pygmies.* New York: Rizzoli, 2000.

White, T. D. *Prehistoric Cannibalism at Mancos 5MTUMR-2346.* Princeton, NJ: Princeton Press, 1992.

Wilson, E. O. *Sociobiology.* Cambridge and London: The Belknap Press of Harvard University Press, 2000.

Wilson, S. M. *The Emperor's Giraffe.* Boulder, CO: Westview Press, 1999.

Yi, Z. *Scarlet Memorial: Tales of Cannibalism in Modern China.* Translated and edited by T. P. Sym. Boulder, CO: Westview Press, 1996.

Yu, C. "Learned Cannibalism in Chinese." *History* (2003).

Zubrinich, K. M. "Asmat Cosmology and the Practice of Cannibalism." In *The Anthropology of Cannibalism,* ed. L. R. Goldman. Westport, CT: Bergin and Garvey, 1999.

Hundreds of informative articles that offered relevant subject matter help to reinforce the research for *Dinner with a Cannibal*. The following periodicals and news agencies aided me in my task.

Archaeology

Biblical Archaeology

Chicago Tribune

Evolutionary Anthropology

JAMA/Journal of the American Medical Association

Le Monde

National Geographic

Natural History

Nature

New York Times

Odyssey

Science AAAS

Science News

Scientific American

Smithsonian

Time Magazine

Wall Street Journal

1999 *Encyclopedia Americana*

1910 *Encyclopedia Britannica*

INDEX

Books Available from Santa Monica Press

The 99th Monkey
*A Spiritual Journalist's
Misadventures with
Gurus, Messiahs, Sex,
Psychedelics, and
Other Consciousness-
Raising Experiments*
by Eliezer Sobel
312 pages $16.95

**The Bad Driver's
Handbook**
*Hundreds of Simple
Maneuvers to Frustrate,
Annoy, and Endanger
Those Around You*
by Zack Arnstein and
Larry Arnstein
192 pages $12.95

Calculated Risk
*The Extraordinary Life
of Jimmy Doolittle*
by Jonna Doolittle Hoppes
360 pages $24.95

Captured!
*Inside the World of
Celebrity Trials*
by Mona Shafer Edwards
176 pages $24.95

Dinner with a Cannibal
*The Complete History
of Mankind's Oldest Taboo*
by Carole A. Travis-Henikoff
336 pages $24.95

**Educating the
Net Generation**
*How to Engage Students
in the 21st Century*
by Bob Pletka, Ed.D.
192 pages $16.95

**The Encyclopedia
of Sixties Cool**
*A Celebration of the
Grooviest People, Events,
and Artifacts of the 1960s*
by Chris Strodder
336 pages $24.95

**Exotic Travel Destinations
for Families**
by Jennifer M. Nichols
and Bill Nichols
360 pages $16.95

Footsteps in the Fog
*Alfred Hitchcock's
San Francisco*
by Jeff Kraft and
Aaron Leventhal
240 pages $24.95

French for Le Snob
*Adding Panache to Your
Everyday Conversations*
by Yvette Reche
400 pages $16.95

Haunted Hikes
*Spine-Tingling Tales and
Trails from North America's
National Parks*
by Andrea Lankford
376 pages $16.95

**How to Speak
Shakespeare**
by Cal Pritner and
Louis Colaianni
144 pages $16.95

James Dean Died Here
*The Locations of America's
Pop Culture Landmarks*
by Chris Epting
312 pages $16.95

L.A. Noir
The City as Character
by Alain Silver and
James Ursini
176 pages $19.95

**Led Zeppelin Crashed
Here**
*The Rock and Roll
Landmarks of North
America*
by Chris Epting
336 pages $16.95

Letter Writing Made Easy!
*Featuring Sample Letters
for Hundreds of Common
Occasions*
by Margaret McCarthy
208 pages $12.95

Redneck Haiku
Double-Wide Edition
by Mary K. Witte
240 pages $11.95

**Route 66 Adventure
Handbook**
by Drew Knowles
312 pages $16.95

**The Ruby Slippers,
Madonna's Bra, and
Einstein's Brain**
*The Locations of America's
Pop Culture Artifacts*
by Chris Epting
312 pages $16.95

**Rudolph, Frosty, and
Captain Kangaroo**
*The Musical Life of
Hecky Krasnow—Producer
of the World's Most
Beloved Children's Songs*
by Judy Gail Krasnow
424 pages $24.95

**Self-Loathing for
Beginners**
by Lynn Phillips
216 pages $12.95

The Shakespeare Diaries
A Fictional Autobiography
by J.P. Wearing
456 pages $27.95

Silent Traces
*Discovering Early
Hollywood Through the
Films of Charlie Chaplin*
by John Bengtson
304 pages $24.95

The Sixties
Photographs by
Robert Altman
192 pages $39.95

**Tiki Road Trip,
2nd Edition**
*A Guide to Tiki Culture
in North America*
by James Teitelbaum
336 pages $16.95

Tower Stories
An Oral History of 9/11
by Damon DiMarco
528 pages $27.95

**The Ultimate
Counterterrorist
Home Companion**
by Zack Arnstein and
Larry Arnstein
168 pages $12.95

	Quantity	Amount
The 99th Monkey ($16.95)	————	————
The Bad Driver's Handbook ($12.95)	————	————
Calculated Risk ($24.95)	————	————
Can a Dead Man Strike Out? ($11.95)	————	————
Captured!: Inside the World of Celebrity Trials ($24.95)	————	————
Dinner with a Cannibal ($24.95)	————	————
Educating the Net Generation ($16.95)	————	————
The Encyclopedia of Sixties Cool ($24.95)	————	————
Exotic Travel Destinations for Families ($16.95)	————	————
Footsteps in the Fog: Alfred Hitchcock's San Francisco ($24.95)	————	————
French for Le Snob ($16.95)	————	————
Haunted Hikes ($16.95)	————	————
How to Speak Shakespeare ($16.95)	————	————
James Dean Died Here: America's Pop Culture Landmarks ($16.95)	————	————
L.A. Noir: The City as Character ($19.95)	————	————
Led Zeppelin Crashed Here ($16.95)	————	————
Letter Writing Made Easy! ($12.95)	————	————
Redneck Haiku: Double-Wide Edition ($11.95)	————	————
Route 66 Adventure Handbook ($16.95)	————	————
The Ruby Slippers, Madonna's Bra, and Einstein's Brain ($16.95)	————	————
Rudolph, Frosty, and Captain Kangaroo ($24.95)	————	————
Self-Loathing for Beginners ($12.95)	————	————
The Shakespeare Diaries ($27.95)	————	————
Silent Traces: Early Hollywood Through Charlie Chaplin ($24.95)	————	————
The Sixties ($39.95)	————	————
Tiki Road Trip, 2nd Edition ($16.95)	————	————
Tower Stories ($27.95)	————	————
The Ultimate Counterterrorist Home Companion ($12.95)	————	————

Subtotal ————

CA residents add 8.25% sales tax ————

Shipping and Handling (see left) ————

TOTAL ————

Shipping & Handling:
1 book $4.00
Each additional book is $1.00

Name_____

Address_____

City_____ State_____ Zip_____

☐ Visa ☐ MasterCard   Card No.:_____

Exp. Date_____ Signature_____

☐ Enclosed is my check or money order payable to:

Santa Monica Press LLC
P.O. Box 1076
Santa Monica, CA 90406